√ *Teague has succinctly described some of the individuals who played major roles in the early years of the flagship campus of the University of North Carolina and Duke, the leading higher education institutions in the state, both exemplifying the early emphasis on higher education in this state.*

SAMUEL H. POOLE, FORMER CHAIRMAN,
UNC BOARD OF GOVERNORS

√ *Randy looks back over his own life and speculates thoughtfully on the future. It is a moving recitation of the tales of woe which not only pushed him to build an array of achievements for himself, but had profound impact on generations to follow through his work with university students.*

ROGER R. REAM, PRESIDENT/CEO,
THE FUND FOR AMERICAN STUDIES

√ *Teague writes with excitement of the earliest days of Virginia. He, Thomas Jefferson and others are descendants of Henry Soane, a Speaker of its House of Burgesses in Jamestown before its move to Williamsburg. Jefferson's niece Phoebe married Alexander Clark, thus bringing the Clarks into their heritages. This is a good read!*

MICHAEL W. THOMPSON, PRESIDENT,
THOMAS JEFFERSON INSTITUTE

To Cathy

FAMILIES

Where We Each Begin

Memories!

RANDAL TEAGUE

Randy April 30, 2019

iUniverse®

FAMILIES
WHERE WE EACH BEGIN

iUniverse books may be ordered through booksellers or by contacting:

iUniverse
1663 Liberty Drive
Bloomington, IN 47403
www.iuniverse.com
1-800-Authors (1-800-288-4677)

and all editions are available through Amazon.com.

ISBN: 978-1-5320-5554-6 (sc)
ISBN: 978-1-5320-5555-3 (hc)
ISBN: 978-1-5320-5553-9 (e)

Library of Congress Control Number: 2018910447

Print information available on the last page.

iUniverse rev. date: 3/6/2019

Also by Randal Teague

Collaborations

Readings on East-West Trade
Editor

A Faculty-Student Inquiry into the Causes of Campus Disorders
Coauthor

A Changing University for a Changing World
Team Leader

To Mom and Dad
and
these teachers of particular importance to me:
Nell Rodgers Croley
Daniel Crum
Faye Dean Evans
Helen Faulkner
David Jones
Walter Swan
Elizabeth Wilson

CONTENTS

Introduction xi

CHAPTER 1   My Journey Begins...1
CHAPTER 2   My Names...7
CHAPTER 3   Teagues in the New World... 12
CHAPTER 4   Durham and West Durham 24
CHAPTER 5   Childhood Continues...35
CHAPTER 6   Religion among Teague, Lasater, and Britt Families .45
CHAPTER 7   More on Britts and Teagues 50
CHAPTER 8   Oli 67
CHAPTER 9   O'Briant and Tucker Families 73
CHAPTER 10   Mom and Her Family 85
CHAPTER 11   Schooling Begins...108
CHAPTER 12   Dad 114
CHAPTER 13   More Durham Memories...132
CHAPTER 14   Chapel Hill 144
CHAPTER 15   Escapes and Vacations...159
CHAPTER 16   Florida, Here We Come!..164
CHAPTER 17   The Note..172
CHAPTER 18   The Wider Door of High School..............................181
CHAPTER 19   The Science Center of St. Petersburg 186
CHAPTER 20   Distant Seas 193
CHAPTER 21   Campaign for Student Council President 211
CHAPTER 22   The Young Americans for Freedom............................215
CHAPTER 23   Awaiting My Call to Washington..............................230

CHAPTER 24 The Washington Years Begin 233
CHAPTER 25 1964 and Beyond..241
CHAPTER 26 What's Next for Me and for You? 265

Appendices...273
Acknowledgments...281
Request..285
Bibliography 287
Index..291
About the Author.. 309

INTRODUCTION

WHAT YOU KNOW ABOUT YOUR FAMILY MAY MAKE YOU feel comfortable or uncomfortable but probably both. What you do *not* know about it can open new pathways of thought and action.

While you might think you know almost everything about your family, you do not. You know little about the years before you appeared on the scene. You know little about what went on when you were early to bed and late to rise or were at school or play. Pluralize your family into families, which reaches back to at least your grandparents, and you know even less about them and the contexts that surrounded them. Ancestry searches give you vital statistics but not their contexts.

An obvious but seldom pondered reality is that life is an assemblage of every moment that shaped it. While those moments occurred in sequence, they are not remembered in sequence. Some we recall with ease, and others we do not, at least not initially. Some we recall accurately, and others we do not, often simply because we never knew all that was occurring. This is analogous to the conflicting accounts of a traffic accident, isn't it? Inasmuch as the brain is a computer, it can bring back long-forgotten memories if we think hard enough around them. The interplay between the conscious and the subconscious brings memories up from their depths, enabling us to shape or reshape the present—not all memories but enough to make it well worthwhile. Recalling long-forgotten memories takes time. It's like digging through layers, each memory recalled serving as a gateway to additional recalls. I think this book sets forth successes in doing that.

With these recognitions, the reader's question becomes, Why should I try to recollect memories long past? The answers are simple but multiple: For what they tell you about you. For what they tell you about your family and families. For what they tell you about what you and others did right and not as right. For the lessons learned. Those look backward. What looks forward is the changed attitude and conduct that can free you from the emotional burdens of the past. That helps you gain greater control of your present and your future.

The reader's next question becomes, Do I have the interest and the energy to do this? Well, it's not easy, but it's also not extremely difficult. It's well within your reach. Taking one step at a time reduces barriers because each one finished leaves fewer remaining. Look beyond yourself and look to your family. There's the greatest of reasons to have the interest and find the energy.

Families are where we each begin. I pluralized that noun because, while we are born into a nuclear family, the very reality that we exist combined two families. That gives each of us, right away, three families: our own, our mother's, and our father's. And they are not our only families, since we have our four grandparents' families to add. They do not stop there, of course, because our descent runs back through recent to ancient families.

Let's look at ourselves within our families in an additional way. We are each a funnel into which vast numbers of ancestors' DNAs were combined to form our biological composition. That is followed by our maturing through childhood and adolescence to adulthood, acquiring knowledge and much else along that timeline. The product of this funnel, that means you or me, is at the bottom of an inverted pyramid of couplings reaching back to the emergence of *Homo sapiens*. Assisted by increasingly accessible research findings, you can learn much about the families that preceded you and the contexts that surrounded them. Who were they? What were their names? When did they live? What did they do? Under what geographical, cultural, social, economic, political, and other circumstances? Then, looking forward, most of us will begin a new pyramid, one as properly righted as an Egyptian pharaoh's, with each new generation creating an ever-widening base from a near to a far distant future. Think of these two pyramids arranged as if they were a geometric hourglass.

This book is about what I did to move forward in my life. It is also about my families and ancestors. It's about who they were and who some still are. It's what you might expect, but I have ascertained, understood, and reported more, occasionally far more, than the expected. It's more than their names, when and where they lived, and what they did and did not do. It's about the circumstances that surrounded them and the opportunities some took. It's about the larger opportunities that a few took. Some lived confined lives, while others freed themselves from constraints real and imagined to experience larger horizons.

To deepen these points, let's look at several examples of my efforts, rewards, and disappointments.

Example 1: Early on in life, I ran for high school student council president, won, became involved in state and national youth politics, grew that experience into the adult world of law and politics, and worked in the executive office of the president of the United States, twice on congressional staffs, and appeared before federal courts, each time putting my and others' shoulders to proverbial wheels to meet my objectives. These efforts generated rewards.

Example 2: I had even earlier become involved in a nationally recognized community science center for students, become its student president, garnered public recognition in marine biology through science fair awards, been invited to participate in a specimen-gathering expedition to the Indian Ocean and southwestern Pacific, persuaded its leaders that I was the right youth for the adventure, and taken summer courses to get ahead of the anticipated loss of months of regular semesters. Yet the expedition failed to secure funding. For me, this had been constant effort, some incidental early reward, including higher visibility for badly needed scholarship assistance at the college level, but I was left with circumstances I could not control and no chance of grabbing this brass ring.

Example 3: After conceding to my four adult children's wishes that

I write this memoir on the earlier part of my life, adding a summary chapter on what happened in later years, I gave much time, much effort, and not inconsiderable treasure to bringing this book forward. But lack of foresight on my part while my grandparents, parents, other relatives, teachers, childhood friends, and others were alive for me to ask questions and extract answers compelled me to research, ascertain, and verify answers that would have been so easily obtained if I had put in the required effort earlier in life. This example's core lesson? Don't wait, for doing nothing seldom generates something.

What do these examples also tell us?

That we each experience results across a spectrum from success to failure, seldom total success or total failure, almost always something in between. They tell us also that, while I could not control the results, I could control my efforts in seeking them. Beyond my own, I asked for and coordinated others' efforts on my behalf, in most cases but not in all bolstering my chances of successful results for me and for them. Someone looking at this might refer to the total effort as a combination of initiative, leadership, and teamwork, but less favorable conclusions can be reached too. You will have to decide for yourself.

If you wonder what follows this page, consider the possible titles and subtitles as choices came to mind as the text evolved. They tell you much about it and about me:

Paths from Home
Run, Randy, Run!
Do It Right
Efforts and Rewards
Meanings
In Praise of Changing Your Mind
Families: Where We Each Begin

I came to believe the last best captures the pages that follow. Here they are, and I hope you enjoy them as much as I did getting them before you.

1

My Journey Begins

DURHAM PARENTS IN MAY 1944 WERE MORE FEARFUL OF losing their sons than of losing the war in Europe and the Pacific. Wartime meat rationing was already ending, even if gasoline, tire, and other rationing would continue until war's end. Not as standing down while other young men were fighting, rather for reasons related to the reorganization of the Piedmont League, the Durham Bulls' bats were silent. Bing Crosby's *Going My Way* was coming to one of its theaters. Duke University students were studying for final exams, and seniors were expecting to graduate in a few weeks. School children were looking forward to the summer. Households were turning on their window and floor fans, as the afternoon heat was already climbing toward summer highs. Ladies were looking for last summer's hand fans, even if they were advertising ploys of churches and funeral homes. New York governor Thomas Dewey locking down the Republican primaries nomination against Franklin Roosevelt seeking a fourth term was largely ignored by North Carolina's nearly totally Democratic voters.

In Europe, Allied troops were pushing the German army up the boot of Italy, and their airpower was pounding its troops, trains, airfields, factories, ports, and cities mercilessly. German officers' attempted assassination of Adolph Hitler had failed, so an earlier end to the war was unlikely. Successes against German U-boats were altering the war at sea in favor of Allied navies and merchant shipping. Stalin's Red Army was pushing Hitler's demoralized Wehrmacht out of Soviet cities and westward across its countryside as Berlin lay increasingly within reach. In the Pacific, the boundaries of Imperial Japan's naval and land forces were shrinking as its island strongholds were lost and its surface fleet's ships and its submarines were sunk.

Amid these events and expectations, one of far less circumstance occurred in Durham. I was born on the Friday morning of May 19.

For anyone unfamiliar with Durham, or 1944, or both, Durham was on the cusp of changes that would follow the end of the war and redefine it. Our family's speck of a place in those years was a duplex apartment on Eighth Street in the city's West Durham. It was less than two blocks from Duke University's East Campus in one direction and two blocks in another from Erwin Mills' textiles plants. It was less than a block in a third direction from E. K. Powe School, where I would attend grades one through four. Eighth Street was populated with lower-middle-class workers at those mills and the cigarette manufacturing plants in the fourth direction about a mile away and part of downtown.

What else is there to know about our neighborhood?

That its families were for the most part good people, loving their nation, fearing their God, and struggling to make ends meet. Our 821 and 821½ Eighth Street housing fit easily within that definition. By a duplex's design, we four Teagues occupied only half of it. Eighth Street was sociologically and economically far from Durham's affluent streets. So much so that years after we had moved from it, Durham's city council renamed it Iredell Street, perhaps in hopes of upgrading it beyond their finally paving and guttering of it. Why Iredell? James Iredell, a lawyer and political essayist, was not only one of the early associate justices of the Supreme Court of the United States, nominated by President George Washington, but his oldest son, a junior, would become the state's one-year-and-four-day governor and twenty-seven-month US senator. The council's awareness of the Iredells' achievements may have been intended to give the street's residents new aspirations. Perhaps they were unaware of such an intent.

What is there to know about our duplex? Framed wood painted white, two small stoops in front, a front yard but a bigger one in the back with ill-fated Dutch elms and Mother's clotheslines. What had been intended by its builder as the living room of our apartment was shared by my brother and me as our bedroom. Our parents occupied the originally intended bedroom between ours and the kitchen. This meant we lived without a living room, an oxymoron of sorts, but with the addition of a few chairs and a radio, our bedroom and our tiny kitchen were most of our living space. Looking from its front door, which was the entrance to the kids' bedroom, windows ran along the left side of the two bedrooms and kitchen. When you came through that front door with your head up, you looked straight through the two bedrooms and kitchen to the back door, a screened-in porch, and that backyard. Bitterly cold winter nights would occasion my father crawling under the unit in predawn hours in attempts to thaw frozen pipes. Dad had to park in the front yard because our unpaved and un-guttered dirt-and-gravel street had no places for parking. Automotive traffic generated the dust found on our furniture, and dry springs and falls lengthened the dust season. With irregular frequencies, the city would spray used automotive engine oil onto the street in efforts to reduce it. Of course, fresh oil on the bottom of children's shoes and feet tracked into households. In rainy weather, the source of airborne dust became the source of mud. Three-to-four-foot-high hedges along the front yard's border to the street did nothing to deter dust, mud, or oil. For several weeks each spring, a lilac bush between the duplex's two front stoops bloomed sufficiently to assure Mother of several handfuls of cuttings. Seventy-plus years later, the duplex is gone. The land under it now supports a recently built apartment and retail complex for those studying at or working for Duke University or in the secondary and tertiary jobs that flow from it. Four blocks away, the Watts Hospital where I was born is closed, but its edifice remains as a statewide school for gifted and talented students.

At Watts on May 19, my mother gave birth to me as I sought to make an earlier entrance than she and the attending nurses had expected. The temperature outside was to get to 84° that spring day, but it was still early morning, and I was presenting. The nature of her and my condition occurred because she was in a bathtub when my eagerness to join the world community compelled their rush into the delivery room before I accomplished the task on my own. I ask myself often, could those moments be a reason for my impatience and my claustrophobia?

Several days later, it was a short car ride to our duplex. I am confident I was held securely in my mother's arms as she sat in the front passenger seat, there being no seat belt for her or dad and no car seat yet invented for me. In the years that followed, it was to be a much longer journey for me from that duplex. Some persons move deliberatively toward their futures. That's certainly true for me, but I also deliberately ran from my past.

As noted, my life's journey did not begin on May 19. It began roughly nine months earlier. That's an interesting notion for me, because nine months earlier, my parents were almost certainly at Carolina Beach, south of Wilmington, or at Virginia Beach on a late summer vacation. I suspect therefore that I am a vacation baby, planned or not on some evening, afternoon, or morning. My mind's ear can hear my father's cigarette lighter clink shut. I doubt if my conception near the ocean gave rise to my lifelong attraction to the seas and a close encounter with nearly becoming a marine botanist, but it's worth a consideration.

May 19

What of May 19?

Every year has one, so let's look at what of importance happened on it in other years. I share a May 19 birthdate with entrepreneur, philanthropist, and university founder Johns Hopkins; Danville,

Virginia–born Nancy Viscountess Astor, the first woman elected to sit as a member of the British Parliament; modern Turkey's founder, Mustafa Ataturk; Vietnam's Ho Chi Minh; African American Muslim leader Malcolm X; Cambodian dictator Pol Pot; writer Nora Ephron; and others from the years that preceded me. From the years that followed, I share the date with Pete Townshend, Andre the Giant, Grace Jones, and Archie Manning.

In American history, May 19 had made its mark: George II's granting of a charter to the Ohio Company to open the Ohio River Valley to colonials, in part to push back against French intrusions from Canada; Mexico's signing of the Treaty of Guadalupe Hidalgo, ending the Mexican-American War and ceding California, Nevada, Utah, and parts of four other states to the United States; the opening of the first department store in the United States; the Homestead Act becoming law in order to open the American West to accelerated settlement; the Civil War battle of Spotsylvania Court House ending in Virginia and Confederate president Jefferson Davis being captured and arrested in Georgia; the Ringling Brothers Circus premiering, and Buffalo Bill Cody premiering his own "Buffalo Bill's Wild West"; the National Football League adopting the college draft to begin in 1935; and Franklin Roosevelt meeting with Winston Churchill to agree on an invasion of Europe, its approximate target date, and the Operation Fortitude schemes to mislead the Germans as to where that invasion would begin.

In English and other European history, May 19 is known for the departure of Pope Eugene III–authorized English crusaders to bolster the siege of Lisbon held by the Moors, a "connect the dots" example for me because I turned eighteen in Lisbon in 1962; Christopher Columbus's selection of his son Diego as his sole heir; Catherine of Aragon's marriage by proxy to England's future Henry VIII to become the first of his six queen consort wives; his second wife, Anne Boleyn's, beheading and the Holy See's consequential canonizing of Sir Thomas More, who lost his head in that dispute; Henry and Boleyn's daughter Queen Elizabeth I's arrest of Henry's first wife's daughter Mary

Queen of Scots, perhaps with the date in mind; the Long Parliament's declaration of England as a commonwealth and republic, the latter of which lasted for only eleven years; the French founding of its Order of Legion d'Honneur; and Oscar Wilde's release from Reading Gaol.

My May 19 birth was only seventeen days before the Allies' D-Day invasion of Europe across the beaches and in the air above France's Normandy coast. The German defense line in Italy collapsed on my birth day. In hiding in Amsterdam that day, Anne Frank would write that she had developed a contained affection for her friend Peter. She had no way to know that 240 gypsies from the Netherlands' Westerbork were shipped by train that day to Auschwitz.

To highlight the obvious, there is nothing in these paragraphs that ties me and *my* May 19 birth to those persons and events other than the coincidence of timing. Roughly one out of every 365 persons among our earth's billions has the same birth date by whatever calendar or language depicting theirs, but knowing these coincidences has added contexts to my life.

2

My Names

WE ALMOST ALWAYS KNOW WHY WE HAVE OUR SURNAME, and a person often knows with certainty the reasons for their given names. That's true if you're a junior, a III, a IV, or increasingly now a V and even a VI. Being named after a grandparent or an aunt or uncle is common. When they are not obvious, we can ask a parent, and he or she can tell us, but sometimes we don't think about this until our parents are no longer with us. Let's examine Randal and Cornell, and then we'll address Teague. There are lessons in each.

The spelling Randal comes to us through its European derivations. The name and spelling of Rögnvaldr in Norse became Raghnall in Celtic, Ranuff in Welsh as in Ranuff de Blondeville, sixth earl of Chester who was Randle, sixth earl of Chester in medieval English, they eventually becoming Ronald, Randal, and Reynold among others. If one wonders how those pronunciations and spellings evolved into Randal, keep in mind the English pronounce Leicester as Lester and Magdalen as Mauldlin. Rögnvaldr was a combination of roots meaning mighty ruler, counselor, and adviser, but the name Randal does not answer my question as to why I am Randal. It never occurred to me to ask my mother or father, and I should have, but those roots set out some of my personality traits, all unforeseeable to my parents at my birth. I later asked others within my extended family, and not a person knew. My own Randal has been misspelled with frequency, but the nickname of Randy was inevitable, at least when not in London, and Rand and Ran emerged in adulthood.

My mother told me that "Cornell" was "the name of one of your dad's friends," and she thought it "balanced well" with Randal. That was the totality of her answer. Was it also because the three names balanced with six-seven-six letters in their respective lengths? It was probably more than all of that, and I have a somewhat logical probability with no way to authenticate it. According to the published history of Durham Dairy, at a time when Dad was at one of several stints there, the company brought in two dairy specialists, V. J. Ashbaugh and C. B. Martin, to evaluate its operations and make recommendations to its owners and managers. Ashbaugh and Martin were from Cornell University. They assessed the dairy's organizational contexts, structure, and operations from field to milking barn to processing plant to customers' tables. It is possible if not probable that Dad was interviewed by one or both and discussed it with my mother. Might their references to Cornell University, rather than a given or surname of a friend of my father's, have been her source of the idea for Cornell? Perhaps it was a lovingly expressed aspiration for my Dad since he may have wished he could have gone to the university but my middle name would be as close to it as would be possible for him. I will never know, that being a lesson learned about the importance of asking follow-on questions.

Years later, my middle name focused me on Cornell University. Our first son, a Junior known by Cornell, had no interest in Cornell University and its winter's icy slopes. He was not yet aware of the area's renowned fly-fishing and downhill skiing across the Vermont border. I took him to the top of Cornell's McGraw Tower when he was about ten or eleven, and, not unlike the devil tempting Christ in the wilderness, I said to him that all he saw from the tower was his for the asking if he worked hard enough for it, knowing that my wife's father

Harold Townsend's and his predecessors' legacies there would be of calculable value in an admissions process. My observation fell on deaf ears. I had not yet learned that the most effective reverse psychology was for me to tell him that he probably could not attend Cornell. I did not then, and do not now, hold his decision to attend the University of Kentucky against him, for it was his life. It was my and his mother, Jessica Townsend Teague's, youngest son, James Keller Burke Teague, who continued the Townsend family's tradition at Cornell, one dating from the class of 1872 and its Abram R. Townsend. Besides, James graduating from Cornell began his own Teague legacy there.

The reason for my surname "Teague" is more readily apparent, but what is a Teague? This spelling stretches back to at least England's thirteenth century, for it was Henry III who formally recognized this spelling at court. Variations on the spelling stretch further back into antiquity, and there are many of them.

Tadhg and Its Spellings

According to one line of research, our surname emerged in the later years of the first millennium in present-day Scandinavia. From there, it was taken by Vikings to the land to which they rowed and sailed. I was informed in Oslo that its ancient Nordic root, spelled "Tadhg" with the "d" and the "h" on the same stem, meant a bard, a poet, or a philosopher. Upon learning of that cluster of meanings, my mother observed it just might mean "bullshit artist." I retorted "one with the gift of gab" as a better summary. Seriously, there are over twenty variations of Tadhg, some easily recognized, others less so, and some far less so. T-e-a-g-u-e is but one of them.

The Swedish second wife of one of our country's directors of central intelligence, Adm. Stansfield Turner, informed me in a dinner conversation one evening that it simply meant "peat moss." I did not take easily to her observation, lowly peat moss being what it is compared to the stature of a poet or philosopher. Sadly, Turner's wife, Eli Karen Gilbert (known as Karen), and others were killed in a chartered aircraft crash in Costa Rica on January 15, 2000. Admiral Turner survived with the amazing coincidence in the crash's timing that I was having lunch at a mountainside restaurant no more than an hour's driving time from San Jose's Tobias Bolanos Airport for private and chartered aircraft, near which the accident occurred almost immediately after takeoff. I was watching a television report on it out of the corner of my eye as Costa Rica's EARTH University president, Dr. Jose Antonio Zaglul, and I were sharing—as this news broke—that we each wondered when we learned of an airplane crash if we would know someone on the aircraft. The apparent cause of the crash was severe side winds flipping the Czech-built LET 410. Because of Turner's and others' presences on it, crash theories to the contrary emerged, especially since the CIA refused initially to acknowledge he was on it, because others from the agency were on it. Admiral Turner had been retired from his CIA position for nearly twenty years, and his wife was with him, which seemed to me hardly a scenario for a James Bond–like thriller in Costa Rica or neighboring Nicaragua to its north or Panama to its south. My defensive posture toward her observation should have ended with that crash, but if so, why am I recalling it here?

According to Francis Collins Porter and Clara Wilson Gries's *Our Folks and Your Folks*, the tadhg pronunciation may have come into the British Isles from a direction quite different from that of the Vikings. It indicates that tadhg originated in what we know now as the Middle East, carried therefrom into ancient Spain's legendary Milesian communities or Scotic race, from there into the ancient Ireland that the Milesians conquered, and then with many spellings throughout the now two Irelands, England, Scotland, and Wales and later to the lands its emigrants settled. In this respect, Wikipedia recounts the legend that Milesius of Spain was a son of Bille mac Galicia, who was himself king of Galicia, Andalusia, Murcia, and Castile and was born in Brigantia in Spain. Milesius became king of Braganza and is regarded as "the Father of the Irish Race."

Those accounts address from where the name may have come, but they do not address definitions that emerged from their uses. We should address several of them. Cornish and Welsh references include "a handsome person," "fair," and "beautiful" but contrastingly "rustic" and "rude." Ancient uses have given way to modern ones. The most intriguing to me is the *Urban Dictionary*'s definition of Teague: "A very attractive man who draws a lot of attention to girls he loves. He loves women and they love him back. He is wonderful in bed and the girls keep coming back. He is very sweet and caring. His smile is like no other and is very unique." I ask at the age of seventy-four, where was this definition forty years ago? For what it's worth, a numerology account has me pegged precisely: "People with this name have a deep inner desire for travel and adventure, and want to set their own pace in life without being governed by tradition. People with this name are excited by change, adventure and excitement."

When I reflect further on the name's Irish spellings, I am reminded of Thomas Robert Tighe Chapman, seventh baronet of Westmeath, who was the Anglo-Irish father of T. E. Lawrence. We recognize that son from his and others' books and from the eight-Oscars-winning 1962 Sam Spiegel–produced, David Lean–directed, and Maurice Jarre–scored movie *Lawrence of Arabia*. T. E. Lawrence's father used his contrived Lawrence surname to conceal his whereabouts as he fled from Ireland with his children's governess to Wales, where Thomas Edward was born to them at Snowdon Lodge. The family quickly moved to Scotland, then to Brittany on the coast of France, then to Jersey in the English Channel, and finally to England's university town of Oxford, where Tom's interests grew. It was to Oxford that he returned after the World War I armistice and the victorious powers' dividing of the Ottoman Empire into the modern Middle East countries whose names and borders we know today. He died in 1935 on May 19 from injuries suffered in a motorcycle accident days earlier. I am reminded that a Taig is a pejorative Irish Protestant term for a Catholic, or at least a Catholic rabble-rouser. I think also of another Irish variation, Tiegs, as in Cheryl Tiegs, the American model, actress, designer, author, and entrepreneur. When I think of McTeague, I recall Frank Norris's novel of 1890s San Francisco, *McTeague*.

3

Teagues in the New World

WHAT DO WE KNOW ABOUT THE EARLIEST TEAGUES TO
America and their genealogical lines? We know that they were
few and most easily described centuries later as "the *southern* Teagues"
and "the *northern* Teagues." In 1840, their largest concentrations were in
North Carolina and Maine. By 1920, their largest concentrations were
in North Carolina and California. Owing to modern society's mobility,
they are now nearly everywhere.

Southern Teagues

An ancestral line appeared along the Maryland and Virginia shores of
the Chesapeake Bay in the 1650s, and it began "the southern Teagues,"
a principal line descended from John Teague (1635–1677). According
to *Patent Book No. 3.*, which is contained in a book entitled *Cavaliers
and Pioneers*, at an entry dated November 27, 1652, John Teague was
entered as one of a party of ten persons transported by Edward Revell
to five hundred acres in Northampton County, Virginia, a neck of land
parted by a branch of Pangotege Creek, from land of Anthony Hoskins.

Northampton County is southwest of Cecil County, Maryland, the latter being on the Delmarva Peninsula, a compression for the peninsula on which are Delaware and parts of both Maryland and Virginia and that shelters the eastern side of the Chesapeake Bay from the Atlantic Ocean. Since almost all travel of distance in those times was by water, the sailing time between Northampton County, Virginia, and Cecil County, Maryland, would have been a day or two across and up the bay. That entry indicates that John Teague was indentured—that is, bonded—to Edward Revell, meaning that Teague was under contract to Revell for a period of time, commonly five to ten years, in exchange for Revell having paid for Teague's transport from England to the New World. This labor system was widely employed in the seventeenth and eighteenth centuries to populate the British colonies in the New World. It was of benefit to indenturer and indentured and morally preferred to and less expensive than involuntary servitude, which we know as the abomination of enslavement. An indentured person's bond could be sold from one holder to another, but when the bond expired, the person was a free person. The growth of tobacco, rice, and indigo and the plantation economies encompassing each of those export crops created an enormous need for labor. This contract labor system most commonly brought young persons to America because they wished to leave the Old World's crowded and impoverished conditions and the severely limited opportunities out of one's own class. Being young, they were more able-bodied to do strenuous labor. As the PBS series *History Detectives* concluded, "A new life in the New World offered a glimmer of hope." We know from Samuel G. Smyth's *Genealogy of Duke-Shepard-Van Metre Family* that this John Teague's son William (1695–1762) and some of his children, including his son Moses (1718–1799), left Maryland for Virginia's Frederick County, which at that time in Virginia's history encompassed four counties in what remains in Virginia, plus five additional countries in what is now West Virginia. Today's Frederick County's seat is Winchester, not the Fredericksburg that one might wrongly assume. We do not know where within those nine counties William Teague settled, but we do know that his son

Moses moved to Orange County, North Carolina, which too was a larger county then than now. Chapel Hill is within the original and the reduced Orange County.

There were other Teagues in the southern colonies and northern colonies in the years following 1607 in Virginia and 1620 in Massachusetts. We know from records that only two days after John Teague was recorded as arrived and indentured to Edward Revell, a John Teagg was recorded as arrived and indentured to Andrew Munroe in neighboring Northumberland County, Virginia. A Dennis Teague was recorded on August 28, 1655, as arrived and indentured to Richard Price and bound for New Kent County, south of Virginia's York River. On March 16, 1657, John Teague co-purchased land on the "North side of Horne Harbour Creek," and on September 25, 1663, George Teague was recorded as arrived and transported by John Lawrence, bound for the "West side of Chawanoke River." Another John Teague was recorded on September 26, 1664, as arrived and bound for property in nearby "Rappahanocke (that is, Rappahannock) County on the North side of Rappahanocke (ditto) River, upon the North side of Rappahanocke (ditto) Town." Others were to follow.

John Teague

My line from John Teague and his wife follows through his son, Edward Teague, born in 1660 at Tegg's Delight at present-day Conowingo in Cecil County, Maryland. This is slightly northeast of where the Susquehanna River flows into the Chesapeake Bay. Edward Teague died in 1697. Tegg's Delight and several additional properties that he added to it are in the ownership of the Girl Scouts of Central Maryland, with few improvements on their six hundred plus acres aside from camp and administration buildings and an impressively restored circa 1868 Gilded Age mansion and sprawling estate known as Bell Manor. The Philadelphia Electric Company acquired the property from the Bells, and PECO's electric power-generating Conowingo Dam on the Susquehanna can be seen from this property. After a half century's delay from when I first became aware of this property, genealogist Brock Bierman arranged for and we visited Camp Conowingo, as the Girl Scouts' property is known, in 2015. We visited Bell Manor, had my photograph taken standing in the hearth of a massive stone chimney whose house no longer exists, and hiked much of the property with its well-informed caretaker. Concerned that this property, situated with spectacular views of the Susquehanna, could be sold by the Girl Scouts in order to raise funds for its other camps, activities, and administrations, I was informed that a formalized agreement was reached decades ago with the US Coast and Geodetic Survey, an agency that among other responsibilities preserves and protects property from private development, to protect the property. I hope a cash-strapped US government does not change its mind in this respect.

There are nine generations between John Teague's and mine. Among them are the referenced Moses Teague (1718–1799) and his first wife, Elizabeth Loftin (1713– or 1714–1759). He became the owner of an Orange County, North Carolina, property, from which he gave badly needed financial support during the War of Independence to the colonial militias in North Carolina, South Carolina, and Virginia. He and several of his sons were Regulators, residents of North Carolina's inland region who believed that "royal government officials were charging them excessive fees, falsifying records, and engaging in other mistreatments." Their opposition resulted in an armed confrontation known as the Battle of Alamance of May 16, 1771. The Regulators lost, and the royal governor and his forces arrested and hung at least one without as much as a military court trial. It is from Moses Teague that I became a member of the Sons of the American Revolution and several other Revolutionary War–era lineal societies. I am descended from Moses and Elizabeth's son Issac Newton Teague (1748–1824). President Barack Hussein Obama and his mother, Stanley Ann Dunham, are descended from Moses and Elizabeth through their daughter Isabella Mary Teague (m. Welborn) (1742–1821). Generally, southern Teague descendants moved from Maryland and Virginia into the Carolinas, then throughout the south, and then westward into Texas and the Indian territory now known as Oklahoma.

If a little humor can be permitted in respect to the word "Teague," that humor comes from the common usage of the sound "teague" among the Native American tribes that the early English explorers found living along the Atlantic shorelines' barrier islands of the Maryland and Virginia colonies. When one drives along these islands on a national park–visiting, fishing, beaching, or other excursion there are road signs to Assateague, Chincoteague, and Pungoteague, and there was a tribe along the Virginia shore by the name of the Gingoteagues. Historians find no connections between these Indian names for themselves and their village areas and Teague-surnamed Englishmen. Linguists assume the English were recording the cognate of an uttered "tig," "tigg," or "tegg" by using the spelling of "teague," a surname known to English scribes. As a frequent visitor to this area, including with family and friends to observe massive bird populations in the estuaries or the wild ponies on Assateague or to fish in the many coves and inlets of the area, I am amused that the Assateague National Seashore on both sides of the Maryland and Virginia shoreline boundary can be jovially construed as named after a Teague's rear end—Assateague—albeit the proper pronunciation of a double *s* in the colonial era was often as a *z*, meaning it should be properly pronounced "Azateague."

Matthew Page Andrews's 1937 book, *Virginia—The Old Dominion*, reports, "On December 25, 1662, Chincoteague Island was granted to Captain William Whittington by Wachawampe, Emperor of the Gingo Teagues, and regranted twice later. Wachawampe's will of 1656 is on file at Eastville, Va." More interestingly, Randall Revell was a witness to the execution of this will when the Indian emperor made his X mark, and it was this Randall Revell who assigned the five hundred acres to his son Edward Revell, who transported among others John Teague, who arrived ten years and a few days before this initial grant by Wachawampe.

What is known about other southern Teagues of note?

Walter Dorwin Teague (1883–1960) and his son W. Dorwin

Teague (1910–2004) would appear from their financial successes to have been northern Teagues. They were not. The elder was an accomplished industrial designer, architect, illustrator, graphic designer, writer, and entrepreneur, often referred to as America's "Dean of Industrial Design," and the younger was also a successful industrial designer and inventor. While Walter Dorwin Teague was born in Decatur, Indiana, his family was a southern Teague family, his Irish-American grandfather having moved in 1840 from North Carolina to Pendleton, Indiana, one of the nation's larger Quaker communities. Walter Dorwin Teague's father became a circuit-riding Methodist minister in those environs, who, though with little money, "ladened" his home with books that his children devoured. That book tradition continues among Teagues.

Congressman Olin Earl "Tiger" Teague (1910–1981) was born in Oklahoma and raised in Mena, Arkansas. He graduated from what is now Texas A&M in 1932, joined the army in 1940 as a lieutenant, and was discharged from it in 1946 as a colonel. He participated in the invasion of Normandy and was awarded the Silver Star with two clusters, the Bronze Star, and two Purple Hearts. The "Tiger" nickname did not come from his actions in those battles but rather from his high school football career. He represented Texas A&M's College Station and its neighboring towns, ranches, cattle, and oil rigs from 1946 to 1978. Those decades saw him champion veterans and their educational, health, and other benefit needs. He served as chairman of the House Committee on Science and Astronautics and its subcommittee on manned space flight. As a recognition of his leadership, he became chairman of the House Democratic Caucus. The original Visitors Center at the Johnson Space Center in Houston, the Olin E. Teague Research Center at Texas A&M, and the Olin E. Teague Veterans Center in Temple were named in his memory. He rests at Arlington National Cemetery.

There was another Teague elected to Congress after Olin and Congressman Charles Teague of California died. Congressman Harry Teague, a Democrat from New Mexico, was elected for one term from 2009 to 2011, to succeed the Republican incumbent who ran instead for a Senate seat and, having lost that Senate bid, defeated Teague two years later. Harry Teague "grew up in an impoverished family of sharecroppers and lived the first nine years of his life in rural central Oklahoma without even running water. His family moved to Hobbs, New Mexico when he was nine years old. He attended Hobbs High School but dropped out at the age of 17 to work in the oil fields to support his sick parents." From the lessons learned in those fields, he became "a small business owner of a company that now employs 250 people and is a member of the New Mexico Oil and Gas Association." Not long after he was elected to Congress, I dropped by his office and left my business card. His heritage, like Tiger Teague's before him, indicates he was probably a southern Teague, but his financial gains tell the story of a successful one. I never heard from him.

Northern Teagues

Another Teague line began in Massachusetts and became a core element of "the northern Teagues." The first recorded Teague surname in that region of which we are aware is Daniel Teague, a taxpayer in Hingham, Massachusetts, in 1719. It is probable that other Teagues by this or other spellings came into the northern colonies before him. After all, 1719 was ninety-nine years after 1620's *Mayflower*'s arrival, but no recordings of any of their vital dates have been ascertained by anyone who in turn passed them to me. We do know a fair amount about those who followed Daniel Teague. Many of these Teagues came from Rockland, Maine, including a J. R. Teague and a G. F. Teague, but not all did.

Northern Teagues seem to have been incapable of engaging in any commerce without doing so successfully. No Teague conceived, financed, nor built New Hampshire's Mt. Washington Cog Railway, but Col. Henry N. Teague acquired and managed it. Inaugurated in 1868, it is the world's first mountain-climbing cog railway, meaning its rack-and-pinion undercarriage secures it firmly to a notched track as it climbs and descends. It remains our nation's longest cog railway and the world's second-steepest one. Colonel Teague was succeeded in this venture by Arthur S. Teague, a business protégé but not a relative, who was in turn succeeded by his widow, Ellen Crawford Teague, who, in doing so, became the world's first woman president of a railroad. It ascends and descends in the state's White Mountains, its summit known as "the coldest place in the continental United States." It was designated a National Historic Engineering Landmark in 1976.

The ancestry of Judah Dana and Evaline Morse Teague of Aroostook County, Maine, was set forth in Porter and Gries's *Our Folks and Your Folks*. Aroostook is the northernmost county in Maine, surrounded by Canada on all but its southern border. These Teagues are the ancestors of the Teagues who made a substantial mark in California's history, for as the nation moved westward, so did they. Their first stop headed west was the newly discovered oil fields of Pennsylvania. They made enough money there to head to Salina, Kansas. Charles Collins Teague's father received letters from his mother's brothers, Charles Collins and Wallace Hardison, then in Salina. They had bought both a bank and a cattle ranch. Charles Collins Teague reports in his autobiography that the "letters told of the wonders of that new country and invited my father to come out there and manage their businesses," and some pages later, "My father thought that Salina, Kansas was destined to be the metropolis of the West. He invested heavily in non-productive city property and incurred considerable debt. Then came the depression of the early nineties and his fortune was wiped out and his health broken. In 1893 he decided to move to California. He died in August of that year, soon after we arrived in Santa Paula." He should have held on to life for a few more years because that son recovered all of the losses and made far more gains in California. A nationally prominent Aroostook County Collins is US senator Susan M. Collins, who served as the New England regional director of the US Small Business Administration and in other public service capacities before entering the US Senate in 1997.

I was told years ago that Teagues were associated with the Missouri-Kansas-Texas Railway Company headquartered in Charles Collins's and Wallace Hardison's Kansas. The Katy was the first railroad to connect north Texas with "the rest of the country" by connecting with "railroad magnate" Benjamin Franklin Yoakum's Trinity and Brazos Railway. The Texas community of Brewer was renamed Teague in 1906 after Yoakum's niece Betty Teague, sister of his mother, Narcissa Teague. With knowledge and New York financier Jay Gould's and others' monies and governments' promises of legislated rewards, Yoakum controlled 17,500 miles of railroad between Chicago and the Mexican border by 1909. Texas now has the most miles of track of any state, and New York now owns Yoakum's Tywacana estate on Long Island as its Bethpage State Park whose Black Course has twice hosted professional golf's US Open. About ten years ago, I drove the hour or so north from College Station to Teague to check such a trip off my bucket list. I would never intend to malign anything named Teague, but the census report of 4,557 people must have counted those in cemeteries, military service, and away at college, plus all the cattle within its boundaries. In the few years since, fracking in and around Teague has fostered a revival evidenced by new public and private construction.

As the nation reached the Pacific and began developing California, so did the Teagues from Maine. They were to contribute significantly to the making of the state as the nation's largest agricultural producer. One Teague family became major cattle ranchers, and Charles Collins Teague's *Fifty Years a Rancher* autobiography published in 1944 captures that era and his and their successes. It did not require a PhD in agricultural economics to know that cattle ranching was not the highest value use of their land, no matter what the profits were. As California was growing, so too were land values. As a consequence, the Teague, Collins, and other families invested in and then became major producers of walnuts for the national market. We identify the Blue Diamond brand of the 3,500 almond growers' California Almond Growers Exchange today with just that, almonds, but these nut ventures began with walnuts. Growing nuts was a better use of land than cattle ranching, but a problem with growing nuts was that they were harvested at the same time each year. The question raised was what else would be harvestable at a nearly opposite time. Citrus fruit was the answer. From these and other families' asset-risking innovations grew a large number of citrus orchards and citrus fruit agricultural cooperatives to address common needs, including marketing, sales, and transportation. Lemons were the first crop, followed by oranges, each with increasingly improved varietals to match California's water and weather realities. Limoneira being Portuguese for "lemon lands," the Limoneira Company had its 1893 beginnings in Ventura County, producing not only lemons but also Valencia oranges and walnuts. It hired in 1901 Charles Collins Teague as its first general manager, and Limoneira corporate history reports, "Teague's leadership and innovation set the standards for farming practices." Teague did not stop to count his rewards. Along with his lawyer, George E. Farrand, and a handful of others, he founded the California Walnut Growers Association, and they and others then founded the California Fruit Growers Exchange. Farrand was succeeded as their lawyer by Stanley Forman Reed, a leader in the cooperative movement and soon to become the United States solicitor general during parts of President Franklin D. Roosevelt's first two terms and thereafter an associate justice of the Supreme Court of the United States. Reed had undergraduate degrees from both Kentucky Wesleyan College and Yale University, and while he studied law at both the University of Virginia and Columbia University, he never obtained a law degree. If that was not enough education, he studied further at the Sorbonne in Paris. The lack of a law degree did not slow his career, for in those days it was not necessary as long as you had "read the law" and passed an entrance examination, often orally, or were otherwise on motion admitted "to the Bar." The bar is a real or imaginary rail or barrier dividing working and public spaces in a court room, separating the judge, bailiff, first chair lawyers, and jury from the not-yet-testifying witnesses, spectators, and press corps. This is another "it's a small world" example, but press clippings from Dad's golfing days include a photograph of him with Justice Reed at a Durham-area golf course.

A large membership cooperative grew from Charles Collins

Teague's and others' investments in fruit production and marketing. It did business as Sunkist, corporately Sunkist Growers, Inc., a play on its advertising agency, Lord & Thomas's, "sun-kissed" recommendation. Sunkist describes itself as "the largest fresh produce shipper in the United States, the most diversified citrus processing and marketing operation in the world, and one of California's largest landowners." Its annual sales and licensing fees have exceeded $1 billion for each of recent years. Charles Collins Teague, our "Yankee from Maine who became a pioneering rancher," became Sunkist's chairman after his brother Milton held that position. As if those successes were not enough, Charles Collins Teague and Milton Teague's uncle, Wallace L. Hardison, became cofounders of the Hardison-Stewart Oil Company, which became Union Oil Company of California, whose gasoline and other products are sold under the brand UNOCAL and whose stations occupy street corners throughout the West.

Charles Collins Teague's son, Charles McKevett Teague, was elected to Congress in 1954, serving from 1955 until his death on New Year's Day in 1974. Because he knew much about the subject, Congressman Teague was the ranking Republican on the House Committee on Agriculture. He served also on the House Committee on Veterans Affairs with Congressman "Tiger" Teague. Because of the fresh fruit relevance, the "Teague Special" at the Republicans' Capitol Hill Club was for many years its dieter's offering, although a waiter once thought it was named after me, probably because he felt its low calories constituted an appropriate meal for me. Charles Teague was a Stanford University and a Stanford Law School double alumnus, practiced law in Los Angeles and Ventura Counties, and served as a director of the McKevett Corp. and the Teague-McKevett Co. He also served from 1942 to 1946 in the US Army Air Corps and was awarded for that service. It was because Olin and Charles Teague were the only Teagues to have served in the House of Representatives that Charles chided me that "Things are supposed to run in threes, Randy. You need to get yourself elected!" when I was working on a congressional committee staff.

22

Understanding Ancestry

Several connected points should be made about understanding ancestry. We each know that a person is descended from thousands of ancestors. If that sounds preposterous, consider that each of us has two birth parents, four grandparents, eight great-grandparents, sixteen great-great-grandparents, thirty-two great-great-great-grandparents, and so on, because each generation doubles the number. This doubling has its limits because there would eventually be a mathematical number larger than the number of persons existing. Why a break in the growth of the number? Because distant cousins marry one another without knowing they are distant cousins, a matter addressed thoughtfully in A. J. Jacob's recent *It's All Relative: Adventures Up and Down the World's Family Tree*.

This doubling means I have about nine thousand ancestors in the generation of the Jamestown colony. It also explains how my first other-than-Teague ancestors in what was to become the United States appeared at roughly the same time as those in Jamestown. I make note here of two of those, Henry Soane and Christopher Branch. Henry Soane was a successful land holder at and near Jamestown, and he served in the Virginia House of Burgesses in 1652–1655, 1658, 1660, and 1661 and as its Speaker. Soane was the grandfather of "the original" Thomas Jefferson who was the grandfather of President Thomas Jefferson. Christopher Branch also served in the House of Burgesses.

How can I comprehend the massive number of ancestors in the distant generations past of Henry I of England, William the Conqueror, Louis I of France, Charlemagne, Charles Martel, and Siegbert I? Does it impress me that I am descended from their lines? Of course it does, but so too are hundreds of thousands of other persons, including readers of this paragraph, some of whom have researched and verified their descents and others who have not yet done so.

4

Durham and West Durham

W HAT IS THERE TO KNOW ABOUT DURHAM AND ITS West Durham?

In his 2002 *Durham: A Bull City Story*, former *Durham Morning Herald* and *Durham Sun* columnist Jim Wise observed that "Durham is a product of coincidence (which some believe is God's way of working incognito) and unintended consequences." There is much to support his conclusion, and there is much to learn as to how he came to it.

Durham city and Durham County were named in recognition of Dr. Bartlett Durham. His gift of four acres to a railroad began its emergence as a city named in recognition of that gift. Bartlett Durham was born in 1824 to William Durham and his wife, Polly (*née* Snipes), in Orange County about eight miles southwest of a township that in 1819 had been organized and named Chapel Hill, which would in time contain the University of North Carolina. Durham never formally enrolled but said he attended classes at the University of Pennsylvania's medical school in Philadelphia. As was the case then with clerks "reading the law" in order to become lawyers, it is assumed that Durham "read" medicine under the tutelage of doctors. Perhaps he could not afford the tuition at Penn. Upon his return to Carolina, he purchased land for $182, on which much of early downtown Durham was to be built. He boarded at Andrew Turner's house on the property of which Liggett and Myers later built their principal factory. He then built his own house, referred to as "Pandora's Box," near what is now Main Street in the vicinity of the later built Durham Hosiery Mill. Upon learning that the North Carolina Railroad needed land for a station and an owner to the north had sought too high a price for his acres, Durham donated those four acres for the train stop. The site would first bear his name as Durhamville, then briefly as Durham Station. As soon as 1853, the US Postal Office network recognized the location simply as Durham. Medical doctor though he was, Dr. Durham became the first railroad agent in the vicinity, an agent with a liquor license, and a part owner of a general store. As proof that politics can be inconsistent, he was elected to the North Carolina General Assembly on a seemingly contradictory temperance platform, one opposed to liquor and his own licensed sale of it. He died in 1859 from pneumonia and still a bachelor at only age thirty-four. Ten years later, the General Assembly incorporated the site as the City of Durham and in 1881 created Durham County out of portions of Orange and Wake Counties. Dr. Durham had been buried at his mother's Snipes family burial ground at Antioch Cemetery in Orange County, but in early 1934 and at the suggestion of Durham civic leaders, he was moved to a burial site with high visibility at the entrance to the city's new extension of its Maplewood Cemetery on West Chapel Hill Street. He rests under a man-high tombstone that lists in chiseled granite an incorrect middle name and erroneous years of his birth and his death. So much for political haste in selling municipal cemetery lots. By the centennial of Durham's founding, it was widely known as a city of tobacco, textiles, and medicine.

Civil War's End Near Durham

Jim Wise also reminds us in his *Durham: A Bull City Story* that a small town can have big stories. Durham attests to that through its Civil War, tobacco, textiles, and higher education places in our nation's history.

Half a dozen years after Dr. Durham's death, the area found a firm place in the annals of the end of the Civil War. Everyone remembers Confederate Gen. Robert E. Lee's April 9, 1865, Palm Sunday surrender to Union forces at Appomattox Court House in southern Virginia, in large measure because it was his surrender to Union Gen. Ulysses S. Grant. Who recalls the larger surrender of Confederate forces that occurred later that month? It was near Durham. James and Nancy Bennett had lived in a farmhouse on its western outskirts since 1846. They were to lose three sons in that war. Wise informs us that Sherman's advance entered the state on March 1, an Ash Wednesday, a day on which its Episcopalians in services read the liturgical text from the prophet Joel: "Let all the inhabitants of the land tremble: for the day of the Lord cometh, for it is nigh at hand," truly a jarring text. He reports it was at the Bennetts' that Sherman, who knew to himself that Abraham Lincoln had been assassinated, and Confederate Gen. Joseph E. Johnston concluded their negotiations for the April 26 surrender of Confederate troops that were not surrendered by Gen. Robert E. Lee. It was that earlier surrender that President and Mrs. Lincoln were celebrating when they went to Ford's Theater on April 14. Lee was the commanding general of only the Army of Northern Virginia and had no authority to surrender the 32,000 under Johnson's direct command or others stretched from the Carolinas to Texas under other commands. This Bennett Place event was the largest surrender of the war. Interestingly, Gen. Sherman, the same man who ordered the burning of Atlanta, accepted such lenient terms proffered by Gen. Johnston that he found himself subjected to such ridicule in Washington that he was nearly ordered by Secretary of War Edwin Stanton to be court-martialed. The Bennett House surrender represented not only the practical end of Union-Confederate hostilities but also the beginning of a slow reconciliation toward a reunited nation. April 1865 has been referred to as "the month that saved America," but Wise points out it was the month that made Durham. A double-columned monument with an impressive crosspiece bearing the word UNITY and erected in 1923 stands near the farmhouse.

Durham's Brightleaf Tobacco

There is a connection between Union soldiers being in and about Durham and the significant increase in national, and eventually global, tobacco use that followed the war. Many of the soldiers knew that Durham was the place from which brightleaf yellow tobacco products had emerged, and they went looking for it, found much of it warehoused, and took it home, which further spread the awareness of its preferred taste and aroma. The tobacco empire resting on brightleaf did not begin with the Dukes or other owners. It started with the quick thinking of an enslaved man. Thankfully, his role has not been obscured.

The story found in Jim Wise's *Durham* tells us that an eighteen-year-old blacksmith named Stephen fell asleep on a rainy night in the summer of 1839 while curing his owner's tobacco for market. When he awoke, the curing fire had nearly gone out. No doubt thinking of the worst consequences for him, he rushed to find anything to restart it. He found a supply of charcoal, used it instead of traditional hardwood, and the six hundred pounds of curing tobacco above him turned yellow instead of brown. As Wise puts it, Stephen had unknowingly transformed the tobacco industry by producing brightleaf by "dumb luck and quick thinking." Proof was in the Danville, Virginia, market when brightleaf brought forty dollars per hundred-weight instead of the customary ten dollars. An auctioneer who benefitted from brightleaf sales in Danville was Chiswell Dabney Langhorne, the father of Nancy Langhorne, the future Viscountess Astor of England. Billions of dollars would be made in the aftermath of this brightleaf innovation as Durham, Winston-Salem, Kentucky's Louisville, and Virginia's Richmond competed to become the nation's cigarette-manufacturing capital.

Duke Family Emerges

While pouch tobacco was processed before and during the Civil War, Durham's George Washington Duke (known as Washington) and his two sons by his second marriage, Benjamin Newton Duke and James Buchanan "Buck" Duke, decided that there was money to be made if cigarettes could be uniformly pre-rolled at factories. They helped found an industry by doing that, made enormous sums of money for themselves, and provided livelihoods for many thousands of others. Duke's oldest of his three surviving sons, Brodie Leonidas Duke, the second son by his first wife, was also to have much to do with building Durham. Jim Wise reports that after Brodie left home following his father's refusal to move the family's business from its country setting into Durham Station, Brodie won the argument when the family moved its business in 1869 into Durham. In the meantime, Brodie had set up his own tobacco business on Main Street with the brand Semper Idem, meaning Always the Same. Against his father's opposition, he built the Trinity Park, the Duke Park, and North Durham neighborhoods on land he bought and developed. He moved successfully into textiles with his Pearl Cotton Mill. In 1878, he built a two-and-a-half-story brick tobacco warehouse, which still stands as a remodeled office building. He expanded into retail stores and furniture manufacturing. According to an 1890 edition of the *Durham Recorder,* his accomplishments were as long as any other of the town's businessmen, including his father's. It was not until he made his own name that in 1879 he rejoined W. Duke Sons & Company. That was not long after its first outside investor, Baltimore financier George W. Watts, had been brought into it. Brodie hated Watts, using that verb publicly. As Wise writes, Brodie was the black sheep of the family, and in the end, his two brothers won the battle for their dad's heart. While they are entombed spectacularly in Duke Chapel, Brodie's remains are in the Duke mausoleum at Old Maplewood Cemetery, along with others from Washington Duke's first family.

Like yeoman farmers throughout the state's midsection, Washington Duke toiled on a farm, not a plantation. If he owned a slave, research and criticisms of tobacco smoking would have ascertained it by now. He did not volunteer for Confederate military service, was conscripted into its navy, and captured by the Union Navy. At war's end, he was taken from a Union prison to coastal North Carolina, where he was put ashore in New Bern to walk to his farm. In the summer of 2015, a reenactor walked from it to that farm, a shorter trek than on the roads of 1865. It took the reenactor two weeks. The manufacture of muslin pouches for pouch tobacco and the production of other cotton textiles, especially hosiery, gave Durham its second postwar industry.

West Durham

The Dukes and Julian Carr caused Trinity College in rural Randolph County to relocate to Durham. The resulting Duke University, its medical school, and hospital were to become nationally renowned and internationally known, and they were located in West Durham. Between their tobacco empire and the renaming of Trinity as Duke, there lay another Duke success. The family's needs for industrial, asset, and income diversifications led them to underwrite financially the experience of William A. Erwin Sr. and his family in the manufacturing of pouches, denim cloth, and sheets, and pillowcases. Erwin Mills was also in West Durham. Erwin's brother-in-law, Edward Knox Powe, known as E.K., helped manage Erwin Mills and laid transformative foundations in Durham's public education system.

Unlike the Dukes, Erwin was not self-made. He was born in 1856 to a wealthy Burke County planter. A two-year graduate of the Agricultural and Mechanical College of Kentucky University in Harrodsburg, now the University of Kentucky in Louisville, he became a salesman with Holt, Gant & Holt, part of the textile empire being built by his uncle E. M. Holt and situated in Burlington. As treasurer and general manager of E. M. Holt Plaid Mills, he acquired in-depth knowledge about the making of cloth. Erwin Mills grew rapidly to become one of the state's largest. Hardheaded businessman that he was, Erwin was "in matters of large public welfare zealous, active and devoted." He earned an "enviable reputation" and income and became a donor to Trinity College, Duke University, St. Mary's School in Raleigh, the Chapel of the Cross in Chapel Hill, St. Philip's Episcopal Church in Durham, and

St. Peter's Hospital in Charlotte. Each received what we refer to now as transformative philanthropic gifts, as did other organizations. When in the 1970s my wife and I owned a farm in the Virginia countryside past Leesburg and Waterford, we met Agnes Gant Harrison, daughter of Roger Gant of Gant fabrics fame and the wife of Burr Powell Harrison Jr. of one of Virginia's most prestigious families, and appreciated deeply their charitable commitments throughout that area.

How had West Durham arisen on the western edge of the original Durham? Preservation Durham's "Old West Durham" narrative details answers:

> The large neighborhood of West Durham began its development as a tiny settlement known as Pin Hook (sometimes described as "Pinhook" – ed.). On the Hillsborough Road (the present W. Main St.) one mile west of Durham, Pin Hook was little more than a traveler's rest when the railroad town of Durham was being established in the early 1850s. It was located southwest of where the Erwin Cotton Mills would stand and consisted merely of a lodging house, camping grove, grog shop and well. By the 1880s, some of Durham's prosperous businessmen seeking a less urban environment were building their homes in the east end of West Durham. It was not until the 1890s that this sparsely settled area began to experience the development that would quickly transform it into the community of West Durham. At the turn of the last decade of the 19th century, the Dukes and George W. Watts recognized that there were tremendous profits to be made in the textile industry. These men were eager to invest their enormous tobacco industry earnings; it was characteristic of them that they should choose to do so at home when there were scores of other good opportunities across the country. In 1892, Benjamin N. Duke secured

William Allen Erwin to be general manager and secretary-treasurer of the new textile enterprise. Erwin, a member of the pioneering Holt family of Burlington, NC, had gained invaluable experience managing the family's mills. Erwin contributed $40,000 of the initial $125,000 capitalization of the new company; the Dukes and George W. Watts provided the balance. The mill was named for the Duke's new business partner, but the product they decided to manufacture – muslin for tobacco bags – was an appropriate complement to their original, successful endeavors. Erwin joined the venture in the spring of 1892, and by the end of the year the mill village of West Durham was taking shape. Erwin oversaw every aspect of starting up the new factory, from purchasing the machinery to selecting the locations for the factory buildings and laborers' houses. Undoubtedly, many houses had been constructed for the workers who manned the 13,000 spindles and 400 looms in the main building. The swift success of the Erwin Cotton Mills may be attributed to a combination of local capital, Erwin's managerial talent, and the low price of both cotton and labor; it resulted in rapid expansion of the factory and surrounding community. Within a year, the mill stopped manufacturing muslin and became the first southern mill to successfully produce denim. In 1895, the mill employed 375 workers. One year later, the main factory building was more than doubled in size to accommodate approximately 1000 workers. The 1898 Sanborn Insurance Maps show that the dye house also was enlarged, cotton warehouses were built, and a large brick warehouse was appended to the office building. Considering that the mill employed 1,000 workers in 1896 and operations continued to expand, it is likely that the Erwin Cotton Mills' approximately 440 houses covering more than fifteen blocks around the West Durham mill [known as Erwin Mills Village – ed.] were completed about the turn of the century. A great number of these houses survive today in neat rows of identical forms situated close to the street, presenting a clear idea of the character of West Durham mill village. The finest houses in West Durham were built by three textile executives who not only were all associated with the Erwin Cotton Mills, but also were related to each other. Around the turn of the century, William Allen Erwin, his brother-in-law Edward Knox Powe, who also was an executive of Erwin Cotton Mills, and Erwin's brother, Jesse Harper Erwin, an executive of the Durham Cotton Manufacturing Co. and one of the directors of the Erwin Cotton Mills, all constructed large houses. Textile mills were characterized by a combination of paternalism and economic sanctions that included long hours, low wages, and poor living conditions. Yet in some ways Erwin, encouraged by Ben Duke, managed to do better than many of his fellow textile manufacturers. Erwin earned widespread notice for reducing the work days at his factories to eleven hours and for refusing to employ underage children. He also provided the West Durham community with a park before Durham had any city parks. Erwin Cotton Mills built Erwin Auditorium in the middle of the park. William Allen Erwin and Edward Knox Powe were known for their interest in the education and religious life of their employees' families. Powe in particular was concerned that West Durham's children receive a primary education; he also assisted many of those who were academically inclined to pursue a college degree as well. The community of West Durham was so large that by around 1910 it had two grade schools.

On Ninth Street, West Durham Graded School No. 2 was in an even larger two-story frame building that had an auditorium on the second floor. This building was later replaced by brick buildings and the school was renamed in honor of Powe. The growth of the local business district paralleled development throughout West Durham. By 1940, the neighborhood had filled out to its present boundaries and had been incorporated into the City of Durham.

As textile manufacturing in search of cheaper labor went overseas decades later and tobacco fell under enormous public health pressures from Washington, Durham slid into rough economic times, narrowly avoiding what could have been far worse times. It was E. K. Powe's grandson, E. K. Powe III, who co-conceived, cofounded, chaired, and helped assure Research Triangle Park. Located between Durham and its Duke University and North Carolina Central University, Raleigh and its North Carolina State University and other colleges, and Chapel Hill and its University of North Carolina, it and they assured a rebirth to Durham. It was not Charlotte with its national banking headquarters, and it was not Raleigh with its state government, but Durham now had a revitalizing economic strategy, tactics, and reality. Powe was joined in that venture by Gov. Luther Hodges, a retired textile executive who went into politics, became governor on the death of Durham County's Gov. William Umstead, and became President John Kennedy's and Lyndon Johnson's secretary of commerce. He was joined in Research Triangle's development by Durham banker George Watts Hill Sr., Winston-Salem's Wachovia Bank and Trust Company retired president Archie Davis and chairman Robert M. Hanes, Greensboro businessman and builder Romeo Guest, UNC-tied sociologist George Simpson, and others who saw to its vision and early successes.

The Triangle now encompasses more than fifty-five square miles of corporate offices, hotels and restaurants, shopping centers, schools, parks, and neighborhoods. It has global attraction to corporate research, development, sales, and attendant management. Its Cary has a population of over 160,000, making it the seventh largest municipality and largest unincorporated town in the state, compared to what appeared to be only several thousand residents when we moved to Florida in 1957 and Durham had a population of only slightly over 70,000. E. K. Powe III brought the area into the twenty-first century of new commerce, education, and technologies.

5

Childhood Continues

W HAT ELSE SHOULD BE WRITTEN OF MY EARLY YEARS?
Well, I survived them, but I had to do so by overcoming
more than ordinary illnesses. Do I recall them? Yes, but not much about
the earliest ones. There is a reason, and it deserves a few words. At a
Renaissance Weekend in Charleston that I was attending, a panel of
neurologists explained that a percentage of brain cells are sloughed off
by the age of two or three, a consequence of which is we have no ability
to recall our earliest years. Their discussion caused me to wonder about
my earliest memories. Over time, I came to the conclusion that my
earliest recalled memory is of an incident on a train bound from Raleigh.
My mother challenged a porter of shortchanging her as we were headed
to Boston to visit her sister and family, and an argument ensued. It must
have been the tension level that locked this into my memory. I would
have been about three. I remember being held over Dad's shoulder on a
bitterly cold, full moonlit night while leaving his parents' house toward
our curbside car. I would much later read in his *Fifty Years a Rancher*
autobiography Charles Collins Teague's theorem that "Experiences of

childhood remain the longest in our memories" because they are the furthest away from our present.

As to my early illnesses, bronchial asthma dominated my daytime and nighttime lives until puberty began. I fought and fought to breathe, and a consequence was enlarged lung capacity. During the first grade, I was hospitalized for what seemed like endlessly boring days with hepatitis. I came out of that captivity with a permanently spotted lung. While walking with my mother near the intersection of West Durham and South Gregson Streets, an automobile broke a u-channeled metal pole at nearly ground level and sent it parallel to the ground into my back and my mother's legs. It was a bizarre coincidence, for we were walking toward an appointment at our Dr. Angus McBride's office. I recall operating room surgical instruments on carts and green-tiled walls before I went under to have my tonsils removed at McPherson Hospital.

While not a memory of an illness, I recall being grilled on my ABCs one summer evening, without the completion of which my parents and brother were not going to take me with them to a movie. I should have reasoned that the odds were in my favor because they were intending to go and had no babysitter if I failed this inquisition. I recalled them in their proper order. Sometime later, my brother, then known by his middle name, Merle, placed an unknowingly live .45 bullet into a toy gun, pulled the trigger, and blew a hole through the front screen door. From where this bullet came no one recalled, because Dad owned no pistol, and the Beck brothers, recently returned from military service and living several houses away, did not hand out ammunition. It provoked considerable neighborhood conversation as parents asked what toy gun had a firing pin. A cap gun came closest. I recall I sold to a scrap metal collector for the impressive sum of one quarter a pedal-powered rusty children's car that Dad had bought for one of us. Dad advised me sternly that evening that it had been a bad transaction on my part. There was a positive side to this in that it was a lesson in knowing value-based price negotiation when the motivation of the other party is to take advantage of you. I remember on many later Saturday mornings being dropped off at the Rialto Theater in downtown Durham for westerns, other serials, and cartoons amid the unchaperoned rowdiness of hundreds of sugar-high screaming kids. It was pandemonium, and we were always admonished by parents to keep our eyes open for "the bad kids" from East Durham. I wonder now if East Durham parents told their children to keep their eyes open for "the bad kids" from West Durham.

I was older when I was allowed to go to Erwin Auditorium and plunk down a nickel to watch full-length movies, walking the dozen or so blocks to and back with my brother and a bunch of other kids. The auditorium was the community center for Erwin Mills' workers and their families and served West Durham's public meeting needs. Its auditorium also hosted concerts, plays, and lectures. When chairs were removed, it served as a gymnasium for basketball and other athletic activities. Those chairs were properly aligned in rows for only a few seconds after its lobby doors were opened to kids. I recall seeing Elizabeth Taylor in *National Velvet* there. Its release date had been less than seven months after my birth, an indication the auditorium did not host first-run movies. It did not survive 1984's construction of the West Durham Expressway.

There were no public kindergartens in Durham as I watched my five-year-older brother head most weekday mornings to E. K. Powe School on Ninth Street, originally named West Durham Graded School No. 2. Families had to have the money for private preschool education, and we did not, so we kids from poorer families spent our days playing in neighborhood homes, yards, and streets and in E. K. Powe's schoolyard after its classes and afternoon athletic programs were over. I learned to ride my first bicycle on the late-December-hardened baseball field and played various ball games there in warmer weather. Soccer had not yet been introduced to elementary school athletics.

When Durham undertook in 1949 the centennial of its 1849 unincorporated founding as Durham Station, I managed to get enough pocket change from my mother and elsewhere to lose all of it trying to win at county fair–like games whose temporary stalls had been set up downtown at Five Points. I would have been slightly older than my fifth birthday. It was a lesson for me on there never being a need to risk monies in adventures in which opposing interests control the outcome.

Sylvia Cayton and her brother, Lawrence Jr., lived with their parents in the other apartment of our duplex. It was Sylvia who told me that Santa Claus existed only in spirit, though her disclosure was far more bluntly offered than my capture of it here can be. Butch Rhew and his family of no known relation to my mother's father's family lived across the street. The tobacco snuff-dipping elderly ladies there would send my considerably underage brother to a store with cash and a handwritten note, one I assume saying that it was okay for the clerk to sell the product to the underage bearer of both.

Directly across the street from us was the Ferrentino family, the breadwinner having come to Durham from Italy to be a stonemason for the building of Duke's collegiate gothic-styled West Campus and the Duke Chapel anchoring its principal quadrangle. I believe he died before either my birth or my age of cognition, but his widow and their adult daughter still lived there.

Two houses from us was the Carson and Virginia Cardon family. I recall easily the smell of fresh-cut cedar in his woodworking shop at the rear of their property. He handcrafted nearly everything, from cedar chests and chests of drawers to birdhouses and toys.

On the other side of the Cardons were the Becks, both of whose sons, Charles and Calvin, fought in the Marines Corps in the South Pacific. They brought back from their training at Camp Lejeune and Parris Island and their battles in the Pacific so much bounty that every boy on the street received something from them. Mine, probably regifted by my brother, was a hard, plastic practice bayonet for an M1 carbine. My brother was like a younger brother to them. His trove included a sword, a helmet with a noticeable bullet-dinged dent in it, and a bugle, the attempted blowing of which while standing on a limb up a tree alongside our duplex caused his fall, broken leg, and five months of confinement, most of it wearing a leg cast. Our cousin, Nancy O'Briant, reported that his fall was made more certain by his new toy cowboy holster and pistols brought back from a shopping spree for family youngsters by her father, Paul, when he attended an Army-Navy football game in Philadelphia. How many hands are required to hold on to a tree when you are calling forth imaginary troops with a bugle with one hand and shooting at them with the other? Three.

Of course there were other families on our street known to our parents but not to my brother and me.

The Dukes' Empire Grows

The Dukes had the business acumen in 1885 to acquire a license from Virginia's James Albert Bonsack to deploy in their manufacturing his newly patented automated cigarette-making machine. A single machine's output was two hundred per minute, in sharp contrast with hand-rolled production of four per minute, the installations of which gave the Dukes 90 percent of the American pre-rolled cigarette market by 1890.

American Tobacco Company was one of the twelve original members of the Dow Jones Industrial Average in its 1896 premier. Their successes in sourcing, manufacturing, marketing, jobs creation, bolstered tax revenues, and dividends to shareholders was too much for Washington bureaucrats to tolerate. They undertook in 1907 during President William Howard Taft's administration to bust the Tobacco Trust. There are lessons here about the unintended consequences of regulation. That busting had by 1911 resulted in the surviving American Tobacco Co. as well as Liggett and Myers, R. J. Reynolds, Philip Morris, Brown & Williamson, and P. Lorillard Co. Not to be bested by this intervention in their business prowess, the Dukes structured an alliance in the United Kingdom through which a merger with British-American Tobacco by BAT's acquisition of the Dukes' residual American Tobacco Co. occurred, resulting eventually in world domination of cigarette markets, particularly in Great Britain, China, and Japan. A massive increase in Duke family wealth and eventual Duke Endowment assets resulted.

BAT's principal global competition became Britain's Imperial

Tobacco, one of whose heirs, Dr. Catherine Mary Hamilton Wills, daughter of Sir Hugh David Hamilton Wills (known as Sir David) MBE and CBE, is a professional acquaintance. We served together on the Salzburg Global Seminar and Twenty-First Century Trust boards, the latter nonprofit corporation having been founded by her father in 1987 and later chaired by Lord Patten of Barnes, Her Majesty's last governor and commander-in-general of Hong Kong before its 1977 handover to the People's Republic of China. I also think of this trust busting when I am in the Taft Dining Room at the University Club of Washington, as the portrait of the only president also to be chief justice of the Supreme Court of the United States stares down at me. When our oldest son, Cornell, was about six, his leg and Will Taft V's leg were in the same burlap sack in a race near Virginia's Chancellorsville battlefield. What a small world it is.

If there is an irony of the forced breakup of the Dukes' tobacco empire, and there is, it requires a fast-forward to 2016. As the war on tobacco raged in the United States, cigarette sales dropped precipitously, an intent of that war. This war would overshadow the war on drugs as movies increased entertainment depictions of illegal drug use and thereby its social acceptability. By 2014, the R.J. Reynolds tobacco empire had acquired American Tobacco and announced its intent to acquire competitor Lorillard Inc. for $25 billion. The combination of these private and public actions resulted in a conglomerate that controlled 80 percent of American cigarette sales. In over a century, the government that had busted the Dukes' near monopoly of 90 percent signed off in 2015 on the creation of an 80 percent duopoly in domestic production. The story does not end there. In 2016, BAT made a $47 billion offer to Reynolds American to buy the 58 percent interest that it did not already own, a BAT move intended to create the world's largest listed tobacco company by market share and revenue. So much for government trust busting in the public's and consumers' interests.

What happened to Durham's tobacco empire? The last of its once thirteen tobacco auction warehouses closed in 1987. Original construction of tobacco plants and warehouses was with brick and mortar, which was the right judgment, as Durham now enjoys its revival. Plants and management offices have been converted to condominiums, apartments, restaurants, and retail shops. Some of them are near the Durham Bulls old baseball field, with the mechanical bull that snorted smoke on the occasions of homeruns, a team, a park, and a bull made more famous in the Kevin Costner, Susan Sarandon, and Tim Robbins 1988 movie *Bull Durham*. The Bulls and bull have relocated downtown.

Duke University Emerges

How do some of these events relate to Duke University?

The Dukes gave the necessary funds, and industrialist Julian Carr gave a gift of sixty-two acres as inducements to Trinity College to move about seventy miles to Durham. What was the attractiveness of Trinity to the Dukes and their colleagues? Trinity had begun in 1838 as Brown's Schoolhouse, a private subscription school founded by Methodists and Quakers under the leadership of the Rev. Hezekiah Gilbert Leigh, an educator associated with the founding of Virginia's Randolph-Macon. In that it had grown by 1841 to two buildings and nearly seventy students, the state issued a charter with a name change to Union Institute Academy. Ten years later, Union was renamed Normal College to indicate its education of teachers, and with financial assistance from the Methodist Episcopal Church, it became in 1859 Trinity College. In 1887, Yale University–educated John Crowell became Trinity's president. He substantially revised its curricula, built a campus-wide research library, and set out to persuade its trustees that the university should relocate to an urban area in order to attract improved faculty, more students, and enlarged financial resources. After considering other proposals, the Duke and Carr offer on behalf of Durham was accepted, and Trinity moved to it in 1892. Trinity's, the Dukes's, and others' interests met in that move. What still required being addressed were how to differentiate this Trinity from the many Trinitys and how to admit women as Oberlin College in Ohio, Stanford University in

California, Washington University in Missouri, and others were already doing.

Carr was to play a pivotal role in the second matter. So committed to women securing the right to vote in public elections was he that Elizabeth Cady Stanton and Susan B. Anthony recognized his importance early. Carr was also instrumental in the education of Methodist minister Charles Soong and the financing of Soong's Shanghai-based Bible-publishing and banking empires. In turn, Soong became active in Dr. Sun Yat-Sen's attempts to establish a modern republic in China and was the father of history's three Soong sisters, each of whom was educated at Wesleyan College in Macon, Georgia, and one additionally at Wellesley College in Massachusetts. One married Dr. Sun, the founder of the Republic of China and its Kuomintang nationalist political party, the KMT; the second married Gen. Chiang Kai-shek, Dr. Sun's successor as head of the KMT, by then in opposition to the Communists, an effective warlord against the Japanese invaders, and the founder of the Republic of China on Taiwan; and the third married K'ung Hisang-his, a wealthy banker of substantial influence. On a 1981 American Council of Young Political Leaders (ACYPL) delegation to China, I visited Dr. Sun's residence in Guangzhou, known to Westerners as Canton. Dr. Sun had been one of Hong Kong University's (HKU) first students when it was in 1887 the Hong Kong College of Medicine for Chinese and returned to it in 1911 after its change in name and status and the Sun-led overthrow of China's imperial monarchy. His statue adorns today a relaxing lily pond at the heart of its present campus. It is at HKU that the Fund for American Studies, whose board of trustees I chair, undertakes its American Institute on Political Economy for outstanding university students from throughout Asia. Again, a small world.

Julian Carr's roles in Trinity College relocating to Durham to become Duke University years later have been widely known. While he advanced women's rights, no record is known to me of him having advanced the rights of racial minorities, including especially African Americans in and around Durham or in North Carolina, the South or anyplace else. He might have strategized the visibility of advancing women's rights to cover his opposition to others' struggles for their rights. Duke University today is not in many ways the Duke University of its founding, but it has taken new measures to acknowledge Carr's roles in its founding as a necessary step, among others, toward its future, including removing recognitions of his roles. In doing so, it has put greater distance between Carr's roles and the university of today. Tomorrow's Duke University will depend on what else it does. When I lived in Durham as a child, its centrally-located junior high school was named in recognition of Julian Carr. I have not lived there since 1954, but Durham too will need to continue to address these issues. It's one of the reasons I make contributions to Preservation Durham.

In addition to tobacco and textiles, the Dukes founded in 1905 the Southern Power Company, an electricity-generating company that through its merger with other Dukes-founded power companies became Charlotte, NC-headquartered Duke Power, now Duke Energy, our country's largest public utility. They also acquired massive land and timber holdings now known as the Duke Forests. Our Teague family photographs on Easter mornings were taken in the Sarah P. Duke Gardens adjoining the university and amid its azaleas, rhododendrons, fountains, and Japanese koi ponds.

A Washington Duke follow-on gift in 1896 to Trinity was made upon the assurance its doors would be open to women. He made the case to the college's board that his daughter could not have attended the all-male Trinity, the national trend was toward coeducation, and the school ought to be in the leadership of this reform. It was not an easy task and took two years for agreement to be reached. Win though he did, his argument prevailed only in part, for while women were to be admitted and educated with the same rights and privileges as men, they were to live and study at a campus separate from men. The second matter, that being there were too many colleges named Trinity, was resolved when this one's name was changed in 1924 to Duke University in recognition of their leadership and gifts, including Buchanan Duke's 1924 establishment of the Duke Endowment with a corpus that would now be $1.4 billion. Washington Duke's sons were involved in these transfers of wealth, among these additional reasons, to honor their father. Their investments and their charitable gifts aside, they used their wealth to build residences on Fifth Avenue across from New York City's Central Park. Two remain, one at 1 East Seventy-Eighth Street, which is now New York University's Institute of Fine Arts.

Cigarette smoking's adverse health effects are now widely known, but little medical evidence of those effects existed in the Dukes' lifetimes, albeit logical deductions argued against smoking. Tobacco smoking had become an American habit during our colonial era, centuries before medical research determined its risks, while another inhaled smoking product, marijuana, became a similar habit centuries later, without the injunction of lessons learned from tobacco smoking. Tobacco sales may be prohibited someday, but marijuana is being increasingly legalized. Popularity is popularity, and habits are habits.

Buchanan Duke's only child, Doris Duke, inherited at age twelve much of her father's estate upon his 1925 death. She was known as "the world's richest little girl" at the time of that inheritance, its present equivalent being about $800 million. She preserved and grew it, even against her own mother's attempts over nearly forty years to peel it from her through various schemes, leaving approximately $1.3 billion at her 1993 death to the Doris Duke Charitable Foundation. Her uncle Benjamin Duke's descendants included Angier Biddle Duke, who was President John F. Kennedy's chief of protocol and President Lyndon B. Johnson's ambassador to Spain and later to Denmark. Few of the Duke family's residences survive in Durham, but Angier Biddle Duke's mother's house remains on a hillside near Hope Valley Country Club.

6

Religion among Teague, Lasater, and Britt Families

Two blocks from our family's Eighth Street house and on West Markham Avenue is Asbury Methodist Church. Dad's parents, Richard Monroe Teague and Naomi Iola Lasater, were married there in 1904. He was seventeen, and she was eighteen. Founded in 1893, Asbury's present building was not the one in which they were married, but the original was, and the new structure is only about fifty yards from where her mother, Jeannette Jackson Burke Lasater, lived at 719 Sixth Street, now 719 Clarendon.

Introducing the subject of religion through the fact of their marriage, some additional thoughts need expression in respect to our families' religions. I regard these beliefs as valuable contexts.

My paternal grandfather, Richard Teague, was raised not only a Baptist but a Southern Baptist, and not only a Southern Baptist but a Freewill Baptist. Their congregants participate in foot washing as acts of penance for sin and humbleness in the spiritual presence of their Lord. My paternal grandmother's birth family was most probably Methodist. I think this because the dominant religions in her childhood's Chatham

County geography were Baptist and Methodist, and she and her mother chose Asbury Methodist for her wedding.

My grandmother's older sister, Martha Ann Lasater Britt, Aunt Matt to us and Mattie to others, was an Episcopalian attending the newly formed St. Joseph's Episcopal Church at West Durham's intersection of Main and Ninth Streets. Aunt Matt's granddaughter, The Very Reverend Martha J. Horne, is not only an Episcopal priest educated at Virginia Theological Seminary (VTS) in Alexandria, the Protestant Episcopal Church of the United States' "missionary seminary," but was also the first woman dean and president of an Episcopal seminary in the United States, that institution being VTS. Through the services of its faculty, students, and graduates, VTS serves the United States and the Church of England Communion globally.

Martha and I had not seen one another since childhood when we met with spouses in tow at a dinner dance at Christ Church Alexandria. Christ Church is known as "George Washington's church" even though it is not alone in that respect. It does have custody of the Bible on which his hand rested when he was sworn in as the new nation's president. It is also one of many churches associated with the Lees of Virginia. Robert E. Lee attended it from the age of three and was confirmed there with two daughters in 1853 at his age of forty-six. Lee had married Martha Washington's great-granddaughter by her first marriage and thereby George Washington's step-great-granddaughter. She was Mary Anna Randolph Custis and an ardent antislavery activist as well as artist and author. In the context of these sentences, my grandparents' marriage across denominational lines recalls that my wife, Jessica Townsend, had been a Congregationalist but felt comfortable in this—new for her Episcopal faith—and in this church. There, she organized Mothers & Others for young mothers sometimes in need of peer communication on their probably frustrating attempted remaking of their husbands and the more vital shepherding of their children. She was elected to and served on its governing vestry for three years.

St. Joseph's Episcopal Church, known as St. Joe's, is where Dad attended Sunday school during his childhood. It was not the only

Sunday school they attended on the same Sundays. How could that happen? Erwin Mills' William Erwin was intent on the founding of an Episcopal church in West Durham because St. Philip's in downtown was too far away in a time when families walked to places and when churches were neighborhood ones. Erwin's early step was to begin an Episcopal mission, a mission being a congregation preceding the formal organization of a church, in a room on the second floor of his Erwin Mills General Store. Affirming his strategy, that room became too small. After the required formalities of organization and construction, St. Joe's rose as a competitor for souls with Asbury Methodist, Greystone Baptist, and even St. Philips, but it took intermediate steps to assure success. It had become apparent to Erwin that there were still not enough children nor their accompanying parents attending St. Joe's. As a successful businessman, he knew the ways of attracting customers to new markets. His solution? Hold Sunday school on Sunday afternoons and give each youngster who attended a bag of candy at its conclusion. In this manner, young boys and girls could attend Greystone and other churches' Sunday schools on Sunday mornings, where they were given promises of hellfire and brimstone for misbehaving, but attend St. Joe's on Sunday afternoons, where they were given far less intimidating bags of candy. Dad and his two sisters found it within themselves to do this double duty for the Lord. In this manner, Dad was exposed to both Baptist and Episcopal instructions on the Word.

Dad's beliefs seemed to me to be those of many Episcopalians. He believed firmly in Jesus's summary of the law and the prophets found in John 13:34, "A new commandment I give unto you, That you love one another; as I have loved you, that you also love one another." That was his wider road to life.

Mother's beliefs were those of Southern Baptists. I would tease her in my adult years that Baptists were theologically more like Orthodox Jews in that they sought to live primarily by strictest obedience to rules, summarized by Jesus for later Christians in Mark 10:43: to wit, "And if your hand offend you: cut if off: it is better for you to enter into life maimed, than having two hands to go into hell, into the fire that never shall be quenched." That is the narrower road in this life and narrower gateway to the promised life hereafter.

I did not regard myself as a childhood theologian, for that would have been an absurdity, but I had worked toward an understanding of the commonalities and distinctions in my parents' beliefs. I appreciated my father's and my mother's points of view and found them instructive. I know and feel my faith, its simplicity and its intricacies. For me, it is summed most rationally and emotionally in George Frederick Handel's lyric: "I know my Redeemer liveth." When I am in London, I try as often as time and circumstance permit to visit St. George's Hanover Church within a short walking distance from his residence. I sit in a pew and listen on my iPhone to *The Messiah* or other Handel opuses.

I recognized my parents' religious views for what they contributed to my beliefs. I was baptized as a youth at University Baptist Church of Chapel Hill, which was more broadly Baptist than Southern Baptist. I attended St. Petersburg's Fifth Avenue Baptist Church when accompanying my mother and attended the Episcopal Cathedral Church of St. Peter when by myself or with classmates. After moving to Washington in 1964, I was confirmed on February 27, 1966, at St. John's Church at Lafayette Square, known as the Church of the Presidents, as it is across Lafayette Square from the White House and sometimes attended by presidents. I attended Episcopal churches in Washington, where the Cathedral Church of Saints Peter and Paul on Mount Saint Albans and Christ Church Georgetown were my architectural favorites. In those years, the Church of Ascension and St. Agnes on Massachusetts Avenue was my connection to that faith. Thereafter, I went to services at Leesburg Virginia's St. James and St. Andrews in Wellesley, Massachusetts. At every opportunity when in England, the Bahamas, Bermuda, Canada, South Africa, and other countries of its tradition, I attend Anglican churches. While London's Westminster and St. Paul's are splendid, I enjoy the smaller churches that populate London and rural communities, many of which have closed for lack of congregants and funds. I attended Roman Catholic churches, particularly when I represented at law one of the largest

Catholic vocational orders, the Salesians of Don Bosco, also known as the Salesian Missions. I attend, as well, other Christian denominations' churches and other faiths' synagogues and temples, mosques and shrines when in the Middle East, North Africa, and Asia. A Georgetown University–accredited multinational institute in Greece of the Fund for American Studies would emerge in 1996 in part from this variety of experiences and their perspectives, not only mine but others. These beliefs and experiences shaped my view that God's essence dwells within our individual nature, and our encounters with him consist of his presence in our daily lives whether we realize it or not.

7

More on Britts and Teagues

GRANDMOTHER TEAGUE HAD SIBLINGS, AND AMONG her sisters was Martha Ann Lasater Britt, my great-aunt Matt. Her husband was Robert Mullen Britt of Halifax County in northeast North Carolina. He was known as Mr. Britt, Robert, Bob, Uncle Bob, or Daddy Bob, depending on the relationship, and he was an electrician at Erwin Mills. The April 1, 1945, edition of its company newspaper, *Erwin Chatter*, reported, "Robert M. Britt has been employed with this company since March 1, 1898. He was born August 15, 1875, and is now 69 years old. Mr. Britt was an electrician at No. 4 Mill for many years and is still with the Electrical Department. He owns his own home at 904 Oakland Avenue, and is a familiar figure to all Erwin Cotton Mill employees."

We have discussed the Dukes, their wealth and their university, including the fact that they were collectively the largest shareholder in Erwin Mills. There is an additional Duke matter deserving our telling, but I cannot vouch for its credibility. It may or may not be true, but if it is, it is quite an account. According to my cousin Nancy Glenn, the Britt house on Oakland Avenue, which I recall going to on occasions, may have held an interesting place in the history of what became Duke University.

As the nineteenth century transitioned into the twentieth, railroad magnate Leland Stanford had in 1885 established what we refer to as Stanford University. John D. Rockefeller had in 1890 funded the establishment of the University of Chicago in the Midwest and in 1901 the Rockefeller University in New York City. Andrew Carnegie had in 1900 established the Carnegie University, which was to merge in 1967 with the Andrew and Richard Mellon–established Mellon Institute to become Carnegie Mellon University. Capitalists had become philanthropists, and higher education was among their beneficiaries.

The Dukes' contributions to Trinity College and the university are beyond dispute. The Duke sons' older sister, Mary Elizabeth Duke Lyon, who was Washington Duke's only daughter, had pressed within the family for the creation of a university. She died in 1893 at thirty-nine years of age, which associates her thought with the reasons for the move of Trinity to Durham. She pressed also for its coeducational nature, as the momentum for women's rights was well under way. We owe it to them and ourselves to recall that this was a period of widening roles of women in our society, as those reforms came from their hard work to achieve them. Any meeting, secret or otherwise, on the question of a new university and endowing it would have been about three decades after Mary Duke Lyon's death and around twenty after her father's. In these contexts, it was appropriate to name a university after their father and place his statue at the entrance of its campus.

George Washington Duke died in 1905. While his legacy in American industry was assured, his legacy in higher education remained inchoate. He had not graduated from a college or university, but he associated routinely with industrialists who had and had not. His sons pondered in the early 1920s, when they were themselves in their seventies, whether they should give an additional gift to Trinity College. Using our era's terminology, it is probable that the Dukes were the focus of institutional development encouragement from Trinity's leadership to make a transformative investment in it by way of major gifts. One or both sons may have felt they needed a gathering of close friends to weigh the question and reach a well-reasoned answer.

Beyond their valuing of the opinions of attending persons, they needed absolute secrecy about the meeting in case the consensus went against the proposed gifts. To have it known that they had considered and not given it would have been bad politics for them within the Trinity College and broader Durham communities. According to this account, the sons decided the meeting needed to be not at their offices or homes. They needed also a host who was known to them for an ability to closely guard the consideration's secrecy. Robert Britt is reported by Nancy Glenn to have been the person chosen to meet the tied needs of secrecy and place. Robert and Matt's house is said to have been that location.

The Dukes answered yes. Their gifts were the creation of the Duke Endowment and their $40 million foundational gift. The latter amount in today's value would be about $552 million. It strengthened Trinity College, set the stage for its transition into Duke University, and provided funds additionally to Furman University in South Carolina and other institutions. Before Buchanan Duke died in New York City in October 1925 at the age of eighty, he made provision for an additional $67 million testamentary bequest, which is now about $904+ million, the two gifts totaling about $1.456 billion in present value. The gifts lived up to donor intent, for they transformed Duke into a nationally and then internationally renowned institution of higher education.

I know of no way to authenticate the actuality of this meeting in the Dukes' and Britt's lives. Its secrecy would have tightly determined who attended it and which other few knew about it. The fact of the meeting was probably never disclosed to Trinity College, for such a disclosure would have undercut the desired appearance that it was solely the Duke family's decision, which, in the end, it was. Consequentially, it would not have become part of Duke's official in recognition of his reporting skills, he was transferred in 1936 to its New York City operations. Preferring foreign news, he moved from its general news desk to its foreign desk, where he in time became AP's foreign news editor. His 1963 obituary reported that he had "an illness in 1943 (which) caused him to reduce his news handling activities, and for a while he worked on the foreign news portion of AP Newsfeatures," not returning to regular duties until March 1947. Among his achievements, his work toward World War II's end in Europe became a foundation stone of his legend. His contacts behind the German-occupied lines kept him informed as to their awareness east of the English Channel of D-Day planning west of it. This gave him a significant scoop as sunrise on June 6, 1944, witnessed the largest armada of ships in a landing force in world history as it stretched along Normandy's coast. This scoop is puzzling to me because it occurred during his absence from the AP for reported reasons of ill health. What follows is sheer speculation on my part but, even so, is worth at least consideration.

Could Roberts's D-Day reporting and all that led up to it have been part of a larger role he had undertaken? Could he have been using his extensive information-gathering network in Europe to inform the US military of what it needed to know, while in cautious return informing the Europeans of enough of what they needed to know to bolster their morale? Could he have been working not for but rather with a US government agency responsible for the coordination for US armed forces as to what he had ascertained about situations behind enemy lines? As a matter of researched fact, he is *not* listed in the US government's December 23, 2010, disclosure of the Office of Strategic Services' personnel, but the OSS's personnel were not the only ones working with it, and the OSS was not the only US government agency involved in intelligence gathering, its analyses, and uses. The Military Intelligence Service is one. How could such a relationship have come about? It could have emerged from our government's awareness of the depth of his knowledge and analyses from reading articles drawn from his European network. Further, R. Harris Smith's 1972 *OSS: The Secret History of America's First Central Intelligence Agency* recounts

Russian "Prince" Sergei Alexandrovich Obolensky's extensive New York City presence, a presence shared with Roberts and their social circles. Obolensky was an émigré from the Russian Revolution to that city and had married quite well, an Astor in fact, becoming both a hotel baron and "the darling of the New York social set." From there, Obolensky headed the OSS's Operational Groups that worked with the French Maquis guerilla forces behind German lines before, at the time of, and after the Normandy invasion. If this conjecture is plausible, and with the war in Europe ending in August 1945, why did Roberts not return to his full-time role at the AP until 1947? Perhaps it was because he remained in ill health as publicly reported? Perhaps also, while military warfare in Europe had ended, political warfare for the future shape of Western Europe remained under way and unsettled until parliamentary elections in France, Italy, and elsewhere ended with assurances of coalition government formations several years after the war's end. Could Roberts's valuable roles have continued as a necessity of Allied governments? Is there anything else that adds to this conjecture? Yes, for despite his senior status, Roberts is beyond ordinarily difficult to research, even within the AP's own and other archives, which can be an indicator of a sanitized role.

Whether ill in health, convalesce, or rehabilitation, or "ill" in order not to have to be at his AP office on a regular work schedule, Roberts's AP reports and analyses were carried nationally and internationally for years. When he died in February 1963, his obituary was published widely for that and at least one other reason. As reported in it, his mother, Margaret, was "nationally known in literary circles as the teacher whom (Asheville's own) novelist Thomas Wolfe described as 'the mother of my spirit'." That is a profound recognition. How did it occur? Wolfe had been a student from the age of twelve at the Roberts' North State Fitting School until he left to enter UNC at age fifteen, not unusual in that era. He graduated in 1920, taking his master's from Harvard in 1922, and teaching at New York University for seven years beginning in 1924 while living a turbulent and often combative personal life. There are three places where Wolfe's and Roberts's lives overlapped:

in Asheville during their youths, although six years difference in age during childhood and adolescence is wide; at UNC when Roberts was there as a student and Wolfe returned occasionally; and during 1936–1938 in New York City. Wolfe died of tuberculosis of the brain in Baltimore at only thirty-seven.

UNC and Chapel Hill were startlingly different in their years there from what we have in our minds about both. Although chartered in 1789 with doors open for students in 1795 and the only public university in the United States to have awarded degrees to students in the eighteenth century, UNC was still a small institution. Wolfe's undergraduate enrollment was less than seven hundred. By contrast, its undergraduates now number over 18,000, its graduate students nearly 11,000, and its total faculty, administration, and staff are over 12,600. UNC reports its "students come from every country in the state, every state in the nation, and more than 100 other countries." Chapel Hill's population was only 1483 at the 1920 Census, in contrast with 2017's estimated population of over 57,000, to some degree having grown through annexations. The point of the much smaller community and much smaller university? Wolfe's and Roberts's opportunities for their discussions, which included UNC's academic departments and its Dialectic Society, newly formed Carolina Playmakers, Pi Kappa Phi fraternity, the *Daily Tarheel* offices, and Golden Fleece honor society as well as at university eating halls, Franklin Street and other restaurants and watering holes, and under many spreading red oaks.

As to Roberts, my cousin Nancy Glenn observed to me that "He was a big deal and also one of the nicest men you would ever want to meet." Manhattan was his and Verna's proverbial oyster, and they were important there. There is no wonder that her aunt, that is my Grandmother Teague, availed herself of opportunities to travel to New York City to stay with them.

Verna Roberts's grandmother and my great-grandmother Jeannette Jackson Burke Lasater died in the Britt's house on February 15, 1941. She was eighty-four years of age and had outlived husband, Robert, by fifty-three years and never remarried. The site of that house is now a parking lot for a neighborhood church.

Dad's Sisters

My Teague grandparents' first child and daughter was Ruby Beatrice, born in 1908 in Danville, Virginia, roughly sixty miles northwest of Durham. In their years, those miles were more daunting than in our age of interstate highways and faster vehicles. Why had the newly married couple gone to Danville? How I wish I had asked either of them the simple question, "Why?" Recollections of their grandchildren older than I are that our grandfather worked at one of the Dan River area cotton mills. Electrical power generated from, as well as water from, the Dan River were critical to it. From Grandfather's standpoint, Danville was also about halfway between Durham and the Mount Airy area, where he had been raised and many relatives still lived. When my father was born in Durham in December 1917, grandfather was working at Erwin Mills.

Their second daughter, Mary Jeannette (known as Jeannette), was born in 1910 in Durham, which confirms my grandparents had returned to it. Confirmation is found in *Hill's Durham City Directory 1905–1906* in which my grandfather is listed as a mill worker, married to Iola, and living at 8 West Main Street, which would have been downtown. His parents had moved to Durham too. They are listed as living only several hundred yards on Guess Road from my mother's and the Rhew family's Rose of Sharon Baptist Church, a coincidence thirty years before that had relevance to either family. One of grandfather's sisters, Myra Jane, was buried in its cemetery in 1912 as simply "M. J. Teague" because she had so disliked her given names that the family respected that attitude at her burial site. The 1931 edition of *Hill's* reports Granddad as a serviceman with Durham Dairy Ice Cream Co. and living at the 1005 Rosehill Avenue address that I know from my years with them. He was living at that address when he died in 1965.

Winston-Salem's Reynolds

Grandmother Teague informed me on several occasions that she knew Mary Katherine Smith Reynolds (known as Katherine) in Winston-Salem, much as she knew Sarah Duke in Durham. Katharine Smith Reynolds was thirty years younger than R. J. Reynolds, but her father, Zachary Taylor Smith, was a first cousin of Reynolds, so R. J. had known her since her childhood. College educated and working for his company as a secretary, she won a national contest for an advertising slogan for Reynolds' cigarettes, and the prize was $1,000, which was an astounding award in an era when most workers' wages ran from one to two dollars a day. It was said by many that R. J. Reynolds "got his money back" not only when he married her but also by the millions of cartons sold under her advertising slogan "I'd walk a mile for a Camel," one of the most famous of American advertising history.

R. J. Reynolds had devoted the early decades of adult life to distinguishing himself. His plants' 1875 combined production of 150,000 pounds of processed tobacco reached millions of pounds annually by 1890. That year and with his brother, William Neal Reynolds, and his bookkeeper, Henry Roan, R. J. founded the R. J. Reynolds Tobacco Company. Preceding Reynolds's innovations, tobacco had been finely cut and sold in pouches, later as individual smokes pre-rolled by women's hands with a top roller turning out about two thousand in an eleven-hour day, and still later as machine-rolled smokes. Reynolds's contribution to the industry was his concept of a *pack* of cigarettes, which he introduced in 1913. Within a year, he had sold 425 million packs, with ten packs to a carton. Technological innovations had taken tobacco from "roll your own" to factory-manufactured single cigarettes to a pack of twenty to a carton of ten packs. Both the industry and the individual smoker had gone from rolling a single smoke to a carton of two hundred factory-rolled cigarettes. While many Reynolds family members enjoyed the wealth created by R. J. and a son became mayor of Winston-Salem and treasurer of the Democratic National Committee, of northwest North Carolina. It is just south of the North Carolina-Virginia border near the foothills of the Appalachians. He was born and remained Richard Teague, which is to say not Dick, Rick, or Rich. You know this region if you know Grandfather Mountain and Blowing Rock to its west. If you recall CBS's 1960–1968 *The Andy Griffith Show* with Don Knotts, Frances Bavier, and the young actor and future director Ron Howard, you know both Griffith's hometown of Mt. Airy and its fictionalization as Mayberry. The original "Siamese twins," Chang and Eng Bunker, died there in 1874 within hours of one other, having purchased in 1839 a farm in nearby Traphill, at which they and their wives, local sisters, would beget twenty-two or twenty-three children, the number remaining in dispute but their gravesite near Mt. Airy not. Granddad was born in 1887 to William Swaim Teague and Mary Frances Durham. His father was born in 1852, a youngster during the Civil War, and a farmer and shoe cobbler in adulthood, and whose descent ran from John Teague's son Edward, born in 1660 at Tegg's Delight near the Chesapeake Bay's northern most reaches. Grandfather was one of thirteen children, not counting several of his mother's sister's children after that sister's death. He was sufficiently late in the birth order that his oldest siblings were more like aunts and uncles to him.

His father told him about his parents' farm being raided by Confederate soldiers for its livestock, perhaps because the family was known to support Abraham Lincoln. Straddling the Blue Ridge Mountains of the Appalachian chain, western North Carolina and eastern Tennessee have been predominantly Republican since those years, sending their members of Congress to Washington when the remainder of those two states were solidly Democratic. You get these years of western Carolina history in Charles Frazier's 1997 novel *Cold Mountain*, which was awarded the National Book Award for Fiction and became an Academy Award–winning and Sydney Pollack–produced 2003 movie. The real Cold Mountain is in the Pisgah National Forest with the Davidson River running along its base, and I drive around it and stop at its fly-fishing shop in as many Augusts as Michael and

Like most grandsons, I got to know my grandfather over time, especially because I had only one living grandfather, my maternal grandfather having died fifteen years before I was born. After our family moved to Florida in 1957, I returned to Durham in the summers of 1958 and 1959 to stay with Dad's parents, most of my day-to-day life there being tied to Granddad's schedule, even though I did spend some of those summer weeks with my grandmother Rhew and Aunts Nellie and Lois in another Durham neighborhood. When at my grandparent Teagues', my typical weekday entailed having breakfast at Ruby's café, followed by a drive to the apron of the tenth tee of Hillandale Golf Course's old layout, where he ran the concession stand. There, he sold soft drinks, premade sandwiches, boiled eggs, packaged snacks, and beer, with me helping him at both often-busy serving windows on all requests except beer, which I could not even touch because of the state's liquor laws and my underage status. At the end of the day, we would return to the clubhouse to drop off the day's receipts and head home, where dinner's contents were anyone's guess. Grandmother felt it was unfitting for her to cook, and my grandfather's skills in that respect were limited to vulcanizing fried eggs. They could have been used repeatedly in skeet competitions or as filler for Durham streets' potholes. This situation would often result in me crossing the street to Aunt Jeannette's to have a second dinner with the Tuckers, for she was an excellent cook. One glass of her sweet tea would keep my energy level up for the evening. At some point, she may have concluded that my flights to her house at dinnertime were becoming too frequent, for one evening her servings were stewed tomatoes, stewed corn, and stewed okra. It was the slimiest meal I had ever eaten, and it did slow my ardor for having dinner across the street. Sometimes Granddad and I would eat at the soda fountain at Broad Street Drug in the 1100 block of Broad Street near Watts Hospital. I'd usually have a BLT and a Coke and then wander around the store as he continued to talk with his friends. The store advertised fountain-served Sealtest Ice Cream, which may have indicated an affiliation from his ice cream salesman years. He was inclined near the end of the day to take a nip from his coat pocket flask, so discreetly I never once noticed it. The store is long gone, its footprint now part of Clements Funeral Service.

Granddad would listen on his bedroom radio to Durham Bulls' away games, but no roar of a stadium crowd was equivalent to the loudness of his snoring soon thereafter. There was no air-conditioning in their house, so we slept with the windows open. My remembrances of those nights include lightning storms on the two horizons visible from his bedroom's windows and the sounds of distant trains and barking dogs, especially on full moonlit nights. Grandmother slept on the hottest of summer nights on the screened-in sleeping porch. I recall vividly smells particular to their house and its age.

My recollections of Grandfather Teague's observations on living include:

- "The number of fish you catch usually depends on the number of hooks you have in the water." This is a valuable point to make, but I cannot remember ever fishing with him. It's most probable that this observation had less to do with fishing than it did with life generally, and that remains so.
- "When you're fishing someday with your own kids, remember that the line the fish hits is your kid's line." Never has there been a more important observation about teaching children the value of and required patience for fishing!
- "Jesus picked a board of twelve, and until he was resurrected, only a handful of them knew what he was talking about, and one was a traitor." This was certainly not an intended second-guessing of Jesus, but it does make an important point concerning boards and committees.
- In respect to matters of religion, when ministers of any faith were caught doing something quite un-Christian like, he would exclaim "The road to hell is paved with ministers."
- "You pay the most attention to a baseball game by listening to it on the radio." And, he might have added, doing nothing

else while you are doing so. If he was not in the Bull Durham's ballpark for a home game, his radio was his link to their away games, and he would sit with cupped ear beside it for the whole game.

- "The most important seat in a car is the front passenger seat. If you don't believe me, ask your grandmother. She's never sat anyplace else!"

- "I'd be one of the richest men in America if I could read tomorrow morning's newspaper today." In other words, he was always within the hours between the New York Stock Exchange closing bell and its opening bell the next morning of garnering enormous wealth, if only he could have reversed the sequence.

- "Some things you just don't buy only one of. You never know when you might need the second. Like cemetery lots." In time, he was buried in a lot that Aunt Ruby had bought in her consideration of this observation or in contemplation of his death, her death, both, or more. Grandmother Teague occupies the second, my dad the third, Ruby the fourth, her son Linwood the fifth, and Linwood's wife the sixth. There is no seventh. I have bought one of two lots in Alexandria, Virginia.

- "No one really needs to see a doctor." He saw very few of them and lived until he was seventy-seven, but he might have lived additional years if he had seen more of them. His family and his neighbors surely wished that he had seen an otolaryngologist.

- "When your time comes, you should die in a really unusual way. It makes a much more interesting obituary for the reader." He died in a hospital bed.

My recollections of Grandmother Teague's observations on how to live include:

- "The worst case seldom happens." Her lesson? Don't let fear of the worst case control you. I think with a similar intent, she would admonish, "Don't worry yourself crazy over a problem you don't yet have."

- "There should be a good reason to get out of bed in the morning, but there sometimes is not."
- "Don't do anything that your husband, children, or household help can do for you, and cooking is best done by someone else."
- "Don't ever turn down an opportunity to visit relatives. It would be rude not to accept their invitations."
- "It's important to know what's going on, even if it means being on the telephone most of the day learning about it."
- "Once your children have left home, what else is there to do except talk with your friends?"
- "A fur coat's better than a cloth coat year-round."
- "A phrase which has opposite meanings that only you know which one you intend is 'It was a once-in-a-lifetime experience,'" ranging from a great experience worth repeating to one so bad you'd never do it a second time.

A Transformative Gift

After we moved from Chapel Hill to St. Petersburg, Granddad decided to buy me a typewriter. I did not know it at the time. Cousin Nancy Glenn told me recently that her mother had shared with her that he felt I was "a good student and wanted to make life a little easier" for me. He bought me an Underwood and hid it under his bed with intentions of giving it to me, perhaps belatedly for my May 19 birthday or as an early Christmas gift. On the 1959 train ride from Florida to North Carolina, I finished reading Charles Darwin's *On the Origin of Species*, that year being the hundredth anniversary of its publication. Maybe that fact impressed him. As Nancy's recollection goes, Grandmother discovered the typewriter and broke it in whatever ways one can break a manual typewriter. I find this hard to accept, for it is a hostile act against me far more than against him. Living almost solely on retirement income, he had to have saved his dollars again and hidden the purchased successor typewriter elsewhere, perhaps at daughter Ruby's.

Without me knowing that it was his second attempt at making this gift, he gave me a Smith-Corona portable typewriter in a tan-colored metal case, and it accompanied me on my return travel to Florida and for many later years. I had no formal instruction in typing, but I worked hard at learning, moving from a very slow hunt-and-peck to a faster two-fingers-and-a-thumb hunt-and-peck that over time became even faster. When I moved from middle to high school, where a typing course was offered, I was automatically assigned to it. I went to the teacher and told her I did not need this course and why, but she had her doubts. I assumed she had heard similar opinions from other students. She gave me a sheet of paper and told me to roll it in and show her what I could do. I was understandably nervous, but I blasted sixty-two words onto paper with only one mistake. She told me only half laughingly to "Get out of here!" I thank my grandfather nearly sixty years later for this gift. It enabled me as I continued through school, university, law school, and finally into a career. Further, it was the mechanical instrument that facilitated moving my thoughts from brain to paper and from myself to others. I do not recall what happened to it, as electric typewriters pushed manual ones into dustbins and personal computers and laptops pushed those electrical ones into dustbins. I hope it made its way to another youngster.

8

Oli

M Y GRANDMOTHER NAOMI IOLA LASATER WAS BORN IN the hamlet of Elam in Chatham County, North Carolina, on September 12, 1886. Iola in Greek is "she knows," but we do not know why it became her name. From childhood, her nickname was *Oli*, and no one seems to know its origins either.

Her parents were Robert Artemus Lasater and Jeannette Jackson Burke Lasater. Elam is now within New Hill, which is south of Research Triangle Park. Robert Lasater was also born in that county on December 19, 1855, December 19 also being my maternal grandmother's and my father's birth date in other years. Robert Lasater was a guard at a North Carolina prison, and on June 20, 1888, at the age of thirty-two, he died there, the victim of an epidemic that had swept through it. My grandmother was less than two years old. Her mother later recounted to her that when his body was brought for burial, she instructed those delivering it to take the lid off the coffin so she would know for certainty and eternity that it was him. Fearing contagion, they refused to do so, so she took a claw hammer and did it herself. It was him. His known lineage ran back to George Leister, pronounced Lester, whose son Thomas was born in England in 1586 and died there in 1636. Robert Lasater was interred in the cemetery at what is now New Elam Christian Church.

I know few specifics of her 1888–1902 years, but at some point in time, Jeannette Lasater and her children moved to Durham, almost certainly to pursue job opportunities at its hosiery and related mills. I believe she worked at the Durham Hosiery Mill's complex of seven buildings in East Durham, now preserved in part as apartments but demolished in remaining part in 1970. By 1910, that complex "was the largest manufacturer of cotton hosiery in the world," but it was "abandoned" in 1922 as manufacturing technologies and fashion changed. Although it was listed on the National Register of Historic Places in 1978, only a single building on Angier Avenue seems to have survived the wrecking ball. She is buried in Durham's Old Maplewood Cemetery.

Naomis

I drove in the late 1960s from Washington to Durham for the weekend, as was commonplace for me in those university and law school years. On this occasion, I drove Grandmother Teague in my right-off-the-showroom-floor dark blue Volkswagen Beetle the forty-five minutes or so from Durham to Elam. We spent part of an afternoon unsuccessfully trying to locate where her childhood farmhouse had been and successfully going to her father's gravesite. She told me the story, again from her mother, that in the morning after her birth, an aging African American man came to that farmhouse. As she recounted, he said that he had had a dream that night that a girl was born and she would still be living on earth at the Second Coming of Jesus, a declaration with high drama to someone of the Christian faith. Whether he said he had been instructed in the dream to name the child, or he asked for it in his own right, I do not recall, but the family consented to his request. He gave her the name Naomi from the Bible's book of Ruth. This account needs background.

The book of Ruth is a scriptural narrative of a love story. Its author's purpose was to demonstrate the nature of the love and faithfulness that

God desires for humankind. Tied to the book of Judges, it illustrates what happens when a nation and its people do not obey the covenant with their God. How so? After the death of Ruth's husband, she remained loyal to her mother-in-law, Naomi, who decided to return alone to her home in Bethlehem. Ruth insisted on not only not leaving her but also adopting Naomi's God as her own. After others had finished an initial harvest, Ruth backbreakingly gathered in the field of Naomi's relative Boaz. Out of obedience to the law, which permitted widows and the poor to gather after an initial reaping, and his compassion, he allowed Ruth to gather the remaining and extra grain he had spread in the field. Sensing why Boaz had added the extra grain, Naomi encouraged Ruth to seek marriage with him. Ruth agreed and asked for her rights, and Boaz agreed, but he observed that he would have to be sure in advance that there were no others with rights to the field. Boaz and Ruth married, and Ruth conceived a son named Obed, who became the grandfather of King David, the founder of the House of David of Jesus of Nazareth. Scriptural commentaries highlight that this narrative discloses three steps of repentance: work, ensuing reward, and restored trust.

I will return to this account of the field of Ruth.

Jamestown Settlement

The settling of Jamestown in Tidewater Virginia is important for reasons far greater than our family's, but it is quite relevant to us. Jamestown and the James River were named to honor King James I, whose attention to ecclesiastical matters within the Church of England brought forward the translation and publishing of the English Bible known as the King James Version. Jamestown's 1607 founding was thirteen years before differently motivated English colonists landed in 1620 at Plymouth Rock, which was within the northern reaches of the Virginia colony as then defined. Delineations resulting in the borders of the eventual commonwealth of Massachusetts did not occur until 1691.

More than one aspect of Jamestown is of significance to us.

The first is that Jeannette Jackson Burke was descended from Henry

Soane Sr. (1594–1632). Of what importance? His son Henry Soane Jr., born in Bristol, England, in 1622, arrived at Virginia's growing Jamestown settlement before or during 1651. This younger Soane received a grant of land in exchange for bringing himself and his family to Virginia, and he acquired additional properties in locations along the James and its tributaries. A member of Virginia's House of Burgesses in 1652–1655, 1658, and 1660–1661, he became its Speaker in 1660, dying in 1661 before its seating for a new term. His largest place in history is he was the great-great-grandfather of the Declaration of Independence's principal author, University of Virginia founder and third president of the United States Thomas Jefferson. Soane's known lineage runs at least to the first Thomas Worger during the life of Elizabeth I. It was a coincidence that I became a founding director of Virginia's Thomas Jefferson Institute on Public Policy. As a confirmed descendant of Soane, memberships opened for me and others in such lineage organizations as the Jamestowne Society, the Sons (and Daughters) of the American Colonists, the Sons (and Daughters) of the American Revolution, and others.

The second importance is set forth through the inscription on the monument erected on the site of Queen Elizabeth's 1957 visit on the occasion of the Jamestown founding's 350th anniversary:

1607

AT JAMESTOWN BEGAN
THE
EXPANSION OVERSEAS OF THE
ENGLISH SPEAKING PEOPLES
THE
COMMONWEALTH OF VIRGIINIA
THE
UNITED STATES OF AMERICA
AND THE
BRITISH COMMONWEALTH
OF NATIONS

1957

The third is two-pronged. The first is that I had the pleasure of being in the company of several thousand at Jamestown for its four-hundredth anniversary in 2007, attended and addressed again by Her Majesty. The second is that I joined Her Majesty and husband, HRH the Duke of Edinburgh, and their oldest son, William, Duke of Cambridge, other members of the royal family, and a different company of several thousand on June 15, 2015, at Runnymede Meadow near London. It was on the occasion of the eight-hundredth anniversary of King John's accession to the demand of certain enumerated rights of barons on behalf of themselves and other English freemen as set forth in what became known as Magna Carta, the Great Charter, of June 15, 1215. This was the "Bad King John" of Robin Hood legends. As the youngest son of the powerful Henry II and his nearly equally powerful wife, Eleanor of Aquitaine, John's father had derogatorily referred to him as John the Lackland because he would almost certainly not inherit any of the royal family's lands. The putdown stuck. June 1215 was near the end of his tumultuous reign, but he did not see what was coming, dying in October 1216 from lowly dysentery. With his enemies trying to kill him in any way they could, it is a lesson that contaminated drinking water or food washed in it can bring down the mighty. As a member of the National Society of Magna Charta Dames and Barons and as a descendant of "surety barons" who guaranteed to John, themselves, and other feudal lords and knights that he would keep his pledges made in it, I was privileged to be in the Society's delegation to that anniversary and various events before and after it.

The fourth is to recall that in *The Journals of Captain John Smith*, published in 1612 but reporting among other things on his extensive navigation of the Chesapeake Bay in 1607 and 1608, Smith reported that oyster shell mounds at Indian villages along the shorelines were ten or more feet high and could run a hundred feet or more in length. My family's many oyster eaters' joke line on Smith's observation is to observe how large those shell mounds would have been if cocktail sauce had been invented. Smith also reported that the oysters found in the bay were as large as a man's foot. This is not tangential information, for I am a member of the Tidewater Oyster Gardeners Association.

The fifth is to encourage the reader to watch the 2005 Terrence Malick–written and directed movie *The New World* starring Colin Farrell as Captain Smith, Christopher Plummer as Christopher Newport, Christian Bale, and O'orianka Kilcher as Pocahontas on Netflix or any other platform. It is a powerful and mostly accurate depiction of the founding of Jamestown through the death of Pocahontas at Gravesend near London on the earliest leg of her intended return to Virginia.

9

O'Briant and Tucker Families

I T WAS CONVENIENT FOR DAD'S PARENTS TO HAVE ONE of their daughters, his sister and my aunt Jeannette, living directly across Rosehill Avenue with her husband, Andrew Lyon "Tuck" Tucker, and their three sons. His other sister and my aunt Ruby lived on Oakland Avenue on the other side of my grandparents' block. When Dad moved back to Durham in the late 1960s, he lived in several locations, but his last was on Englewood Avenue at the north end of my grandparents and their daughters' block. The four families lived within easy walking distance, not usual even then and quite uncommon now. It was a middle-class neighborhood of one- and two-income families then and probably remains so now.

The O'Briants

Aunt Ruby and her husband, Paul, lived with their son and daughter, Paul Linwood O'Briant Jr. (known as Linwood) and Nancy. Their house was spacious and well furnished. Its telephone from the years when all one had to do was pick up the receiver and click it for the operator to respond rested in its hallway cubby hole for decades after it was functionless. The fireplace mantle held a massively heavy classical mirror that I had for a period of time after her death and which our daughter Mary Robb Durham Teague Wilson now has in Northern California. I recall a gigantic magnolia in their backyard next to a beautiful stone outdoor grill, which I never saw used even once. Ruby loved to play bridge with neighbors and other friends. Her 1948 four-door sedan Chrysler had a floorboard between the back of its front seats and its rear seats, seeming large enough to set up a card table. Family photographs taken in her living room at holiday seasons still rest in our homes. And who among us can forget her spats with Aunt Jeannette as they both grew older and cantankerous, each losing enough of their hearing that it probably did not matter to the other what they were saying.

Linwood was a sophomore at Davidson College when he was drafted into military service during World War II. Yet his brief time there determined the direction of that service by causing whoever determined that direction to send him as a military policeman (MP) to the United States Military Academy at West Point because he was perceived to be smart enough to understand its cadets. He returned to Davidson, graduated with honors in history with a concentration in religion, became a certified public accountant, and, in addition to his accounting practice, taught at a Columbia, SC, community college where he helped many students straighten out their career goals and find jobs. Nancy attended the Women's College of the University of North Carolina, now UNC-Greensboro. Ruby and Paul eventually divorced, but our family would occasionally see him in the Durham area.

Ruby's family and friends traveled most years to New York City to see Broadway plays and, according to Nancy, "walk, walk, walk" in their sightseeing. When Linwood was stationed at West Point, they would go up the Hudson River to see him and once kept going northward to Canada. Gasoline, tire, oil, and other commodities were rationed during World War II because our troops needed them, but Paul sometimes traded the café's access to food supplies for oil and gas ration cards to meet the café's vehicular needs. Other times, they'd take a train from

Raleigh to the then architectural jewel of Penn Station. If Broadway plays in New York City were not enough theater, Ruby would take Nancy to professional performances at Duke and UNC. Nancy recalls seeing the Metropolitan Opera's coloratura soprano Patrice Munsel at Duke and film and television actor Richard Boone at UNC's Playmakers shortly before he began the *Have Gun, Will Travel* CBS television series in 1957.

Ruby's Cafe

Ruby owned and managed a café at 712 Ninth Street in West Durham. It was across from Erwin Mills and its large workforce. This part of Ninth Street is the several-blocks-long commercial section parallel to Erwin Mills' footprint. In my childhood, this section began with a filling station and bank near its Main Street intersection and continued, among other retailers, with Dean's fabrics store, Couch's furniture store, Cheek's Dry Cleaners, McDonald's Pharmacy, a barbershop, I think a beauty parlor, and a hand full of eateries, ending at Barnes Supply, from which my parents bought Eastertime chicks and an ABC (for Alcoholic Beverage Control) retail store for the state's monopolized sale of alcoholic beverages, proceeds from which were earmarked by law for state expenditures in education and transportation.

There were three reasons for Ninth Street's many eateries. There were hundreds of workers at Erwin Mills. There were Duke University students in search of food better than cafeteria fare. Before Interstates 40 and 85 skirted Durham, Ninth Street was part of the business segment of US 70, an interstate primary road running from Globe, Arizona, to the Atlantic coast of North Carolina, which routing meant families and truck drivers looked for affordable places to eat and patronizing those diners they had come to appreciate for good food and value.

Readers of industrial history typically believe mill towns existed solely for factory owners to collect rents from wages paid to their employees. They could be right in part, but there were additional reasons. One was the proximity of workers to their work before broader ownership of automobiles and availabilities of public transportation. Erwin Village houses were well built and on half-acre lots and close to the street so each had enough property for children to play and adults to raise vegetables and perhaps fruit trees in their backyards. Neighborhood security was effective because neighbors knew one another and went together to schools, churches, and neighboring stores. Because conversations' laughter and anger traveled out of open windows about two-thirds of the year, self-control was required. Further, management's warning was like an invisible workplace poster: if you commit a crime, you are out of a job, and that means out of housing for yourself, your spouse, and your children. As a result, crime in West Durham was almost nonexistent. It was a place where children could walk in day or night without fear beyond that of a ghost or goblin from a grandparent's tale.

The *Durham City Directory 1934* lists Ruby and Paul as working at West End Lunch, which was probably their Ninth Street cafe. We know from city records that its wooden framed building was built in 1930, this date adding to this probability. Sometime in that decade, it became Paul's Place. Because nearby Camp Butner soldiers were furloughed and its civilians were off work on weekends during the war years, Paul and Ruby stayed open twenty-four hours a day then, although onsite beer sales were probably proscribed during certain hours and altogether on Sundays. German, so-called German, and Italian prisoners of war at Butner numbered about six thousand, with the so-called Germans consisting of Austrians, Czechs, Dutch, Frenchmen, Luxembourgers, and Poles and "a single Lithuania" captured in German uniforms because they had been forced to fight for their captors. As time went on, so-called Germans were allowed to work out of camp as long as in civvies. The café's signage proclaimed "O'Briants," but it was known to its customers as "Ruby's." Her acquisition of the café in her own name was not without careful maneuvering on her and Linwood's part.

In 1951 and for whatever reasons, the café was to be sold at public auction. Ruby sent Linwood to the auction with a fistful of $1500 in cash to bid on it. Her fellow Ninth Street businesses and other customers knew Ruby wanted to keep the café for herself, meaning without Paul, but did not have enough money to win a spirited bidding. Some were husband-and-wife enterprises, and many ate their breakfasts or lunches at Ruby's. A crowd gathered for the auction, and a fellow showed up who intended to win the bidding. Ruby's supporters swung into verbal action and made it clear to him that if he won, they would see to it that he had few customers. He must have regarded their promise as credible because he took a walk, Linwood prevailed, and Ruby's café had a new beginning.

Ruby's chief of the kitchen was Maybelle Bagley, and this African American woman could cook the best food and do so with a combination of careful planning, quick preparation, and a smile. Customers from Erwin Mills had only forty-five minutes to leave their workplace, walk to Ruby's, review a new daily menu, decide and order, be served, eat, pay for it, and return to their work station or receive a harsh word or get docked. I reckon the time between entering and leaving Ruby's was twenty-five to thirty minutes maximum. Maybelle was assisted by the able Percy Tenney.

With customer-loving recipes in their heads, Maybelle and Percy were of great value to Ruby. Every now and then, someone in our extended family would decide he or she needed to replicate one of Maybelle's dishes. With Ruby's and Maybelle's permissions, they'd go into the café's kitchen, watch Maybelle or Percy, write down each ingredient and guestimates as to amounts, go home, and try to duplicate it. They failed nearly every time. Chef Bagley had her secrets.

The café had a bar counter with only ten stools and only four or five booths for four persons each. Two waitressing out front and two cooking in the kitchen could have between twenty-six and thirty-two customers at the same time, nearly all ordering within a few minutes of each other. Ruby's daughter Nancy recalled that at one time Ruby was charging thirty-seven cents for a meat, three vegetables, a cornbread muffin or a roll, and a drink. Extra soft drinks were a nickel or dime, and beer was probably a quarter. Despite those prices, Ruby managed to net and save enough of it to send Linwood through Davidson and Nancy through UNC-Greensboro as well as own her home and meet living expenses.

Nancy's first out-of-high-school work was at Ruby's, waiting on tables that summer and "hating it." While Ruby covered the counter and the cash register, Nancy waited on the booths. Ruby paid her thirty-five dollars a week, but withholding tax and Social Security deduction left her with $25.27 of which Ruby insisted Nancy "save" twenty-five dollars, leaving her with twenty-seven cents each week, less than a penny an hour! No wonder Nancy hated it! As required by Ruby, the twenty-five dollars was banked, but instead of it remaining in the account to accumulate interest for Nancy's future years, it became her $300 check to UNC-Greensboro for the fall semester.

My brother and I were limited in our experience and biased in our judgment, but we knew that Ruby's café was the best place for a hot dog with mustard, chili, chopped onions, and lots of black pepper. Coney Island never had a tastier one! The café was open only for breakfast and lunch. It did not stay open for dinner or on Sundays. As a child, I was struck by mill workers from the night shift coming into the café for their breakfast with a beer before heading home, for their hair and clothes and, now we presume their lungs, were covered with cotton dust.

The café came to its end as a café when Ruby could no longer secure kitchen help to follow Maybelle and Percy. No one seemed to want to work in a kitchen with all that heat, urgencies of filling orders, and most probably for so little income from it. Ruby also knew as her birthdays were growing in their count that she could collect monthly rent without having to work so hard. It became in succession Navajo Trading Post, Devil on Ninth Street as in the Duke Blue Devils, and Native Threads and is still there, a feat of preservation in that few believed it would survive the occasional hurricane to hit Piedmont, North Carolina. It is amazing that the heat from the 1968 firebombing of neighboring Couch's furniture store did not spontaneously ignite it. Not long before Ruby's closed, I was there on a trip from Washington and ordered lunch, including a beer. It was legal to serve me, yet Ruby made it clear that I could get any beer I wanted down the street. Her sliding metal door to the beer cooler was closed to me. I had a soft drink instead.

Preservation Durham's website has a handful of early to recent photos of Ruby's and modest improvements to it through the years, but that website also has interesting commentaries from those who chose to recall it, for example:

> However small and un-dense the structure may be, it adds a quaint interruption to the masonry storefronts and a reminder of the early 20th century transition of wood frame commercial and residential structures to the more substantial masonry structures.

And in recalling Couch's furniture store and its 1968 firebombing:

> ... or the tiny wooden building next to it – 35 years older, but a simple part of the community rather than being caught up in a national wave of protest. Does it make a difference if someone met their future spouse in this restaurant?

And from one of my second cousins, Amanda Tucker O'Briant, on April 25, 2012, as she was fighting a losing battle with colon cancer:

> This was my grandparents' restaurant. It was a modest place with booths and a counter. They served home style cooking and the best pies in West Durham. My family has many happy memories of this place.

Let me add something else. That she owned her place of business was my first awareness of business ownership and what it meant. It was from listening to discussions in the family about the seemingly never-ending issues associated with its operation, including finding and keeping good help and making sure that her customers were happy with its food, service, and price. I became aware of the laws of supply and demand and the price point fulcrum between income and expense, making a living or losing it, though I would not hear those economic terms for years. I was proud that she owned her café.

What Nancy imparted to me as a major difference between West Durham then and now was it had been a virtually crime-free community. In her words:

> I remember being raised in a crime-free area—people's jobs and homes were on the line—however I remember on Fridays there was a lot of traffic on 9th Street. During the war, Camp Butner gave weekend passes so the military arrived—now a lot of those men were West Durham natives waiting to be shipped out. If you will remember, there was an alley way between Cheek's Dry Cleaners and Morgan's Restaurant that led back to 8th Street. One of the men who lived on 8th Street was going home late in the evening and someone stepped out from behind either Cheek's or Morgan's restaurant and grabbed him and stuck their finger down his throat and scratched his tonsils (which the medical profession was not in the habit of removing at that time). Shortly after that the Durham Police stationed a walking patrolman to 9th Street 24 hours a day. I can see him but can't pull up his name right now because, bless him, he stayed on that duty until Erwin Mills was sold to Burlington (in 1974). I assume Burlington did not have the same rules/threats that Erwin Mills had. That was the only crime I ever heard of while growing up.

The Tuckers

Aunt Jeannette worked at Erwin Mills for forty-eight years, rising in responsibilities and retiring as a sewing room supervisor. Erwin Mills was in the early 1900s one of the largest producers of denim in the world, and industry historians believe its denim was the first to reach

China. She was at Erwin when Abney Mills acquired Erwin Mills No. 1 and No. 2 in 1953 and when what remained was acquired by Burlington Industries in 1962. By that latter date, the mill was primarily producing sheets and pillowcases. Erwin's workers enjoyed some of the better working conditions among fabric-producing mills, even though they had to threaten to strike to secure them. We are prejudiced in her favor, but our family believes Jeannette would have been promoted into management had she been a man. We know also that, while wage and benefit numbers are relative as to the years in which they are earned and paid, her salary and benefits as a supervisor of a sewing room floor at Erwin Mills were less than they would have been if she were a man. Evidence of this is that upon her retirement, management presented her with a startling $30,000 bonus for those years.

Her husband, Tuck, was a field supervisor with the North Carolina highway department during much of his working life, but he had been a jazz musician in younger years. That might be how the two of them met. He was twelve or thirteen years older than she. Greystone Baptist Church was more than a Sunday-morning service for them, for they were immersed in its roles within families and neighborhoods. It was a recognition of the place of faith in their daily lives.

The first television among my Teague grandparents and their three children's families was at the Tuckers'. Three generations would gather in her living room most Sunday evenings to watch the black-and-white screen that flickered on as its vacuum tubes warmed up. The most popular Sunday-evening show was CBS's *The Toast of the Town*—more popularly, finally, and officially *The Ed Sullivan Show*. A variety show, it featured the *New York Times*'s entertainment reporter, Ed Sullivan, and a broad range of talent from opera and ballet, plays and musicals, singers and their ensembles, jugglers and other circus-like acts, comedians, and aging vaudevillians. It had the eight o'clock slot. It was on this show that the Beatles first appeared in the United States. Another of its most watched nights was Elvis Presley's national TV debut.

It's hard to believe in the digital era of one thousand or more cable channels and streaming on every other kind and sized screen that watching a movie in those years was done either on the big screen of movie theaters or on the small screen of televisions. Full-length movies on the small screen were popular reruns from the big screen. Hallmark Hall of Fame and General Electric Theater on Sundays provided sometimes live broadcasts. UHF stations added educational features. Sports occupied most of Saturday's afternoon and often evening broadcast time, well at least until the Grand Ole Opry in Nashville came on.

For nearly fifty years, I recalled Richard Harris's outstanding performance in Paul Gallico's *The Snow Goose* and Richard Boone's live performance in an adaptation of the medieval morality play *Every Man*, originally *The Somonyng of Everyman*, which is to spell today *The Summoning of Everyman*. As to the first, in December 2014 I went to the Paley Center for Media on West Fifty-Second Street in New York City, next door to the 21 Club, where I had attended an inspiring luncheon of the United States Olympic Endowment, and watched on a computer screen that production of *Snow Goose*. I was as moved by it then as when I had first seen it. It remains an effectively told account of the heroism of the English people during the Second World War and of the spoken and unspoken relationships of them as they step-by-step defeated Nazi Germany and for the earliest years without the badly needed total commitment of the United States. Several years later, as often turns out to be the case in our digital age, Harris's and Jenny Agutter's *Snow Goose* became available in streaming formats.

As to Richard Boone's performance in *Everyman*, the Center did not have a video recording of it, and, further, I have found it impossible to verify my recall. I do know that the birth hour of the globally famous Salzburg Festival (Salzburger Festspiele) was August 22, 1920, when Hugo von Hofmannsthal's morality play *Jedermann* was performed on Salzburg's Cathedral Square in an outdoor staging by the Austrian-born theatrical legend Max Reinhardt. Hofmannsthal's play encompassed the original medieval play but with updated material garnered over the centuries of humankind's struggles with life and mortality. Reinhardt's Salzburg residence, Schloss Leopoldskrom, is now the convocation center of the Salzburg Global Seminar, and I served on its governing board of directors. I have almost abandoned finding this Richard Boone performance.

Discussions at the Tuckers' over what to watch were sometimes spirited. A Sunday-afternoon football game versus ice skating finals is an example. The week's single prime time movie ran on Sunday evening in CBS's nine o'clock slot, which two hours would take the viewer to eleven o'clock local news. Seldom was I permitted to stay up that late, Sunday being a school night. There were only four VHF channels, with educational television confined by federal regulations to UHF channels, every channel change accompanied by getting up from a comfortable seat or uncomfortable floor, going to the TV, and manually turning its channels dials, the invention of the remote and then voice recognition being decades away. Grandmother and Granddad on one hand and Aunt Ruby on the other soon got their TV sets, but we Teagues did not get our first until we moved to Chapel Hill. Inasmuch as a television set required an outside antenna prior to the introduction of coaxial cable for mountainous regions where line of site telemetry could not reach many rooftop antennas, driving around a neighborhood and spotting TV antennas affixed to chimneys or metal poles would indicate which houses did and which did not own TVs. Rabbit ears sitting on top of the TV worked less well, even if you attached sheets or strips of aluminum foil to pick up more broadcast signal.

While attending Durham High School, their oldest son, Andrew Leon Tucker (known as Leon), worked the second shift at Erwin Mills, finishing at 11:15 each evening. That's not easy for anyone, but perhaps anticipating college tuitions, his parents told him the family needed more income, including from his labor. Leon began the study of engineering at North Carolina State in Raleigh, but he went into the army as part of the armed forces buildup tied to the Korean War. He excelled in basic and advanced training and became an Airborne Ranger, the army's premier raiding force and one trained to infiltrate enemy lines by land, sea, and air. He fought in that war, as Rangers parachuted into pitch-black darkness and made their way onto equally dark beaches from US submarines on subzero cold and moonless nights. He has great pride in never losing a member of his squad while doing "the dirty work" required of them. His was a claimed record of no man killed, no man taken prisoner, and no man otherwise missing in action. He survived those combat missions only to be badly injured in a regulations-required periodic parachute jump out of Fort Benning, Georgia. A strong wind gust after he had landed resulted in a broken ankle requiring years of rehabilitation. Near the end of his service in the 1960s, he was stationed in Panama where he witnessed turbulent anti-American demonstrations and from which he informed family on both their nature, who was fomenting it and for what purposes, and how it was being ignored by our government and national news media.

Jeannette and Tuck's two youngest sons, Richard and Robert, are twins. Richard and his wife, Carrie, were successful in the highly competitive women's clothing wholesale business, not an easy task for two southern Protestants in an Old Testament–dominated line of commerce centered in Manhattan as manufacturing was already moving to Asia. Perhaps it helped in New York City that our Richard Tucker bore the identical first and last names of the Metropolitan Opera tenor, a son of Bessarabian Jewish parents. That Richard Tucker's monument is in Lincoln Square near the street corner named for him, they having the effect of reminding donors to the Richard Tucker Music Foundation on their ways in and out of Lincoln Center's Metropolitan Opera performances of the continuing need for their charitable gifts. This coincidence of names and timing and his reasonably acquired knowledge of Yiddish phrases worked well for Richard. Richard and Carrie also imagined, designed, and pursued the taking of American rodeo, along with country music entertainment and Western culture and art, to China, but they were blocked by the powerful there who felt it would give the United States too favorable an image. They continue to pursue educational exchanges intended to reach younger generations. Richard established the Andrew Lyon and Mary Jeannette Tucker Legacy Scholarship at Tyler Junior College in Texas, it being his and Robert's alma mater. Robert worked as a property liquidator based in Kansas as well as for Richard.

This is an appropriate place to shift from Dad's paternal and maternal parents' families to Mom's paternal and maternal families.

10

Mom and Her Family

M Y MOTHER'S FATHER, WILEY PRESTON RHEW, WAS born in 1878 and died on September 19, 1929, after a nearly yearlong struggle with pulmonary tuberculosis. His death from "the white plague," as TB was then known, was unfortunate timing for his widow and children, for it was ten days before the September 29 collapse of US stock markets and the beginning of the Great Depression.

Censuses and North Carolina cemetery records show scores of Rhews in Lebanon Township in north Durham County and bordering Orange County. Later generations spread across North Carolina and elsewhere. His father was William L. Rhew (1840–1880), and his mother was Elizabeth Frances (Fannie) Holloway (1839–1922), and her parents were William F. Holloway and Elizabeth Caine. His father's parents were Irby A. Rhew and Artelia Browning. Wiley Preston Rhew was eighteen years older than Bertha Mae Rippey when they married on October 10, 1915, and their first child, my mother, was born on August 10 of the next year. A September 20, 1929, obituary was captioned "Well Known Man Dies in Lebanon: Wiley P. Rhew, Prominent Farmer, Succumbs."

The surname Rhew is not related to "rue," meaning "street" in French. Rather, Rhew appears to be a German spelling of the French *rieu,* meaning "little river," and appears as a surname in French and German spellings, perhaps because this duality was a practical need in Alsace as it was either within France or within Germany, depending on which had prevailed in the last Franco-German conflict. The assumption, but not yet a confirmed fact, is that Wiley's first Rhew ancestor to arrive in the States had an Alsacean heritage. There is some evidence that he arrived in the States from Ireland, but Ireland was often a transit point to the United States, much as Bristol, Plymouth, and other English ports had been during our colonial era.

Mom's mother's birth name was Bertha Mae Rippey, a surname spelled in census and other records accurately and inaccurately with an *e* and without one. Wiley and Bertha were married when much of America was trying to avoid entry into World War I, then in its second year among its European combatants. In that he was thirty-seven, he was not a prospect for being drafted into the army. In their married life, they lived north of Durham on a small farm that she had inherited. It is leftward off of Guess Road about a half mile north of its crossing of the Eno River. The farm came from the estate of Henry W. Jackson, who had come into it from the Cates family. Wiley was fifty-one, and Bertha was in her early thirties at the time of Wiley's death. His death left Grandmother with five girls between the ages of one and thirteen. How they survived the Great Depression is unimaginable to me. The raising of food at the farm and the harvesting of naturally grown plants of field and forest may have contributed to their survival, but even a successful year of harvests would have been marginal to their total needs. Keep in mind that farming in those days meant wringing a chicken's neck, cutting off its head, and degutting and plucking the feathers off before cooking it, not to mention painstakingly moving water by buckets full from the Eno River in order to save wilting corn and every other plant during droughts, and laboriously canning vegetables and fruits to have them on fall and winter tables. This near impoverishment required her to earn income from working off the farm, with relatives taking care of her brood when she was at work. She managed to survive for herself and them, and she seems to have done a commendable job of it because mother and daughters came out of the experience as fine women. I heard her daughters tell her often how much they loved her, and I hope they also told her how much they appreciated all that she had done for their survival. As children, they may have hardly noticed the severity of their situation.

Emotional depression seemed to run in Rippey genes, and its consequences were sometimes evident. It affected some but not all of her daughters, but that evidence reaches further back. Grandmother and her brothers and sisters were raised from her age of four by her spinster great-aunt Eliza Cates, because each of their parents, Daniel and Geneva Couch Rippey, had committed suicide in 1900 as a consequence of their addiction to laudanum and their inability to obtain it. Laudanum is a tincture of opium that could be ordered through Sears Roebuck and other mail order catalogues and elsewhere until Congress enacted tightened restrictions. The preceding Romantic and Victorian eras were marked by laudanum's widespread use in Europe and the United States, including by George Washington to relieve dental and gum pain, Mary Todd Lincoln to fight depression, and the English poet Samuel Taylor Coleridge in a struggle against anxiety, depression, and almost certain undiagnosed bipolarity. The knowledge of widespread use by others did not help either of them overcome their withdrawal when it became unavailable in rural North Carolina. The question for us is whether their addiction arose from their attempts to overcome depression. How will we ever know an answer? We probably won't.

Near Grandmother's flat-boarded, tin-roofed farmhouse had stood a log cabin in which relatives had lived. During her childhood, aging aunts gave an account of when their father returned from wherever he had been when the Civil War ended in April 1865. As his wife and children saw him approaching, they raced down the farm road to embrace him, but as they came near, he told them empathetically not to touch him. When he arrived at the cabin moments later, he started a sizeable fire, took every stitch of clothing off, and shaved his entire body, throwing clothes and all else into it. The lice and other vermin on him had been that bad. It was probably the case for tens of thousands of returning soldiers.

My brother and I enjoyed going to her farm on weekends, over holidays, and during the summer, especially if we could spend the night when our parents were traveling or just wanted peace and quiet. In our years, she lived there with unmarried daughters Nellie, Annie Bell, and Lois, until A.B. married. Our enjoyments of the fields, forest, and Eno River were especially true after my five-year-older brother got a BB gun, after which we learned that crows counterattack when you shoot at them. It was not a painted house in that paint was a cost that could not be met. Its boards had turned a dark brownish gray and dried to a dangerous level. It had a porch on the right side and one on the back. The latter overlooked the spring from which came all of their water, one heavy bucket at a time as it was carried up a short slope, whether it was liquid or hatchet-chopped ice. There was never a hand pump for water. There was a massive oak in front with a swing and a circular driveway around her Canna lilies. I can still taste in my mind the tomatoes in which she took much pride. Dad would cut our Christmas trees at her farm, and Merle and I would walk with him as he took them to and tied them on top of our car for transit to Eighth Street. I have on the floor of my balcony a stone from the farmhouse's chimney as well as an anvil-wrought nail pulled from its soil.

The probate of H. W. Jackson's estate in 1915 was in large measure in respect to this farm. It itemized among other chattel property one horse, two cows, two pigs, one buggy and harness, and one wagon and harness. Presumably, the one horse had to alternatingly pull the buggy or the wagon. When we were children, the only farm animals were chickens and, maybe a little earlier, a single milking cow. I can remember the childhood-felt discomfort of taking our chicks originally from Barnes Supply on Ninth Street, after they had become unruly in the weeks following their Easter-morning gift to us. Our discomfort was related to having fried chicken there months later. We were always assured that it was not one of our chickens. My brother and I thought,

Yeah, right. How would they know? And where else would our chicks have gone but the frying pan or the stew pot? An answer to that question is their chickens were sometimes stolen, once nearly all of them. In an attempt to change the subject, Mom's sisters would tell us our chickens were producing the eggs we had for breakfast, never mind that by logic half of our chicks would have matured as roosters. The lesson? Children sometimes know things parents don't think they do. The farmhouse's tin roof was a delight, relaxing to listen to during gentle rain and terrifying to hear in a hailstorm. The house was heated with a single stove. They did not have a second stove on the back porch, as some rural homes did for cooking in hot weather. It had a dark cellar where preserved foods were kept and where I was scared to tread for fear of black snakes said to be there to reduce the mice population.

In years preceding even my mother's childhood on it, this farm had housed at least two stock animals, as witnessed by this news account in the *Durham Recorder* of February 19, 1909: "Mr. W.P. Rhew had an accident this week: His cow put her tongue through the crack of the stable in her efforts to get some fodder and the horse [on the other side of the crack] bit the end of the cow's tongue off. The cow is getting along very well but has some trouble in the eating." There must have been a lot of newspaper competition in 1909 for this incident to have spurred this coverage. Perhaps any news was treasured in those days.

The farm was sold in the 1950s, her farmhouse torn down, and suburban houses built upon it. A Rhew family cemetery sits amid them. Rural cemeteries are protected by North Carolina law and county sheriffs. Known in North Carolina cemetery census records as the Jeff Rhew Family Cemetery, it is named after Jefferson J. Rhew whose farm may have encompassed it. There are reported in the Durham County Cemetery Census to be thirteen marked graves in it, all but one with rocks as headstones, such was the extent of rural poverty in those years. The names of only seven of those thirteen are reported in that census, itself a product of research by Doris Tilley, I assume of the neighboring Tilley farm's family or its descent. The seven known by name are Rhews, but the family questions the accuracy of that census, for several of those named are known by family and within church records to be buried elsewhere. There could be more unmarked graves here, for, while most adults would not move a stone at a burial site, who knows what a passerby might have done over the decades. We know from Aunt Lois that a man who drowned in the adjacent Eno River is buried there.

I noted one weekend afternoon some years ago that several neighbors had encroached on the cemetery by keeping excess building materials on it. I had no need to be angry about it in that the encroachment may have been without awareness of its boundary, so there was no need to call the sheriff's department. Instead, a telephone call to the funeral home that serves the Rhew family, the funeral home's directors' discussions with the neighbors as a polite reminder of cemetery laws, and a sizeable memorial stone purchased by me ended the encroachment. At least we hope so. I scripted the stone's text with these words and design:

RHEW CEMETERY
THE KNOWN AND UNKNOWN HERE
REST IN THE PEACE OF THEIR LORD

Nearly each time I am in the Durham area, I drive past it. I sometimes see that some one or more neighbors was kind enough to clear out its underbrush. I noted recently that the memorial stone had been moved about four or five feet further from the roadway but believe that was to move it off the right-of-way and make the immediate area easier for lawn mowing. It is more fitting in its slightly new space. Rhew family descendants appreciate the respect and care given to this cemetery by its neighbors on Heritage Drive and hope it will continue.

Farming was not making ends meet for the Rhew women. Grandmother had to work elsewhere, for there was no viable option not to do so. She worked during World War II at a US Army installation, known then as Camp Butner and located just north of Durham. Part of the Butner facility was used as a prisoner of war camp for German POWs. I can recall only one recollection from her as to those years, and it was of their constant begging of her for cigarettes, which she readily ignored as a nonsmoker and patriot. Dad would occasionally drive us on a Sunday afternoon past the by-then-abandoned camp where guard towers were leaning and weeds and young trees were growing in exercise yards. The Butner Federal Correctional Complex of the US Department of Justice's Bureau of Prisons now occupies the site. Grandmother later worked at a facility that packaged sandwiches for retail sale at area convenience stores. We would wait for her on Sunday afternoons when she got off work in order to drive her home. During later years, she enjoyed sitting on the living room couch with her feet up and watching our children, that is her great-grandchildren, play games, wrap Christmas and other presents, do school projects, and share what they were doing in their Alexandria lives. That later house's original dining room was Nellie's sewing parlor, so we ate our meals at a table in the kitchen. It was so small we ate lunch in two shifts, and the food always seemed tastier than the same food served elsewhere, especially the salted, peppered, and buttered hot biscuits or rolls encapsulating sliced tomatoes that had been in the garden only moments earlier. In that the world is never static, this is true of neighborhoods. Hers of those later years is now predominantly Hispanic. The drugstore where we would get ice cream is now an appliance store. Our favorite hot dog stand now sells tacos.

Grandmother died on May 4, 1988, at the age of ninety-three. She had outlived her husband by nearly fifty-nine years and never remarried. I had seen her only a few days before her last illness. I had driven to Durham from the Research Triangle. There we had an American Council of Young Political Leaders (ACYPL) debate tussle with representatives of the Committee of Youth Organizations of the Soviet Union, a percentage of whom were known to us to be KGB or other Soviet intelligence operatives. When I met with her, I had the beginnings of what became a severe sore throat, perhaps caught from an ambient bacterial strain or virus from one of the Russians breathing and coughing in our spring air. Who knows from where comes a sore throat? Upon returning to Alexandria, I was admitted to Georgetown University Hospital in Washington with an acute case of epiglottitis, a swelling of the throat that reduces air passage to the lungs. From the gurney on

blonde, she was twenty-one and he was twenty when they were married by the Rev. Lawyer J. Rainey on Easter Sunday. She had graduated from Wiley P. Mangum High School and worked as a department store clerk prior to meeting my father and after they were married. She was to live and work also in Chapel Hill and St. Petersburg, Florida. She is buried at Rose of Sharon Baptist Church's cemetery on Guess Road where the family had attended church services during her youth. Her tombstone epithet is "Our Mumsie," and hers is next to her parents' gravesite, the familiar name Mumsie having been given to her by her sons in the 1950s. According to the state of North Carolina–required cemetery census, there are fifteen surnamed Rhews in that cemetery, but there must be more under other married surnames.

Mother was followed by Nellie Rivers Rhew. Born in 1919 and dying in 2003 only nine days short of her birthday, she was unmarried and a seamstress. She seldom increased her prices for original and alteration work over decades of that service to others. Consequentially, she had a land rush–like clientele because her prices just kept getting better as they remained flat and inflation devalued the dollar. She had polio as a child, and it left her with a need for a built-up shoe. Nellie and her unmarried sister Lois took loving care of their mother. After Grandmother and Nellie died and Lois broke her hip, it was time for Lois to move to an assisted living facility, which she did in nearby Cary between Durham and Raleigh. Grandmother and Lois had saved almost all of their small salaried incomes and Social Security checks, and Nellie had saved most of her income from sewing. We know this to be true, for we found in grocery store plastic bags in not well-hidden places in their house nearly $70,000 in stashed cash when it came time for Lois to move to that facility. It was surprising, welcomed, and nearly comical, but it better positioned the economic viability of Lois's move. We decided to forget immediately the checks the grandchildren, nephews, and nieces had sent them not only for holidays and birthdays but also as we thought about their needs compared to our capacities to help. If it helped give them additional peace of mind, all the better. Nellie's tombstone epithet at Rose of Sharon is "Now Sewing for the Angels."

Nellie was followed in birth order by Elizabeth Frances Rhew (known as Fran). Fran married Earle J. Sherr, a career US Army officer in its Quartermaster Corps who served in various locations in the States, as well as in France, Japan, and perhaps elsewhere. He rose to the rank of lieutenant colonel and continued to serve his country in a civilian capacity after his retirement from the uniformed service. A graduate of Northeastern University in Boston, Col. Sherr served during World War II, the Korean War, the Cold War, and the Vietnam War and died at Walter Reed Hospital in northwest Washington. Fran had attended Salem College, then named Salem's Women's College, in Winston-Salem prior to her work in Richmond and their marriage in 1946. Their children—Sara Jean (Jeannie), now married to Col. George McVeigh (USAF Ret.), Deborah, now married to Dr. Gary Blank, a forestry department head and professor at North Carolina State University in Raleigh, and David—believe their parents most likely met when Fran was working in Richmond during World War II. Earle was probably stationed at nearby Fort Lee, the Quartermaster Corps' headquarters, in nearby Petersburg. She was first known within family and among friends as "Fannie," as was her Elizabeth Frances Holloway aunt after whom she was named. She became "Fran" during a posting in Europe. She died of heart failure in 2002 at the age of eighty. Earle had died of heart failure in 1986. They are interred in Section 66 at Arlington National Cemetery at a gravesite whose headstone looks toward the Pentagon and Washington. They were always quite kind to my brother and to me.

Fourth among the five girls, Annie Belle Rhew was born in 1924. A.B., as she was sometimes known, was a secretary at an interstate moving company office in Durham for much of her working life. She married a Dickens, puns intended. In later life, she was a hoarder, which trait may have been a consequence of being raised without much of anything. Maybe she had simply misinterpreted the adage, "Hold on to what you've got!" After all, the sisters' Christmas presents during their childhoods were little more than a few fresh oranges, some nuts, and a few candies. Her ashes are kept by her only child, Tammy, who lives near Rose of Sharon Church.

The youngest is Ruby Lois Rhew (known as Lois), born in 1928 and "always our baby sister," as her sisters lovingly referred to her. Lois worked at a Durham laundry much of her life, taking the bus in and out of the city each of her working days. She has gently threatened the living to be an unfriendly ghost haunting the life of anyone who puts "Ruby" on her tombstone. For when that time comes, we have pledged it will be only Lois Rhew, her vital dates, and the epithet "Always Our Baby Sister." She has been affected by failing eyesight, and as an avid reader, this has been an unfortunate circumstance. Thank the Englishman Roger Bacon for the invention of the magnifying glass, for she has relied upon it.

According to Lois, Mother and her sisters attended Holt Elementary and, as noted, Mangum High School north of Durham. That information contains no middle school, but perhaps a two-tiered system then preceded our three-tiered system. After all, the two-tiered system grew from one-room schoolhouses.

Mom and Connie Gay

Our family attended in 1955 a family-styled afternoon segment of Mother's Mangum High School twentieth reunion. I knew little about her school years because not much had been shared by her. In 2017, I came across photographs of her and her classmates on the school's steps. They were in a box that my brother and his wife, Barbara, had sent to me following her 2000 death. One was taken in 1935 near graduation, and another at that 1955 reunion. Mother's comments to me had included that French was her favorite subject, perhaps because it was a way to pretend being in Paris, but that is my thought. She enjoyed math and physics, and her tutoring of me confirmed that. There was a press clipping that she had won the National 4-H Club Congress's Gold Medal for Durham County for the best dress design. Neither the medal, the design, nor information on whether she crafted a dress based on it was in the box. I hope she did. The folders contained a printed program from her senior class's April 26, 1935, production of the three-act farce, *Here Comes Charlie*, and she is listed as one of its two business managers. Its pages are replete with advertisements, so the two must have done a good job in that respect. The program is now with our son, Robert Townsend Teague (known as Townsend), whose career focuses among other things on the financial management of Broadway and other plays and other entertainment media. It's nice to have such intergenerational interests and experiences validated in such unexpectedly ways.

It is out of the ordinary to write about a parent's "serious friendship" before marriage, especially when this writer is without knowledge appropriate for defining the singularity or combination of those two words. A fuller telling will inform us of at least the friendship.

The "he" for her was Connie B. Gay, and he was almost exactly two years older. They met while she was in high school, although what follows does not make the case that it was necessarily there. Let me have Wikipedia further tee up this matter by incorporating here its text of Gay's life, career, and legacy:

> Connie Barriot Gay (August 22, 1914 – December 3, 1989) was renowned as a "founding father" and "major force" in country music. He is credited for coining the country music genre, which had previously been called hillbilly music. Gay was the founding president of the Country Music Association (CMA) and co-founder of the Country Music Hall of Fame. The CMA established the Connie B. Gay Award to recognize outstanding service to the CMA by a member not serving on the Board of Directors.
>
> Gay was an entrepreneur who leveraged his musical insight into a profitable empire that extended his legacy into the modern era. He was responsible for discovering some of the talent that now resides in the Hall of Fame, and was himself inducted in 1980, for significant contributions as a music executive.

Gay was born in Lizard Lick, North Carolina [about 20 miles east of Raleigh] on August 22, 1914. His parents, John William Gay and Mary Etta Ferrell Gay, owned a 17-acre tobacco farm where Gay worked as he grew up. He was prepared to carry on the family operation after his parents retired, and most of his efforts were focused towards that end. He supplemented his income and farming knowledge through employment as a farm extension agent in Caswell County, North Carolina. However, instead of farming, Gay became "a major force in country music" known as a "media magician" and a "leading entrepreneur of the 1950s."

Gay graduated from North Carolina State University in 1935, receiving a Bachelor of Science in Agricultural Education. He then worked a variety of jobs including a soil surveyor, a proponent of the Rural Electrification Program, even a stint as a carnival barker, where he depended on making sales to succeed.

In 1938, Gay became an employee of the US government, working for the Farm Security Administration (FSA) in various areas. He became a news commentator in 1941 for a recurring radio broadcast called the "National Farm and Home Hour." The show was broadcast daily throughout World War II. Gay, learning media operations during those years, decided to pursue it as a vocation. In 1946 he left his government employment and ventured into the private sector, ultimately becoming a success in the field of country music.

From 1946 to 1960, Connie B. Gay was a disc jockey [at WARL in Arlington and WNBW in Washington], concert promoter, artistic talent scout/manager, owner of radio and television stations, and music executive. In 1946, Connie B. Gay persuading Frank Blair, the program manager of WARL, a radio station in Arlington, Virginia, to let him do a half-hour show at noon each day. Gay offered to forgo a salary in exchange for a percentage of the advertising revenue, and an agreement was reached. His show, "Town and Country Times" was promoted as offering "a little bit of town and an awful lot of country" and broadcast six days a week. Gay had the business sense to register his program's name as a trademark, an important factor in measuring his financial success. The endeavor was very successful, growing to a three-hour program that was syndicated across the United States and to some international markets on the Armed Forces Network. Because Gay owned the rights to his Town and Country moniker, all negotiations related to its use required his assent. Connie Gay realized lucrative gains from brokering the programs syndication.

In 1954, Connie B. Gay began broadcasting a televised version of "Town and Country Time" on WMAL-TV in Washington, DC while continuing to syndicate the audio portion to the more than 1800 radio stations signed on to his network. He would discover Jimmy Dean and Patsy Cline soon after, and both became regular cast members of the TV program. By years end, the TV program was being syndicated to 40 different stations.

By 1956, Town and Country Time was airing in 50 urban markets, including Spokane, Tulsa, Houston, Los Angeles and Detroit. Gay had formed a company under his moniker called Town and Country Enterprises to manage his assets which had grown to include radio stations he then owned, and artists he promoted and managed. By years end, Connie B. Gay had amicably severed all ties with WARL, giving his full attention to his own enterprise and was a leading contender for

Billboard's Tycoon of the Year award, with an estimated annual gross of $2 million.

Connie Gay was involved in promoting new talent through his broadcast medium, and booking acts to an array of live events. Several country artists that Gay managed, like Patsy Cline, Jimmy Dean and Roy Clark, became inductees to the Country Music Hall of Fame. In March 1956, Gay booked a young, relatively unknown singer, who was described as a "devastating combination of Frankie Lane, Johnnie Ray, and Bill Daniels" in Dorothy Kilgallen's syndicated column. Fifty years later, that night, when Elvis Presley performed for over three hours, had become "the stuff of legend."

In 1958, Connie Gay helped found the CMA and served as its first president. Gay called for a meeting in his hotel room with Wesley Rose, Hubert Long, and Dee Kilpatrick, to discuss the defunct Country Music Disc Jockey Association. The meeting culminated with plans to create a new association that would cater to all aspects of country music, and the CMA was born. Gay also helped organize the Country Music Foundation, which operates the Country Music Hall of Fame and Museum. In 1963, the CMA instituted the Connie B. Gay Award as an honor of high prestige. Gay funded the award with his personal assets and established a trust, in his will, to ensure perpetual viability beyond his lifetime. Now called the Founding President's Award, recipients include Roy Acuff, Johnny Cash, Martina McBride and Brad Paisley.

Gay retired in 1972, selling his business assets and terminating his executive endeavors in country music. Gay's career total gross earnings are estimated to be $50 million [in 1972 dollars – ed.]. Connie Gay died from cancer on December 3, 1989 at the age of 75. His legacy endures, as he is considered "a true founding father of present-day country music."

Let me add an additional description of Gay's business acumen and personal strength. Gay not only proposed the formation of the Country Music Association, he wrote the first check to move it from his idea to a reality. Margaret Jones in her 1995 biography, *Patsy: The Life and Times of Patsy Cline*, tells the reason why that name change was of critical importance:

> Gay became one of the first to coin the term country music, in place of the less flattering connotation of hillbilly. But to succeed in the postwar years, Gay knew he had to dispel the connotation that it was the music of ignorant, toothless, barefooted, inbred white trash; it had to become smooth, or smoother.

His decision to offer his own "Town and Country" radio show of country music beginning at 10:30 on Saturday evenings and its success became a model for country music broadcasts. He fired Patsy Cline, and he did so for her "unreliability, rebelliousness and drinking" deemed by him to be "out of hand." Of course, Cline had her response to that firing by making it clear to all who listened that Gay had his problems too. Gay also had a falling out in 1959 with Jimmy Dean, whom he had helped make a national figure, but Dean over time acknowledged that Gay's take on Cline was mostly right, and Dean was reported in country music and his sausage making to have his problems. Gay was particularly good to those who were good to him. He assisted Winston-Salem's and UNC-Chapel Hill's George Hamilton IV's career, including opening the Grand Ole Opry door for him. In a significant knocking down of a racial barrier, Gay helped Charley Pride from Mississippi become in 1967 the first black performer on the Grand Ole Opry stage since harmonica-playing DeFord Bailey was last there in 1941. Pride went on to become the CMA's Entertainer of the Year and Top Male Vocalist in 1971 and the latter again in 1972, both bolstered by Gay's support. Gay also booked the first country music event, starring Eddy Arnold, at the Daughters of the American Revolution's stately Constitution Hall in the nation's capital, nearly in the shadow of the Washington Monument.

Connie Gay and Washington Area Airports

An additional example of Gay's boldness demonstrated how far he was willing to push an idea with potential monetary gain, and it emerged in the postwar suburb of Falls Church, Virginia. It combined terrifying excitement with his firmly held belief that the Washington area was full of hillbillies who needed that excitement and a loosened grip on their dollars. Gay brought in 1949 an aptly named "Hillbilly Airshow" to that suburb, one featuring country music singing stars and a North Carolina air circus, complete with acrobatic planes and airplane wing walkers.

It's unclear how much money Gay made or lost on the airshow, but it did make political noise when the mayor of adjacent Alexandria complained that the event demonstrated how dangerous it was to have it in the air over Falls Church's Washington-Virginia Airport within minutes of flying time from Washington National Airport on the Potomac River and Bolling Field across the river from it, as well as too near to Beacon Field Airport for private aircraft and Hybla Valley Airport for US Navy pilot training on US Route 1 immediately south of Alexandria. I could not find if he also included Fort Belvoir's Davis Field not far south of Hybla Valley's. The mayor had a good case to make that five or six airports within a few minutes' flying time of each other was inherently dangerous to those in the air and his constituents and others on the ground. Today, only Washington National survives among the first five as an airport for fixed-wing aircraft, and it does so as the renamed Ronald Reagan Washington National Airport, which is DCA on your luggage tag. The otherwise inexplicably named streets of Beechcraft Drive, Convair Drive, Fairchild Drive, Fordson Road,

Lockheed Boulevard, Northrup Road, Piper Lane, and Stinson Road are on the north end of the Hybla Valley Airport site. In that patchwork of streets, Grey Goose Way exists in a possible recognition of Gray Goose Airways and its attempts to perfect an aircraft with a swirling disc rotor. Gray Goose's search for funds involved relocating its headquarters to 1225 New York Avenue, NW, in downtown Washington. There, they were only twelve city blocks from Congress and only three-plus from the White House. In the nation's capital city of appropriated public funds, human conduct has changed little over decades if not two centuries. I rush to add in fairness to Gray Goose leadership's vision that Leonardo da Vinci's late-fifteenth-century design of an aerial screw had encouraged Gray Goose's leadership, and Igor Sikorsky's early 1940s successful invention of the first vertical lift aircraft, which we know as a helicopter, showed their idea was not crazy. But, back to mother and Connie Gay.

Connie Gay, FDR, and Country Music

Mother told me that she thought Gay had been the radio announcer for one or more of President Franklin D. Roosevelt's thirty fireside chats, even though they were not by a fire, Gay presumably intoning, "Ladies and Gentlemen: the president of the United States." I sought to verify this, but I could not, yet what emerged was close to what she thought. In Jones's *Patsy* is a description of what Gay really did in respect to those fireside and other FDR chats:

> Gay's admiration for Roosevelt inspired him to go to work for the Farm Security Administration. During the war he worked on the USDA's "National Farm and Home Hour," one of the biggest network shows of its time. Like radio announcers everywhere, Gay was a jack-of-all-trades, handling everything from writing agricultural tidbits for FDR's fireside chats and Victory Garden slogans to fielding phone calls.

His association with the president, White House staff, and Department of Agriculture leadership could not have cooled his ambitions. To the contrary, Gay had taken Washington by storm, so to speak, and as Jones recounts in *Patsy*, he

> realized that despite its cosmopolitan veneer, the nation's capital was at that time "the biggest city in North Carolina." The residents, half of them transplanted from the hinterlands of the South, brought with them a thirst for the whining of fiddles and the crying of steel guitars and the adenoidal laments of white soul that went unquenched because D.C. did not then have a radio station that catered to hillbillies.

Gay was to satisfy those needs in big ways, and *Patsy* is an informative read in respect to his combination of knowledge, intuition, and bravado, as well as the advent of country music in the nation's capital and nationally. In a late-1940s carve out of territories in the country, Gay pulled the proverbial wool over the eyes of his two competitor-collaborators, one of whom was the legendary Col. Tom Parker of later Elvis Presley fame. As Gay put it in his own words as Jones recounts them:

> I got Washington and the Northeast. They thought the East was the short end of the stick, but that was where the money was, in the media. There were big men in the East who understood the media, but they didn't understand my muscle and they left me alone. They could have squashed me like a bug, but to them I was a penny waiting for change.

Gay had figured out the commercial relationships not only between radio and television on one hand but also as to how they related to increasing the draw and resulting gate for live country music events.

As Jones described this in *Patsy*, Gay's ticket prices "were considered outrageously expensive—$ 3 to $ 6—but Gay believed the steep price would add to the cachet of 'country music,' and sure enough, senators and cabinet members attended."

I did not in the late 1960s know this much detail about Gay, but I did know the broad outlines of his life story. I certainly knew who he was, because he was frequently mentioned in news reports and social pages in respect to radio and television in and out of the nation's capital. He owned radio stations in Washington. WGAY coincidentally embodied his surname whether it was his station or not. Washington area radio buffs believe WGAY was derived from Washington Government And You, which predated both Gay and the far off in time social and political action movements. His WQMR stood for Washington Quality Music Radio. He owned other stations as well, and as *Patsy* points out, they were throughout the country.

My mother was coming to Washington for some time with me. I got in touch with Mr. Gay and brought him up to date as to who I was as it related to Lottie Rhew and her pending visit to Washington. He agreed to have lunch with the two of us if I could get her to agree. I wondered from that inference if he had figured out decades earlier Mom's bashful behavior patterns. With that inference in mind, I did not tell her what I was up to. Instead, I reserved a table at the Capitol Hill Club behind the Cannon House Office Building. I knew he was a dyed-in-the-wool FDR Democrat, but I regarded him having lunch at a Republican club as needed bipartisanship. We arrived at roughly the same time and moved to the dining room. After five or ten minutes, I signed the eventual chit next to me, a convenient advantage of a private club, excused myself with a brief explanation of what was under way, and left them alone to talk for what was about an hour. As surmised by me, Mom had been quite shy about the matter when she realized what was occurring, but I figured his personality would overcome that. I asked her later how it had gone, and she summarized it with one word, "Fine." She went into no details, and I did not pry. I have no knowledge as to whether they ever communicated further, but I received several days later a nice thank-you note from him, which I forwarded to her. He may have sent one to her.

Connie Gay and Jimmy Dean

I'll make a final comment on country music careers. It also underscores a point made by genealogists as to family history being all around if a person is sufficiently knowledgeable to connect the dots.

On one hand, Gay and Jimmy Dean, a Texan by birth but a deeply felt Virginian by choice, had their parting of the ways, although I do not know the breadth of their divide. On the other, Jimmy Dean's Dean Foundation, which was established by him to support education and was later administered by his daughter Donna Dean Stevens and her husband, gave a significant matching grant of $100,000 in 2015 in honor of her father to the Henricus Foundation in support of the Henricus Historical Park on the James River east of Richmond.

This reenactment park site is built on the site of the Sir Thomas Dale–founded Citie of Henricus. Founded in 1611, four years after Jamestown, Henricus was established upriver as "a convenient, strong, healthie and sweet site to plante a new towne." Henricus became the site in 1614 of the first hospital (Mount Malady) in English North America as well as the first college (Colledge of Henricus—that is how its "college" was spelled) to educate both colonists and Native Americans in what would become the English New World. Henricus's location on a deep-draft section of the James River made it safer for other English settlers to locate and for John Rolfe and others to cultivate and export tobacco, known to colonial history as the "golden weed," at first exclusively to England. It was that export which assured the economic survival of the Jamestown colony. It was between Jamestown and Henricus that Rolfe courted and married King Powhatan's daughter Pocahontas.

Henrico County became in 1634 one of the eight original shires, the English term for counties, of Virginia and occupied a vastly larger territory than it does today. Sections within the original land patent were sold to newly arriving other English families. One was the Jefferson family, and it was here that "the original" Thomas Jefferson, the same being President Thomas Jefferson's ancestor, was born in 1677 at the family estate of Snowden. So what is my connect-the-dots point here? As a descendant of that original Thomas Jefferson through his son Field, who was President Thomas Jefferson's uncle, I passed these Henricus and Snowden sites near Interstate 95 between Richmond and Petersburg many times without knowing until 2016 that I was passing them.

My recollections of my mother's observations on living include:

- "Wait till your dad gets home!" It was intended to strike terror in me, my brother, or both, and it usually did.
- "Have you done your homework?"
- "You're lazy!" I trust this was intended to spur me forward, not a revealed truth, but it stung nonetheless.
- "We each choose how we die." I usually heard this when I was unscrewing the lid of the mayonnaise jar.
- "Fri-i-i-ied chicken!" And did her grandchildren ever chuckle upon hearing this exclamation and enjoy its obvious reference as well as her accompanying side dishes and desserts.
- "Better get used to it." In much of my adult life, I have written in a pocket calendar the names of persons known to me who died in that year. I do this to recall their names for All Souls Day, set forth with other parishioners' recalled names in the church's Sunday bulletin most immediately before November 2. For me, 1998 bore witness to a high number of deaths. I mentioned this in a telephone discussion with her, presumably looking for sympathy. She listened, there was a pause long enough that I wondered if the connection had been lost, and she responded with those words and an observation that the lists would get longer. I quickly expected her to add that there would be a year in which my name would appear on someone

else's All Souls Day list, but she did not have to say it, for it had already occurred to me.

- "I think your dad still loved me and knew how badly he had hurt me but just had no other way out of his situation." She went to her grave believing, or wishing deeply to believe, this about their divorce. Hopefully for her spirit's sake, she was right.

11

Schooling Begins

M Y FOUR YEARS AT DURHAM'S E. K. POWE ELEMENTARY
School were not customary. While their contexts give us four
corners of a framework, they were as much under medical doctors'
extraordinary controls as teachers' ordinary ones.

Aside from that reality, a source of my angst was the too slow
pace of teachers' study plans, an impatience that led to my disruptive
behavior. I have wondered during adulthood if those disruptions had
come from what we now know as attention deficit disorder, yet that was
never diagnosed—or if it was, I was never informed of it by teacher or
parent. I was then, as now, able to complete lengthy and complicated
tasks, which is not characteristic of that disorder. Teachers had patience,
because they were required to have it, but I did not.

What is there to write about first grade in 1950–1951's academic
year? I recall in which classroom this was and could walk right into
it now. My report card indicates I was absent a startling one-third
of its nine months. My absences were caused by hospitalization from
hepatitis, repeated bouts of severe bronchial asthma, and the usual colds
and sore throats. Excused though they were, they had adverse impacts.

When mother brought me to the classroom after one of my protracted absences, I clung in the hallway to her, whereupon she picked me up and carried me into it. I was frightened because I had no idea how to fit into where they were in their work. My dreams to this night often reflect this fear of not catching up with persons or situations or both. It amazes me that I was nonetheless given three As in writing, arithmetic, and effort and two Bs in reading and conduct. Ah, there's that conduct matter. I have no facial or other recall of either of that year's two teachers. I do have two written remarks from them in my report card, the first being at the end of the second month: "Randy is doing good work and is a fine boy."

Is it startlingly that the second entry does not appear, after six blank comment spaces covering most of the academic year, until the end of the school year? It is "I have enjoyed Randy. I hope that it will be so that he can read library books this summer. This should help."

This should help what? Presumably, catching up with my classmates. Perhaps also getting ahead of them in case I had continued illness-based absences during the second grade? I responded to that challenge. If anything from those years was a direct by-product of my sicknesses, it was my converting my hours alone into reading hours and then the trivia interests that can come from maybe too much reading. I read, I read, and I read.

One of my favorite early childhood books was *The Story About Ping* by Marjorie Flack and Kurt Wiese, commonly referred to as simply *Ping*. Published in 1933, it is an illustrated account of a domesticated Chinese duck lost on China's fabled Yangtze River, and it became a nearly instant children's classic. In the context of an eighty-five-year lookback, it is an historically accurate depiction of China then, now politically incorrect, or both. Years after my encounter with it, Captain Kangaroo or his friend Mr. Greenjeans read *Ping* weekly for seventeen years. Soupy Sales, Howdy Doody, Shari Lewis's sock puppet Lamb Chop read it on air too. As I was planning in 1981 my first trip to mainland China, as that adjective was less off-putting than Red China or Communist China depictions of the official Peoples Republic of China, I bought a new copy for Jessie and me to read to our children. I was not only on a boat on the Yangtze River where it converges near Shanghai in coastal China with the Huangpu during that first trip, but Darlene McKinnon and I were on it in central China for three days in 2015.

A later childhood book heavily influenced me. It was *History's Hundred Greatest Events* by writer William A. DeWitt and illustrator Samuel Nisenson. It generated interests in American and world history. Little would I have suspected at the age of ten or eleven that five of those events involved my direct lineage ancestors:

- Charles Martel, that is Charles the Hammer, as to his AD 732 defeat of the Saracens near Tours in what is modern-day France, as the Saracens were pushing northward from Moorish Spain;
- Charlemagne, Charles Martel's grandson Charles the Great, crowned Christmas Day in AD 800 in Rome as the first holy Roman emperor;
- William the Conqueror's AD 1066 victory at Hastings over King Herald and his army of footmen and horse, the latter worn out from a forced march from Herald's victory over Vikings at Stamford Bridge only days earlier, in order for this Norman duke to subjugate its people and for him to become their William I;
- the AD 1215 sealing of the Magna Carta by a reluctant King John before twenty-five surety barons acting on their own behalf and that of others throughout the realm, this Great Charter laying the foundation of common law in both England and its later British empire, including especially America, at least ten of those barons being my ancestors; and
- Jamestown's 1607 settlement as the first permanent English colony in North America and the beginning of both the British Commonwealth and the independent United States of America, some of its settlers being my ancestors as well as members of the new colony's governing House of Burgesses, and one of its Speakers.

When I had finished other books in our Eighth Street rooms, I tackled a thousand-plus-page, green faux-leather one-volume encyclopedia, which poor families could afford, the name of which I do not recall. I am confident that my trivia interests arose further from its pages. I did add the Bible to my reading, though I do not profess to having read it page after page, but not a single page of which was as vivid to me as it was to be after I started traveling within the holy lands nearly annually for about fifteen years. Visiting the well-documented and other "by faith believed" locations described in the Bible and noting their geographical, cultural, faith, and other historical relationships are in my opinion without parallel in biblical study. I recommend fervently the experience to anyone within and without the three Abrahamic faiths of Judaism, Christianity, and Islam, that being the chronological sequence of their emergences. Some of these readings came later in elementary school, so let's return to the second grade.

My second-grade teacher was Elizabeth Wilson. Miss Wilson had been my father's second-grade teacher, and she would be my half sister's. She lived on the same block as Dad's parents and two sisters' families, and when he moved back to Durham around 1960, he lived across Englewood Avenue from her. It is hard to imagine a teacher being more attentive to a second-grade student than she was to me. It did not start out that way, but a single incident changed our relationship. She requested each in our class to draw a self-portrait. Perhaps she had attended a teacher workshop on student self-awareness being ascertainable in part through self-portraits? Well, I drew a completely dismembered me: there was my body with one hand, one arm, one foot, one lower leg, one upper leg, and a part of my torso cut off. I am amazed now at this depiction, for I was a reasonably happy child, albeit often an ill one. It must have unnerved Ms. Wilson, for from that day forward, she paid much attention to me. That had its immediate effects. I got five As in reading, spelling, arithmetic, conduct, and effort and two Bs interestingly in language and writing. Shockingly, especially in light of what is here disclosed, there is not a single written comment on any of the first eight months of our nine together, with only "I have enjoyed

111

having you in my room this year" at year's end, a line that she may have written to every student except those most incorrigible.

My third-grade teacher was Mrs. W. M. Jenkins, and I do not recall her. My report card shows five As and two Bs, in each instance with a slight shift in which disciplines they were earned. I had been absent fifteen days compared to sixteen in the prior year. Her written remarks are noteworthy. After the first month: "Randal could do neater work. He has a nice attitude." After the second month: "Randy speaks out too much. He has a nice attitude but forgets too quickly." I assume the latter sentence's real meaning was that I continued to speak out too much after I was told more than once not to do so. After the seventh month: "Randy can do good work but he likes to talk and play at the wrong time. He writes too small and could do neater work. He is a happy child but needs to be a little more serious at times." She failed there to note the emerging of someone with a sophisticated sense of humor who could see the world for some of what it is, often a joke, and say something to others about it. At the end of the ninth month: That darned "I have enjoyed teaching Randy this year" appeared again as it probably did for all others.

The fourth grade in 1953–1954 was my best elementary school year. I began the year with Faye Dean Evans as my teacher, and as the days unfolded, I fell madly in love with her—I mean the highly intense love that only a ten-year-old can feel. She was remarkable in every way, but what would it ever accomplish to have such love at such an age? What wasted emotions there could be, but they weren't a waste to me. Her first, fourth, and fifth written remarks show recognition of my chronologically measured progress within her classroom, whether from love or some other potential maturation: "Randy is beginning to settle down and work, without so much talking. I have tried to help Randy catch up with his work. He has done a fine job and has worked so hard. I believe he deserves these grades. I'm pleased with Randy's new self-control of expression. He has been a fine student."

Then a shoe fell, and it fell hard and right on top of my emotions. She was getting married! Worse, she was marrying someone of derived importance, a grandson of John Daniels, the photographer at Kill Devil Hill on the Outer Banks of North Carolina who on December 17, 1903, took the often-published photograph of man's first flight in a heavier-than-air machine. There was Orville Wright on the stick with his brother Wilbur running alongside the flimsy but airborne aircraft. John Daniels was from the nearby lifesaving station at Kitty Hawk and had taken that iconic photograph. Then, my situation got even worse! Not only was she getting married, but she was also not returning to school after their wedding. Was she moving to where he lived? Were they moving to a third location? Was she choosing something else to occupy her day than teaching? I was left holding her marriage announcement in the Durham newspaper. She was succeeded by Barbara D. Smiley for the sixth through the ninth grading periods, a woman whose face I do not recall and whose surname I found irritating, since who could ever smile under my circumstances? The reward for my unrequited love appears to have been improved grades: only one B with all else As. That summer we moved to Chapel Hill, and I was to learn immediately and over time that its elementary education system was quite different from Durham's and in very favorable ways.

12

Dad

R OY TEAGUE WAS THE ONLY BROTHER OF HIS TWO SISTERS.
Born on December 19, 1917, he grew into a widely regarded,
handsome man. That observation came in part from his slightly dark
complexion, brown eyes, and height of six foot three inches. He
made friends easily in his private life and at work. The "Names in
the News" column of Atlas Constructors' June 27, 1952, edition of its
the *Construction Stiff* referred to him as a "genial fellow." A *Durham
Morning-Herald* retrospective referred to him as "always a gentleman on
and off the golf course." He was an engaging conversationalist and had a
sometimes demonstrated keen sense of humor. He managed employees
tightly, but their recognition that he worked harder than they reduced
workplace tensions. When it came to evidence of self-control, he died at
the age of fifty-two at nearly his high school weight. He was successful
in these ways.

Dad spent much of his teenage years pursuing amateur sports
opportunities. He pitched for Durham High, and news articles report
he was good at it. An athletic scholarship was his only path to a college
education, for his father's income as a wholesale ice cream salesman

was inadequate to cover its costs, even if he lived at home to avoid room and board costs. His interests in Duke University appear tied to their sports. Duke was then more a regional university, having not yet attained national and international reputations. While I have this knowledge of his baseball, I do not know at what age he began playing golf. If successful in tryouts for both, he would have had to choose only one, for both were spring sports.

Following a strong junior year baseball season, he injured his pitching shoulder during a senior year football game. Doctors concluded that the injury's severity would preclude him from pitching competitively. His response was to abandon hope of a baseball scholarship and consequentially any interest in college. If my recollections are correct, he dropped out of school in the fall of his senior year. He appears to have refocused his sports interest toward golf. Had his shoulder heeled with far less damage than the doctors anticipated? I ask this because I find their conclusion about baseball and his success at golf to be inconsistent in that shoulders are quite relevant to golfing. In a *Durham Morning Herald* photograph, he is in an Erwin Auditorium baseball uniform, so he had continued to some degree in that sport. I should have asked him about these inconsistencies. After his return to Durham years later, he turned to family and neighborhood tennis. Perhaps he did that because there were public tennis courts right out his house's back door and across a lane.

When he shared with me his not finishing high school in the fall of his senior year, it seemed downright stupid to me, but the decision may not have been his. It may have been his mother's. This was during the Depression. Further, I did not know until researching this book that his making it to the twelfth grade was three-plus grades more than his sisters. I can imagine a conversation between Dad and Grandmother that, if he were not going to college, he should start full-time work, but that is deduced from what she told his sisters. I did not know until this research that Aunt Ruby's first job was making muslin pouches for cut tobacco. I believe Aunt Jeannette's total career was with Erwin Mills.

Not finishing high school during the Depression was not uncommon, but I never shared this with my classmates, almost all of whom had fathers who were college graduates. I would never have described him as a "high school dropout," rather as "one who did not go to college," for both characterizations were and are true. Concealing the first was more difficult in Chapel Hill, as much a university town then as could exist. I acknowledged that Dad was the manager of the Dairy Bar on East Franklin Street, a job, not a profession, in that this was common knowledge. Two of my three best friends' fathers were professors at UNC, and the third's was the owner of the portrait photography shop that had the yearbook contract for UNC and Chapel Hill High in addition to most weddings, anniversaries, and other special events. That father made homemade wine from grapes grown on his sloping field across Hillview Road from our house. It could have raised eyebrows among his Baptist neighbors, but I assumed they also did not know of his weekly poker games there. Maybe they knew both and could have cared less.

In the hindsight of over half a century, I should have been easier on Dad for not finishing high school. In addition to not knowing about his sisters having been pulled off their education tracks, I did not know that Sunkist cofounder Charles Collins Teague had not finished high school. I learned on a 2015 tour of the Thomas Edison and Henry Ford winter estates in Fort Myers, Florida, that neither of them had gone beyond their eighth grades. Those were different times.

After leaving Durham High, Dad worked at an ice cream parlor and, instead of the risks of idle hands, he was flipping pancakes, fried eggs, hamburgers, and whatever else at the Toddle House several blocks away. *Hill's Durham City Directory* for 1934 reported Dad as a clerk at Southern Dairy on West Main Street and his father as a salesman there, leading me to surmise that his father may have secured this job for him. I am intrigued by his father's job description as a "salesman" because I recall him as a man who drove a refrigerated truck full of five-gallon drums of ice cream for their delivery to retail ice cream parlors and shops, restaurants, hotels, and Duke. I suppose the number not returned to the dairy at the end of each day

116

was how many he had sold as a salesman. Either Southern Dairy became or was acquired by Durham Dairy, or Dad found a successor job with Durham Dairy Co. There, he was at first "the second man" on a horse-drawn home delivery milk wagon for its route, which was the way most pasteurized milk and related dairy products were distributed in those years. It must have given him the required sense of the job. It also gave him a sense of horses' capacities to remember in that they knew their routes as well as dairymen knew them. Yes, while far less known than another, Tevye in *Fiddler on the Roof*, my father was a milkman. His early morning rise and start and the resulting early finish gave him time for nearly daily afternoon golf, especially during months with daylight savings time.

During World War II, Dad had been a coal-stoking fireman on steam-driven locomotives of the Seaboard Air Line Railway, a combination of his lifelong asthma and his fatherhood having precluded him from military service. A single document survives in my files on those years. I discovered on the worldwide web the image of his Selective Service System registration card in his own handwriting, with no date on it because there was no place for it. Alternate civilian service was a requirement when a man could not undertake military service, and that was fine with him because he supported the war and expected he had retreat expectations back to Durham Dairy. My mother told me years later that when Dad returned home from stoking the locomotive's boilers, his denim jeans were so encrusted with his own body salt from perspiration that they would almost stand on their own. It was not an easy job, especially for an asthmatic.

Near the end of the war, he returned to Durham Dairy, this time as the driver on a home delivery truck and later as a supervising route foreman. One of the fun summer events for Durham Dairy employees and their families was the annual late-afternoon-into-evening picnic at Duke Park on the north side of Durham, not to be confused with the Sarah P. Duke Gardens adjacent to Duke University. The event's seemingly endless food and drink were quite special for a child. After

Durham Dairy was acquired by Meadow Gold, a division then of Beatrice Foods Co., now Beatrice Companies, Inc., those picnics ended.

Dad and French Morocco

Dad then chose a dramatic redirection in his work life. I have no knowledge of how he became aware of the opportunity, and it may have been from advertising by Nello L. Teer Company. Founded in 1909 as a general contracting company, Teer was headquartered in Durham and had become one of the larger regional construction companies. This new job embodied opportunities to acquire additional skills, earnings, and savings from an appreciably better salary and to work out in his head whatever other issues may have been there. The opportunity was not in the city, the county, the state, or even the United States. It was overseas, specifically in western North Africa's French Morocco, which was a long way away in those years of turboprop airplanes. The job also held out for him the long weekend and holiday opportunities of Western Europe, which he had not experienced as had the World War I and World War II veterans with whom he routinely played golf, including particularly France and Spain, from which to escape the heat of the Moroccan desert and the dust and sounds of military airfield construction.

This job centered around the prime contractor Atlas Constructor's and associated companies' building of the US Strategic Air Command's (SAC) base at Nouasseur near Casablanca as well as several additional US Air Force facilities in the Atlas Mountains and the Sahara Desert. French Morocco did not become Morocco until it won its independence in 1957, but it had developed a fondness for America and Americans as a consequence of the Allied landing on its beaches in November 1942 and its success in ending its compelled ties with Nazi-friendly Vichy France. This was the real Morocco of the fictitious movie *Casablanca* and its Humphrey Bogart and Ingrid Bergman characters preceding that liberation. Operation Torch, as the military campaign was code-named, was the opening phase of the Allied assault on Nazi Germany by way of sustained attack across North Africa as a gateway to southern Europe.

The Allies' supply line of troops and material pushed eastward through Algeria, Tunisia, and Libya toward Egypt, but it began in Casablanca and gradually other Moroccan ports. Teer was a subcontractor for its specialization in highways, roads, and other paved surfaces.

This undertaking's contexts are important. The Cold War era's SAC bases in the North Atlantic formed a crescent from Greenland through North Africa, and other US air bases completed it in their stretching to southeast Europe's Turkish border with the Soviet Union. In the early 1950s, SAC had formulated the Operation Reflex strategy between other bases and Morocco with B-36 and B-47 air wings rotating to North Africa for extended temporary duty as a staging area for bombers aimed ultimately at the Soviet Union. The Nouasseur Air Base was critically important for SAC because its 12,000-foot runway could support the landings and takeoffs of SAC's heaviest aircraft. In 1958, Mohammed V insisted the United States withdraw its SAC bases in Morocco as a consequence of the American intervention in Lebanon, an intervention opposed by Islamic nations. The delayed closure in 1963 appears to have been in at least chronological coordination with other SAC base closures in that crescent. Secretly negotiated and agreed to in 1962 by the Soviet Union's Nikita Khrushchev and President John F. Kennedy, certain US airbases were closed and our Jupiter missiles withdrawn from Turkey in exchange for the Soviet Union's pledge to not install offensive missiles in Cuba. The closings and withdrawals may have been Khrushchev's initial motivation for installing Soviet missiles in Cuba, or these opportunities may have emerged during subsequent negotiations. Today, Nouasseur is Casablanca's Mohammed V International Airport, and I have landed and taken off from it.

Dad's job was not widely different from what he had done in Durham, drive a truck, except that he was paid more for doing it, and his loads were markedly different. Instead of driving milk and other dairy products from the plant to homes and empties on the return, he drove "mail" from its arrival points to construction sites and vice versa. I put mail within quotation marks because it was not just business and personal letter mail and packages but also light freight arriving by air or ship to Casablanca, Tangiers, and other air and sea points of entry. This gave him much time in his truck, and his routes covered much of this exciting country. It also involved a fair amount of spare time. Dad brought back many photographs of Morocco from the time of its Roman occupation and a few mosaics, the latter no longer permissible. I have eight of his photographs framed on a hallway wall. Instead of undertaking this work with no Arabic and little French language skills, he had Moroccan aides riding with him.

Dad's golfing prowess became relevant there, and it involved King Mohammed V. The word had gone out discreetly to the American diplomatic community and from it to contractors that the sultan had an interest in learning how to play golf better. He was the sultan, not becoming king until 1957 as a consequence of Morocco having negotiated its independence from France, but he was his Morocco's number one man. He knew both its long experience with golf and its connection to attracting foreign tourists. He knew of General Dwight Eisenhower and other Western leaders playing it while there. He may have wanted to make sure of all of its possibilities before he built his own eighteen-hole Robert Trent Jones Sr.–designed Golf du Palais Royal d'Agadir "very private" course at his palace at Agadir. It is at nearly the opposite end of Morocco from the 1917-built Royal Tangiers Golf Club near the Mediterranean and distant from the 1937 Royal Mohammedia course. The combination of his reasons may not have been known to Dad, but it did not matter. Inquiries were made as to who among the companies was known for having exceptional golfing skills. Dad was agreed upon, but I do not know if it was him alone or among several coworkers. What resulted was Dad alone or them giving golfing instructions to the sultan. In descriptions of "golf courses in Morocco," King Mohammed V's son, King Hassan II, is described as "a real golf enthusiast."

My memories of Morocco are from my participation in an international observer delegation to its 1993 election, regarded as an important sign of democratic movement in this Muslim kingdom. They are of a radically changed landscape from Dad's time. The beach near

Casablanca during Dad's years looked much as it had in the newsreels of 1942's Allied landing. By contrast, it looked during my trip like most other high-rise, upscale beach communities. It is also now the site of the Hassan II Mosque, the largest in Africa and with one of the world's tallest minarets, in which mosque Hassan II, Mohammed V, and others are now entombed. The mosque can accommodate 105,000 worshippers in a hall so large that it would umbrella Notre Dame Cathedral in Paris or St. Peters Basilica in Rome. Near it is one of the largest McDonald's on the African continent.

Dad seemed to return a different man than the one who had left for opportunity, income, and their stabilizing influences. If he was not ill at ease upon his return, he was at least uncertain. There were no immediate job openings at Durham Dairy. There followed a period of his doing little besides playing golf and reducing his savings. He became a salesman for Diamond Crystal salt and worked briefly for City Dairy, Durham Dairy's competitor. Both seemed to just mark time for something else. At Eighth Street, nothing came of consideration of their buying Grandmother Rhew's farm, even though they had sat with paper, pencils, and ruler designing a house to replace hers, could have bought it and sold lots for sufficient income to finance their own house's construction, and truly a missed opportunity and probable financial reward from it. If they had bought it, Dad could have made the commute from it to Chapel Hill. This must have added to Mom's disappointments.

After we moved to Chapel Hill, Dad considered acquiring a parcel of undeveloped land between it and Durham. It was on the southwest side of US 15-501's Mt. Moriah intersection with Interstate 40 as its western extremity. He wanted to build a golf driving range and a putt-putt course to occupy kids while their parents were instructed by him on how better to play golf. With his area reputation for golfing skills, he would have given lessons to whomever sought them but particularly to Duke, UNC and other students. Nothing came of his idea. That land's value is now enormously higher than then. Outback, Bob Evans Farms, Cornucopia, Habitat for Humanity, a cancer treatment center, and a

121

significantly sized law firm occupy its road frontage, and additional business and commercial development are behind those retailers and service providers. Whoever owned that land made a fortune; another missed opportunity for Dad.

Dad's Golf

Dad's internal balance for over twenty years seems to have been derived principally from his golf.

Tournament scoring in those years was usually based on match play, not the stroke play with which we are now most accustomed. Each hole is a contest to win and in so doing, all else even, to get "one up" in holes won. If you had a birdie four and your opponent shot par, you won the hole and were that one up. Near that round's final holes, if you were three up with only two holes remaining, the match was over, for the golfer three down did not have the holes remaining to pull even and force one or more extra holes to determine the ultimate outcome. Unless it was the final day, that day's winner played the next day against another winner from the prior day, and the loser was out of the tournament. By example, in Dad's championship flight, the top ranked of all that tournament's flights, only sixteen men would have begun on the first day, their number down to eight on the second day, then four on the third, and then to two, known as the finalists, on the fourth and last day, almost always Sunday. There is a structural analogy here with today's basketball March Madness. The initial sixteen would be in that championship flight because of their qualifying scores being better than those of first, second, third, and other flights above them in scores. By contrast, in the modern era's stroke-based scoring, a tournament winner is the one with the lowest cumulative score over the typically seventy-two holes of four days' competition of eighteen holes each day, also almost always ending on Sunday. Interestingly, match play is being slowly reintroduced in professional golf.

On the local level, Dad won in 1936 his first Hillandale Club

Championship. He was eighteen. He won that championship another four times over the next ten years. He won the more prestigious Durham Herald-Sun Tourney Championship in 1949 and 1954. He missed by only one stroke what would have been a third win, which would have retired its perpetual trophy. This tournament became the renamed Durham Amateur Championship. He was Low Gross at Chapel Hill's First Annual Amateur Golf Championship medal play. On the state level, Dad was Low Gross at the First and Second Annual State Industrial Golf Tournament medal play. On the regional level, he was Low Gross Runner-Up at the Carolinas Golf Association's tournament at Pinehurst and held the low medal honors by an amazing four strokes over the runner-up at the Carolinas District Qualifying for the United States Golf Association's 1950 National Amateur Public Links Tournament. On the national level, he played at the USGA's Silver Anniversary Amateur Public Links Championship at Seneca Golf Course in Louisville, Kentucky. If he had won that tournament, he could have attracted the attention of sponsoring investors in going professional, but he did not. Dad's other golfing achievements include three holes-in-one, two at Hillandale and the third at Hope Valley Country Club.

When the singer Perry Como, the actor Danny Kaye, and other celebrities were in Durham in the 1940s and 1950s to perform at Duke, he and other top local golfers played golf with them. He played in pro-ams with professional golf legends. I have a 1949 news clipping with a photograph of him at Hillandale with Associate Justice of the Supreme Court Stanley F. Reed. Justice Reed had been an attorney for the Teague and Collins families, which cofounded the nut and fruit cooperatives in California that became Blue Diamond and Sunkist. I wonder if Reed inquired of Dad as to whether he was related to those Teagues. Duke University golf team captain and later touring and seniors pro Michael Souchak improved his putting under Dad's coaching, as did others. Some of his amateur golf trophies, photographs from his childhood and adult life, and news articles about him are gathered as my "altar" to his memory in my Alexandria, Virginia, condominium. I acknowledge him almost every morning coming out of and almost every evening going into my bedroom when I am there.

When Good Was Not Good Enough

We should address several intertwined questions about Dad and his golf. Why was he not able to join the ranks of professional golfers? Was it because professional golf in the 1930s and 1940s and income from the circuit were tiny deltas of what they were to become? Was it a lack of sufficient golfing ability and promise to attract investors in him because playing in the National Amateur was not equivalent to winning it? Was it a lack of business knowledge, including on how to syndicate himself, as to which a lawyer could have advised him?

We can surmise at least elements of answers to these questions. He was so burdened by the expenses of a growing family that he may have felt he could not take a risk. Neither he nor his parents appear to have had the business acumen to think beyond that awareness. Durham had many successful businessmen, many of whom knew of his golfing skills, interests, and lack of personal financial resources. Some played golf with him. Maybe he was just an outstanding champion at a public course and city champion in too minor a city? Those observations, newspaper clippings, and his trophies reinforce this son's opinion of his father as an exceptional golfer, but they were not enough in a highly competitive sport.

When Dad died in 1970 at the age of fifty-two, the *Durham Sun's* sports writer of many years, Hugo Germino, wrote in his August 29 column:

> Back there in his playing days, he was a milk route salesman. He never missed a day's work during a tournament. He merely gotup a couple of hours earlier than usual – so he could deliver milk along his long route. And then he had the rest of the day free – to

take to the links to turn back one foe after another. He had a great sense of humor. On one occasion, after he had reached the finals of the championship flight, he delivered a bottle of milk to the doorstep of one foe's residence. He put a note on the bottle. "Better drink this milk for nourishment – because you're going to need it out there on the golf course against me today," the note said.

Germino closed his thoughts by quoting from an interview of Dad from only the week before's Tareyton Classic, a pro-am tournament played at Duke:

That was the last time we had an opportunity to chat with Roy Teague. He was sitting in a chair under the trees around the ninth green – watching iron shots to the green and pulling for the pros when it was their turn to putt. "Boy, I just wish I could get out there and play," he said. "You never realize how much you miss the game until health prevents you from playing. Golf has been my first love. I enjoyed every round I ever played. And I have this bit of advice for the men who are playing today: Take advantage of the opportunity, for there will come a time when you have to go to the sidelines like I have done. I just thank the good Lord that he gave me the strength to play golf as long as I did. Yes, it has been a good life – and golf has been a big part of it."

Because he did not regard golfing as a recreation, but rather as a competition, once the competitions stopped, he stopped playing. That startling awareness first came to me in writing this account. He left his sport at the top of his game, leaving golf as a recreation to others. Other than family, those attending his funeral were for the most part from his years on the links.

Family Finances

When Dad worked as a milkman, he was paying rent, buying groceries, paying for the car's gas, oil, and repairs, paying life and other insurance premiums, covering my substantial medical and pharmaceutical bills, buying our clothing and other requirements of life, paying for his physical and mental health with whatever dollars the green fees were at Hillandale, and more. When he was in Africa, his income was two or three times greater than when on the dairy routes, but it was still blue-collar income.

His financial situation was closely held by him. He lived it himself for what it was. While he must have discussed it and probably frequently with my mother and perhaps occasionally with his parents and sisters, I do not think he shared his situation more broadly. He never proposed the government in Washington improve his situation by taking income from others through taxation. To the contrary, he was an advocate of equality of opportunity, not of income or of assets. He believed in effort and reward in one's own work. As he became a route foreman, then a restaurant manager, and then a manager of seven restaurants and stores, his income grew but only incrementally. My brother and I agreed decades later that we had great Christmases and acceptable summer vacations from so little income available to him.

Did this lower-middle-class income level make me feel different? Certainly not like the words "did not finish high school" made me feel exposed. I knew Dad worked hard for what he earned and his financial insecurity was in large measure of his own making, but its emotional preoccupation was passed to my brother and to me. It has hung sometimes more than others like a darkened cloud over my own life and its search for economic security. In that stress, I passed it to our children. I regret that, except to the degree it is a welcomed stimulus to them, but I knew no way to avoid it.

As a practical matter, our duplex apartment on Eighth Street was never short of food, although Thursday evenings got close to having an empty refrigerator. Friday afternoons heralded the week's shopping at the A&P half a block from Durham Dairy. While we did have baloney in the refrigerator for school day luncheons, Dad would buy a beef steak, run it through his hand-cranked grinder, and add egg, chopped onions, and spices. We would have Paris-quality steak tartar, albeit between white sandwich bread. Dad was also a lover of oysters on the half shell, baked with or without garnishes, or in a creamy, oniony stew, an oyster tradition passed to me and by me to our children and by them to our grandchildren.

How Mom cooked meals in the small space of our Eighth Street kitchen is beyond me. Weekend meals were more elaborate and often a part of either the Teague or the Rhew extended families' recipes or other experiences. I marvel at how she had enough room to prepare holiday meals for larger gatherings. She had her prohibitions against cooking cabbage, fish, or liver, their smells being her objections. She said if you want it, order it when eating out, ignoring that we seldom ate out. She enjoyed cooking pork roasts, and we loved making sandwiches from its cold leftovers. In those days, someone had to drive a nail into a coconut to drain it, clobber it with a hammer to break it open, carve the meat from the shell, and grate the coconut meat, all for one layered cake for which the layers had to be mixed and baked in layer pans. She grated cheese, she peeled and cut or diced our fruits and vegetables, and she shelled our peas and beans.

Our screened-in back porch had a small potbellied black iron stove of unknown origins. Mom would sometimes fire it up and plop biscuit or dinner roll dough on its hot surface. Blackened on the bottom, moist within, and awaiting whatever we chose to put between its buttered or mayo'd slices, no restaurant ever had better ones. Our Chapel Hill kitchen was larger and better designed, but we had to wait until our St. Petersburg house to have breathing room in a kitchen.

There is one thing from our Durham years that made me feel guilty as a child. It was the doctor, pharmacy, and hospital bills Dad had to pay from my asthma and all else afflicting me. I was frequently in doctors' offices and occasionally in hospitals. I fought for breath many nights, struggling to get air into my lungs, with a vaporizer steaming Vicks Vapor Rub into our bedroom's air. I overheard gentle Doc McDonald at McDonald's Pharmacy on Ninth Street encouraging Dad to be more current with his account, me knowing that it was overdue because of expenses incurred for me.

When my wife, Jessica, and I were sitting in a pediatrician's office in Alexandria with a sick child or two during the 1980s, I read a wall poster's message directed at me. The message? My chances as a childhood asthmatic and nonsmoking adult of contracting lung cancer from household secondary tobacco smoke were forty-three times greater than an undefined norm. I reasoned that, if I contracted lung cancer, it would be a direct consequence of my labored asthmatic breathing in of Dad's ambient cigarette smoke. As if it were an alarm clock, the first sound I heard most mornings was the metallic click of his cigarette lighter as he moved from bed to bathroom. Did that poster give me heightened angst? You bet. Would I blame Dad if I contracted lung cancer? I think yes as to the ridiculousness of inhaling chemicals-laden smoke into his lungs. The public policy war on tobacco was in its infancy, although one of mother's cousins-in-law, Wade Carlton of the research staff at Liggett & Myers, helped to develop a cigarette with less health risk by reducing its tar. It met that objective, but its filter was so tight that surveyed smokers compared it to trying to suck yokes out of not a raw egg but rather a boiled one. Carlton was its brand name, but that was a coincidence, for it was almost certainly named to associate it with a London hotel. This was Durham, and we lived within a mile of the cigarette plants producing hundreds of millions annually of best-selling Lucky Strikes, Chesterfields, and other brands. Even the mulch around acid-loving azalea bushes in Durham was tobacco stems, not the pine straw used throughout much of the South.

After his divorce and remarriage in Nevada, Dad returned to Durham. He had his parents, sisters and their families, as well as lifelong friends and other acquaintances there. It made better sense than returning to St. Petersburg. Over the decade or so that he and his new family were in Durham, he worked first for Long Meadow Farms, the principal competitor to his prior Meadow Gold–acquired Durham Dairy. One might consider that employment as an act of disloyalty to his long relationship with Durham Dairy, but recall that he had begun his dairy affiliations with Southern Dairy as a teenager and that, more importantly, he needed immediate income. Long Meadows' operations were on James Street, and he and his new family lived close to them. He then managed Harvey Rape's Harvey's Cafeteria on East Main Street, demolished with neighboring structures in the late 1960s so that Duke Power's, now Duke Energy's, new Durham offices could be built on that city block. At Harvey's, their three girls would accompany him on Sunday evenings to make doughnuts and pastries for Monday morning's early customers. Mr. Rape had the food services contract for the employees' cafeteria at the nearby American Tobacco Co.'s cigarette-manufacturing plant, so Dad had that responsibility too.

Dad's next-to-the-last job was managing Biscuit King at 816 Ninth Street, known in its environs for its "enormous biscuits" and located by coincidence only forty yards or so behind what had been years before our Eighth Street duplex. His wife, Barbara, was at his side there in seeking to make it a success. Biscuit King was several retail doors from Rinaldi's, a family-owned restaurant that had one of Kentucky Fried Chicken's earliest franchise rights and, as a consequence of negotiations with Col. Harlan Sanders's company, was able to remain Renaldi's while advertising and selling Kentucky Fried Chicken fare. Along with Burl Ives, Buddy Hackett, Lorne Greene, Shelley Winters, and other famous and not famous patients, Sanders was a participant in Durham's Rice Diet Program. He would sometimes appear in full costume at Rinaldi's and surprise the heck out of its customers. Duke University had already severed its relationship with this diet program, but it closed in 2013 after seventy years of offering its methodical way to lose weight. It had been surpassed in public choice by the Atkins, South Beach, Paleo, and other diet programs.

Dad's last position was managing one of UNC-Chapel Hill campus's student cafeterias. So many of his fifty-two years were spent within blocks of or on the campuses of Duke and UNC, he must have continued to enjoy students' presences. Perhaps it helped give credence to a thought that under different circumstances he could have been one of them. He was back with UNC students for the first time in thirteen years. Unrelated to that thought, a childhood memory is of him hitting a bag of golf balls with his short irons on a Duke East Campus field at Broad Street and West Markham Avenue. It was only one block from Eighth Street and much cheaper than a driving range. In fact, it was free. That area is now a nearly fully developed collection of athletic fields. He died on August 27, 1970, and several days later joined his father in Durham's Maplewood Cemetery to await his mother there in 1976 and his sister Ruby in 2000.

Nearing fifty years after his death, I miss him, his observations, and our conversations. I see his successes and failures differently now than I did during his lifetime and even during the earlier years following his death. He took pride in his work and the abilities that grew from it. I live with regrets, but I think that observation is true in many, perhaps most, father and son relationships. I see in my own mistakes patterns from his, and, mistakes though they were and are, perhaps recognizing them unites us in an additional way.

My recollections of Dad's observations on living include:

- "You can't always control outcomes, but you can control your efforts toward them."
- "Do it right the first time and don't cut corners. They're good work habits to have. And they'll impress your boss and others."
- "Finish what you had in mind to do when the day began. Tomorrow will have another set of its things to do."
- "You are seldom the smartest person in a room. But you can most of the time be the hardest working person in that room, the first one there, and the last to leave. Others will note that."
- "The beauty of God's creation can be as appreciated on a golf course of fairways, forests, and streams as any cathedral made by man."

- "If you want to be a good cook, you have to be willing to experiment, to think through what was probably in a recipe unknown to you and how it was prepared. You also have to be wise enough to acknowledge a failure at it, throw it into the garbage can, and take the family out to dinner."

- "On highway trips, always stop at the restaurant which has the most cars out front. The one with the least may have the shortest line and be the fastest service, but that shorter line is for a reason known to the locals."

- "If there are only local cafes to choose from and you are unsure of their food, have a fried egg sandwich on toast. No one ever died from one."

- "Sometimes, you have to be bold." Sort of like when it was late on a Sunday afternoon in a Hillandale golf tournament on its second extra, therefore twentieth, hole. The sun was beginning to set, so he drove his tee ball over the tall pine trees on a four-par dogleg left fairway, and it landed nearly on its green for him to then chip and putt his tournament-winning strokes, my reference here being to the second hole of the originally designed Hillandale course when the clubhouse was on the northeast corner of Hillandale Road and Club Boulevard, that second hole now being the redesigned course's thirteenth hole.

- "Don't ever own a restaurant. Don't ever manage one either."

13

More Durham Memories

I HAVE DISCUSSED RUBY'S CAFÉ AT LENGTH, BUT WHAT about other Durham eateries? After all, there are culinary reasons why southerners, especially men, die at younger ages than others. That fact relates in some measure to the required preservation and preparation habits of their food. Prior to electrical refrigeration, southern meats were usually smoke cured, and its fish were salted. Country ham comes to mind as representative of a salt, sugar, and smoke-curing process. Fried chicken preceded its fast food offerings by centuries. Then, there were fried potatoes, fried eggs, fried fish, fried oysters, fried anything. A joke line about southern cooking is "They'd fry lettuce if it didn't wilt!"

The priciest restaurant in West Durham after World War II was the Saddle & Fox on Hillsborough Road. It was built and opened in 1946 by Charles Haynes Jr. as the Saddle Club. Haynes was at age thirteen the city's youngest Eagle Scout. He became a member of the Duke University football team, which played the 1942 Rose Bowl at Duke Stadium because of West Coast fears so recently after the December 1941 Japanese attack on Hawaii's Pearl Harbor. The restaurant's name came from its proximity to the Hillandale Stables of

Durham's fox-hunting gentry. The Haynes family owned many West Durham properties, and what they did not, John Sprunt Hill mostly did. In more recent years, the Saddle & Fox's ownership and branding changed to Cattleman's in an apparent attempt to bring the Southwest to Durham, but its quality must have been found wanting, for it was torn down in 2009 to be replaced by O'Reilly Auto Parts. My cousin Nancy recalls that when her husband, Donald Grunert, a Duke medical student who died far too young, was in medical school, his parents sent him thirty dollars spending money each month, and his favorite "splurge meal" upon receiving it was at a restaurant on Chapel Hill Road where two pork chops, french fries, a lettuce-and-tomato salad, and a drink cost a single dollar. Today, they might cost the better part of that whole thirty dollars!

Sharing with Ruby's a distinction for superb hotdogs was Amos 'n' Andy's on East Chapel Hill Street around the corner from downtown's Carolina Theater. Although the once-popular radio show and then television show are cringe worthy today, Durham loved this eatery's dogs. Why was this hole-in-the-wall so named and famous? Because the creators of the Amos 'n' Andy shows, Freeman Gosden and Charles Correll, met in Durham in 1919 while working in a theater production at the Temple Building a block away. Both were veteran vaudeville actors. Correll was told to confer with Gosden about a staging problem, so they met. That is fact, but it has never been proved that they met for the first time at this eatery, and even if they did, it would not have been named Amos 'n' Andy's. But, first, second, or later meeting, they did meet there, and its new name emerged from that happenstance. Gosden and Correll worked together for fifty years, but the café did not survive Durham's urban renewal programs in the 1960s or '70s.

Bullock's Barbeque off of Hillsborough Road was a popular place for barbeque during my childhood and remains one. Its entrance walls are covered with autographed photos of the famous from the worlds of sports, television, country and other music, and politics. Not to do business on the Lord's Day and to assure their employees a five-day work week, Bullock's is closed on Sundays and Mondays, a lesson learned and necessarily relearned in my adult years. Their vinegar-based chopped pork BBQ and their Brunswick stew are exceptional, and the chocolate pie is extraordinary. Their tea is sweet enough to ricochet a child off the ceiling.

The Angus Barn near the north entrance to Raleigh-Durham Airport is halfway between Durham and Raleigh and convenient to diners from both cities and those in between. It's a country store-fashioned restaurant where state government officials and lobbyists can feel at ease and where families with small children can do the same. Proof of the effectiveness of that strategy is that this 1960s steakhouse is still serving.

The Ringling Bros. Barnum & Bailey Circus, which came to Durham each November, pitched its big top tent in the Durham fairgrounds field near Hillandale Stables and marched its circus wagons and animals from its train to that field to the delight of children and adults. There's another "it's a small world" example here, for the Bailey in that circus's name is from the once independent circus owner and his training site at what is now Bailey's Crossroads in suburban Virginia.

Repetitive Nighttime Dreams

I had three sets of repetitive nighttime dreams, and I had another so unusual, the fourth, that I recall each sixty-plus years after their occurrences. Like nearly all dreams, the origins of each were then and remain now more than difficult to comprehend. The uniqueness of the three sets is that each's rerun dream was the same as its premier one. If I worked on a director's guidance for Hollywood films, I could have storyboarded each. Further, there were months or more distances of time between each's first and second. None was an awakening followed by an immediate return to sleep and the continuation of a dream, and no set overlapped with another.

In the first set of two dreams, I was a child holding hands with a woman whom I felt to be my mother but not with the physical appearance of Lottie Teague. She had on floor-length winter clothing, and her head was wrapped in a shawl. We were with a few others in a darkened warehouse-like building with a large opening to the nighttime outside and with high stacks of sewn large bags against a wall. A militarily uniformed man on horseback and with a drawn sabre rode quickly toward us. From their attire, it was in Russia.

In the second set, I was engaged in a tank and infantry battle in a snow-covered, heavily forested area in which I was quite aware that I was at a high risk of being killed as I emerged from a tank turret. I do not know if the tank had been hit. My and other tanks were moving from left to right on the dream's screen with a moderately high hill running along behind our earthen roadway. The indication that this dream was connected to the Second World War was the design of the tank.

In the third set, I was coming out of the front door of a brick house on the south side of the 400 block of Hugo Street off of Roxboro Road in north Durham where lived a cousin of my mother, Carolyn Rippey, and her family. As I walked at nighttime out of that door, I looked eastward at a bright full moon seen beyond Carolina long-needle pine trees in their neighbors' front yards. I saw an enthroned, seated figure silhouetted against a full moon surrounded by silver-bright clouds as the moon turned blood red. I understood it both times to be the beginning of a Second Coming of Christ. I was terrified and awakened. Thoughts of this dream occurred to me years later when my grandmother Teague told me of what the African American field hand had told her Lasater family on the morning after her birth, that she would be alive at the time of Christ's return to earth. I think of this dream every single time I pass Hugo Street. It has never left me, and pine trees are still standing there.

The fourth dream I had only once, and I think I know some of its contexts, for they range from scriptural to eventful. The scriptural is Jacob and his ladder as described in Genesis 28:10–19, and the eventful is it occurring during the night of April 7–8, 1956, before I was baptized by emersion at the Baptist Church of Chapel Hill on the afternoon of the eighth. There was a ladder resting at the apex of our family's 1208 Hillview Road house roof in Chapel Hill, and every so many rungs had on each side figures standing seemingly in space, not on it. Angels? Not if wings are within the definition. Saints or prophets? How would I know? With musical accompaniment? No. I never shared the fact of this dream with my family, but I am confident that, if I had shared it with my mother's mother, she would have said I was being told I should become a preacher, for she would sometimes observe that I then looked like a young Billy Graham. No wonder she was distraught at my becoming a lawyer, which vocation she regarded as an assured pathway to hell.

Raleigh's Pullen Park

While I am recounting memories, another is of the extended family's annual get-togethers at Pullen Park in Raleigh. This park is in west Raleigh, which is toward the Durham side of the state capital. The Teague-O'Briant-Tucker family would gather there on Sunday afternoons for what to a child was seemingly endless food and fun. For all our ages, there were the usual southern picnic foods of country ham and biscuits, fried chicken, dozens of deviled eggs, and far more. We were a Pepsi family, not a Coke one, owing to the owners of the Pepsi-Cola franchise for the Durham area, the Burnetts, having lived as next-door neighbors to the Tuckers when they were building that franchise. Speaking of soft drinks and permitting a digression, I became a Coca-Cola drinker after our move to Florida, but my favorite soft drink there was Vernor's ginger ale, an English-like "hot" ginger ale. If anyone desires a hot ginger ale, locate and buy Blenheim's pink cap variety, as to which the US manufacturer refers to as a red cap, and the British refer to that cap or top as a crown. If you do, you may never return to only the faint taste of ginger in carbonated water, which is now the prevailing formula.

In that I was increasingly interested in history, a Pullen Park attraction in those years was the birth house of President Andrew Johnson, a small, one-story house with a loft, which had been moved to it from its original location in downtown Raleigh. It was later moved to Raleigh's Mordecai Historic Park.

As to other North Carolina presidents, General Andrew Jackson had been born in 1767 at the Waxhaw, an area encompassing the present town of Waxhaw in Union County on the North Carolina-South Carolina state line. On which side of the present state line has never been authoritatively determined, but North Carolina claims the stronger case. Jackson's political career is more associated with Alabama, Florida, Louisiana, and Tennessee. Similarly, President James K. Polk of Tennessee was born in 1795 in Pineville, North Carolina, and while his higher education was at the University of North Carolina, his career is associated primarily with Tennessee. In such respect, we should not ignore that the territory that is now Tennessee was originally that most western part of the original North Carolina between the Appalachian Mountains crest and the Mississippi River. Jackson is buried at the Hermitage east of Nashville. Polk is entombed on the State Capitol grounds in Nashville, although he may be moved owing to renewed debate over his position on slavery. Johnson, Jackson, and Polk were North Carolina's presidents of the United States, and if you do not believe me, tour the State Capitol grounds in Raleigh. Their statues there were among my first awareness of presidents of the United States.

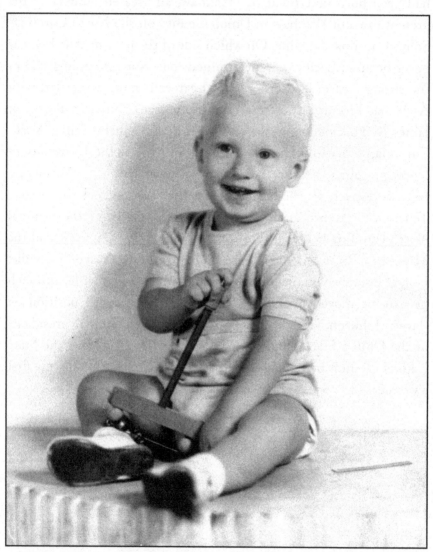

The first known studio portrait of me, taken around the age of 18 months.

Roy Merle Teague, my father, in
his early twenties. [1917-1970]

Lottie Mae Rhew, my mother, in
her early twenties. [1916-2000]

821 and 821 ½ Eighth Street,
the ½ was on the left.

We lived only one block from Duke
University's East Campus, its original
campus site. Here, James Buchanan
Duke's statue stands in from of the
West Campus's Duke Chapel.

E.K. Powe School where I attended
grades 1 through 4. Mr. Powe
was a successful advocate of early
childhood public education.

It was in Chapel Hill's atmosphere
of academic challenge that I
came to know the ties between
learning and giving back.

Three generations at my Grandparent Teague's
50th wedding anniversary celebration.

My brother Roy in the summer of 1957 loading up Dad's Oldsmobile to cross the state to Deland's Stetson University. Dad's Olds was large enough to transport me and my middle school's cheerleaders to soccer games.

A major part of my responsibilities as Student President of the Science Center of St. Petersburg was to teach youngsters about the marine biology which surrounded our city.

One of my marine botany projects was undertaken in part on the second floor of this U.S. Department of the Interior's Bureau of Sports and Commercial Fisheries laboratory on St. Petersburg Beach.

Hard at work in the laboratory during my study of the adverse effects of water pollution on the reproduction of the red algae *Gracilaria verrucosa*.

This 1964 portrait photograph was taken several months after I arrived in the nation's capital in the closing days of February 1964.

Florida Congressman William Cramer, future Senator Edward Gurney and I discuss President Eisenhower's hearty endorsement of YAF's October 1963 testimonial dinner for the Congressman.

My first job in Washington was on the Minority (that meant Republican) staff of the then-named House Committee on Public Works, whose ranking Republican member was Rep. James C. Auchincloss of New Jersey and next ranking member was Rep. Cramer. Technically, I was on "the loaned staff" of its chairman, Rep. Charles Buckley, the head of New York City's powerful Tammany Hall faction within its Democratic Party, because neither Auchincloss nor Cramer had a staff position open for me. That made "The New York Times" that fall. My specific position was at the Republican Clerk of the committee's Subcommittee on Watershed Development, overseeing an early flood protection program. Rep. Fred Schwengel of Iowa was its ranking Republican member. A strong man in a Midwest farming sense, he was a gentle soul, loved his country, and acted at times as if he might be the reincarnation of Abraham Lincoln. Upon his November 1964 defeat in the wake of the Lyndon Johnson landslide victory, he founded the United States Capitol Historical Society and remained in Washington until his 1993 death. Auchincloss was a 1921-1938 Governor of the New York Stock Exchange and introduced at a dinner party his step-niece, Jacqueline Lee Bovier, step-daughter of Standard Oil heir Hugh D. Auchincloss, to Sen. John F. Kennedy, though some historians attribute that to one of several of their introductions.

14

Chapel Hill

WHILE I RECALL DURHAM AS THE PLACE OF MY childhood, I remember Chapel Hill as the place of my adolescence. We moved to it in the summer of 1954. It was a pleasant community in which to continue growing. It was smaller than Durham then and smaller than Chapel Hill now. The growth of its University of North Carolina, support services to UNC, its permanent population, and the retirement communities southward toward Pinehurst had not yet mushroomed. Today, Chapel Hill and Durham have grown together, Chapel Hill and Carrboro have grown together, and Durham, Chapel Hill, and Raleigh have almost grown together as a consequence of the Research Triangle. Mother worked at Chapel Hill's Dairy Bar on weekdays with Dad. Dad being the manager, his hours were less predictable, longer, and frequently inclusive of weekends.

Chapel Hill was more of an intellectual community than Durham because UNC occupied a larger thought space within it than Duke did in Durham. The expansiveness of UNC within the compactness of Chapel Hill is my reference point. Its Playmakers Theater housed UNC productions and other performances. It was later surpassed by the larger

Paul Green Theater in the University's 1976-built Center for Dramatic Art. Memorial Hall, only several hundred yards from Playmakers, housed a large auditorium, probably the largest non-sports seating facility on campus. It hosted many nationally popular entertainers, and I remember the performers, trios, and others from their vinyls' 33 1/3 jacket covers. The Forest Theater east of Playmakers had been dedicated in 1916 on the occasion of the three-hundredth anniversary of William Shakespeare's death, and I recall *A Midsummer Night's Dream* performance there.

Our house on Hillview Road was an improvement over our Eighth Street apartment's three rooms. It had a better layout and was in a neighborhood of homes owned in large measure by UNC professors and Chapel Hill small business owners. Returning to Chapel Hill years later, we saw this house had gone downhill, so badly that it was in need of great repair, perhaps by a bulldozer. It's why I was surprised in a spring 2015 drive-by to see that at least some repair work had been done, albeit heavily surrounded by the forest, which had moved up its hillside as if in response to Shakespeare's command of Birnam Wood in *Macbeth* to move to Dunsinane. A chainsaw seemed to me to be in order, starting near the curb and working back to the 1957 tree line. Alas, that task is someone else's project, although I would volunteer for it even now if it were not in tick season.

Our house was across the street from school friend Joe Moore's house and its arbors for his father's annual growing of grapes for his homemade wine and its enormous oak tree behind the house. On the other side of that oak tree's canopy and down a sloping driveway was school friend Barrett Graham's house. At the bottom of Hillview Road was a family headed by a UNC music professor. They went during the summer of 1956 to Italy, and they were on the SS *Andrea Doria*'s return to the States when the Italian ocean liner was struck by the Swedish MS *Stockholm* and went down off Massachusetts's Nantucket with the loss of fifty-six persons. Thankfully, they were not among the fatalities.

The hill of Hillview Road was our sledding hill. It was a dangerous one because its steep slope ended abruptly at a T-shaped intersection

145

with Plant Road and its ninety-degree-angled curb. The survival strategy involved the sled's front edge slamming into that curb and its momentum propelling its rider into the front yard of the house. Actually, it was more complicated because the sled had to hit the curb between a telephone pole and a fire hydrant about six feet apart, elsewise you were going to be either dead or paralyzed. In further fact, it was more complicated than those possibilities because the final approach and rocketing off the sled were between screaming kids and neighborhood dogs barking at full voice. Somehow, we survived unscathed.

Schooling Continues

Mom enrolled me in Chapel Hill Elementary School on West Franklin Street, and Mrs. Rebecca A. White was my fifth-grade teacher. Unlike the Durham school's traditional A-F grading system, Chapel Hill's seems to have been a nearly bizarre pass-fail system consisting of "+" for "doing satisfactory work according to ability," "−" for "not doing satisfactory work according to ability," and "√" for "improving" presumably between the other two measurements. Any one of those three choices could be applied by the teacher, first to eighteen categories of "Citizenship" defined as "Habits and Attitudes Desirable for Good Citizenship" and next to nineteen "Progress in Studies" measurements in reading, language, writing, spelling, arithmetic, social studies, and science. That was markedly different from the more judgmental grading in Durham, but our expectations were high because Chapel Hill's school district was known to work closely with UNC. In my first year, every single one of the thirty-seven report card boxes had a + in it. After Mrs. White's first written "Suggestions from the Teacher," to wit: "Randy is a very good student. His work is nearly always neat and accurate. When he finishes his work he finds something constructive to do. The only suggestion I have to make is for him to continue to do the same type work."

I also have her next entry, making me wonder if she had another Randy in mind: "Randy's work is being done very hurriedly. As a result he doesn't always follow directions and he becomes too careless. For example, he guesses at the syllables in his spelling words and then he doesn't check to see if they are correct. As a result errors such as these occur: study-ing instead of stud-y-ing, ba-na-na instead of ba-nan-a, travel-er instead of trav-el-er. Sentences such as 'We live in a local.' And 'I studed each item carefully.' Wouldn't occur if he were to read his sentences after he wrote them. Even though he had more plus (+) grades than minus (-) grades, I want him to be aware of his faults and avoid them." Sixty years later, I noted her reference to purported minuses in that I had not a single minus in her 148 boxes where + resided in each. I noted also that my error in "studying" did not deter, perhaps it spurred, my successful quest for five university degrees, three of them in course, which required a considerable degree of "studying" and writing and other paths to those recognitions. Further, that my error in slicing "banana" into correct syllables did not undercut my role in EARTH University's farms producing nearly a million shipped boxes of them annually for Dole, Whole Foods Market, and other grocers in the US, European, and local Costa Rican markets during my service on its board of trustees for twenty-nine years and ten of them as that board's president. Or, that my error in "traveler" did not undercut my traveling to over 110 countries by last count.

I can only assume that a recalled discussion with my mother worked in respect to correctness's priority over speed, for Mrs. White's next grading period's entry is "Randy has maintained his academic standards." How could I have maintained them if I did not have them? Or does this mean my subpar standards from the previous grading period remained subpar? With the ability of that line to be read with two totally separate meanings, she should have been a lawyer or a politician or both.

My sixth-grade teacher was Mrs. Barefoot. Perhaps her not disclosing a first name on my 1955–1956 report card was her prescient way of keeping me from finding her in future years' search for answers unknown to me. This was an exceptional year for me, for it began my transition to university because UNC became a part of my life in key ways. I doubt I will ever know what occurred behind closed administrative and faculty doors. Either my effort to learn more than the rest of the class or my negative disruption of it, or both with no longer a discussion on my report cards, were to change my life. It was to accelerate my emotional escape from Eighth Street. I was not absent a single day, all my studies were graded +s, all but two of my citizenship boxes were +s, the two that were checkmarks being improvements in refraining from unnecessary talking, and all my independent study was creating additional excitement in the world before me. Yet I was still having concerns about whether I was a good or poor student.

How could I have known in those years that Charles Collins Teague had written in *Fifty Years a Rancher* that "I am sorry to say I was not a particularly good student"? I also did not know that neither his school years' weak academic performance nor his not finishing high school had held him back in life or career, in that he cofounded and headed Sunkist and received an honorary degree of doctor of laws in 1924 from the University of California. It would have been easier in my own mind in respect to my father not finishing high school if I had known those facts. Poor student in fact or not, it was going to get worse for me at the beginning of my next school year but then sharply reverse itself onto a new confidence-building and life-changing track.

Early Experiences with University-Like Life

My seventh-grade teacher was Mrs. Jane Hook. It took only a few weeks for me to conclude that this was not going to be an easy grade. My challenging of her on why she wanted us to study Napoleon, when Julius Caesar would have been a more appropriate historical figure to study, one giving us a chance to read from the classics, must have been the final straw for her. As a consequence of whatever my and other teachers thought and sought, about a dozen of us from several seventh-grade classes were extracted several weeks later, interviewed at separate times at UNC's New West building, which housed its education or psychology department or both, by adults not identified to us by name or title to administer IQ and a battery of additional tests.

The product of that testing was what we believed to be an experiment in what later became known as "gifted and talented" programming, GT for short. I had no idea then and have no idea now as to how this arose from interactions between the school, the school district, and the university, but it was in hindsight clearly to my benefit. I thought it liberated me from an overly structured rote education for an experience in independent study. I thought for many years that this meant the powers that be had concluded that we were smart. Yet it occurred to me in writing this memoir that perhaps they had determined to the contrary, that we were uneducable. Each of us remained in our regular classes, which was more annoying than ever, but after the "School's out!" bell sounded, we could each, for these were individual undertakings, not group ones, sit quietly in the back of a lecture hall, listen, and watch what went on in a chemistry or other laboratory, sit in the medical school's surgical observation domes, or watch rehearsals for plays and musical performances. It made the nature and content of university studies accessible, thereby moving me toward an expectation of university studies.

Having made this mental and emotional leap into university-level studies, albeit without measurements, nothing seemed to me to be a bigger waste of time than the seventh grade. I paid the price for that attitude. I ended the year with less-than-stellar grades, but Ms. Hook's comments were not as scathing as I anticipated they would be. Instead, they were so formal that they were probably reproduced as an enclosure for each student's final grading period. I read an imaginary "Good riddance!" between the lines.

Little did I know that the future songwriter, musician, and singer James Taylor was learning somewhere in or out of our classrooms to play cello, from which he did not switch to guitar until he was twelve. No, we did not know one another, and the social lives of our parents were at opposite ends of Chapel Hill's social spectrum. His father, Issac but known to his friends as Ike, was an assistant professor of medicine at UNC's School of Medicine where he would become its dean for seven years, beginning in 1964. The Taylors spent their summers on Martha's

Vineyard, and we spent our summers at 1208 Hillview Road in Chapel Hill as we did every other season, excepting a single week at the beach.

I would most often be driven to school by Dad, whereupon I would unload my bike from the car trunk for the afternoon downhill ride to home. This gave me the independence required to spend hours on campus. As I left the several city blocks that constituted Chapel Hill's business district, I would note to my left the Dairy Bar and its next-door book and record shop, then Morehead Planetarium to the right, followed by the Chapel of the Cross, the university president's official residence, and almost immediately the former big band swing and jazz era bandleader and radio personality Kay Kyser's house.

Kyser deserves several words about him, his short career but long life. Born in Rocky Mount, North Carolina, and a cousin of the *Wall Street Journal*'s Presidential Medal of Freedom and Pulitzer Prize twice-winning editor of its editorial page, Vermont Royster, Kyser had graduated from UNC as its head cheerleader and its senior class president. There had to have been a popularity connection between those recognitions. When this James Kern Kyser was invited by Hal Kemp to take over his Carolina Club Orchestra when Kemp moved north and eventually to California to further his own music career, Kyser adopted the initial of his middle name for its alliterative effect. Kemp was a renowned jazz alto saxophonist, clarinetist, and bandleader and would become a composer and arranger of note. Kyser in turn is regarded by music and entertainment historians of that era as a better bandleader, announcer, and even comedian than a clarinetist, but his band was regarded as excellent in its own right with eleven number one records. Although Kyser was not as successful as Tommy Dorsey, Benny Goodman, or Glenn Miller, those who sang with his orchestra included Jane Russell before she became a movie star, Frank Sinatra, and Dinah Shore. Kyser and his band appeared in several motion pictures. His "Kay Kyser's Kollege of Musical Knowledge" format filled many a nightclub and dance hall and sold many radio ads on Mutual Radio and then NBC Radio from 1938 to 1949. He passed in 1985 at the age of eighty.

Further down the hill that led away from campus, I had my nearly daily encounter with a heel-snapping dog determined to end my biking if not me. At a steeper downward angle that followed, I would pass the house on the left, which was one of my friend's, then another's across a triangulated intersection, then past the entrance to a newer development on the right, and finally a quick turn right into our sloping driveway. It was a hill nearly impossible to bike up.

The university community was continuing its long tradition of left-of-center political activities however defined. The Cold War confrontation with the Soviet Union had our nation jittery over what students were being taught about the USSR and its support of Marxist-Leninist movements, including in the United States. Communist Party of the United States cells sometimes existed on or around colleges and universities. Dad told us one morning that the FBI had notified him only a few moments before it began the night before that the basement of a property near the Dairy Bar was to be searched because it was reported to house a printing press that was publishing allegedly subversive tracts. In our years of true news, alleged fake news, or unquestionably fake news, I have no idea, and Dad probably did not know then, what the FBI found or did not find, perhaps something, perhaps nothing, and it was never clear if what occurred in the basement had anything to do with the business above the basement.

The books and records shop next door was my favorite in a town of several. In it were soundproof booths where one could take a 33 1/3 vinyl record and listen carefully to it. I used much of my allowances to buy books and records there. I can still smell in my mind's recollection the building materials that assured that soundproofing.

One of Chapel Hill's most outstanding offerings to me was Morehead Planetarium, now known as the Morehead Planetarium and Science Center. I spent many afternoons and evenings there. Designed by the same architects as the Jefferson Memorial in Washington, it opened in May 1949 as a unit of the university and is now one of the largest planetariums in the country. Three million dollars for its construction were donated by UNC alumnus, former mayor of Rye, NY, and former

US ambassador to Sweden John M. Morehead III. The Moreheads were among the state's more notable families, and its coastal town of Morehead is named for them. This Morehead had made his fortune at Union Carbide Corporation. Like many industrialists, he donated much of his wealth to charitable causes, including especially to higher education. The planetarium served as the celestial navigation training facility for US astronauts Neil Armstrong, Buzz Aldrin, Frank Borman, Scott Carpenter, Gus Grissom, John Glenn, and scores more. Together with attending lectures, observing experiments in laboratories, and sitting in the surgery ward's observation dome, the planetarium nurtured my interests in science and is among the reason why I responded readily to our St. Petersburg next-door neighbor's inquiry as to whether I would like to visit and become active in the work of the Science Center of St. Petersburg whose stories, it and mine, are told in these pages.

Our family would have been honored to have UNC name its Teague Residence Hall on Stadium Drive, nestled among trees across from Kenan Stadium football field, after our family. It was more appropriately named in appreciation of the life and service of Claude Edward Teague, the university's business manager from 1943 to 1957.

War Games

Keeping in mind that the Second World War was only slightly more than a decade past, a large wooded area behind our house became our reenactment zone.

The neighborhood took advantage of its terrain and our improvements to it. We unknowingly abridged a neighboring farmer's riparian rights, they being the rules at law for allocating water among those who possess land along a watercourse. It was a consequence of our attempt to create a swimming hole by damming, widening, and deepening a stream. With picks, shovels, rakes, hoes, and dogged determination, we set about the task. We did not succeed for three reasons. It was too big a task. That farmer was dependent in part on the flow of this water, even though we felt once the swimming hole had filled, the overflow would continue to meet his water needs. We kids did not own the land we were improving in order to negotiate a reallocation of such rights. This area is now covered with houses and their landscapes.

Building our clubhouse required identifying four trees forming a square and close enough to one another that abandoned saw mill's partially barked boards nearby would reach from one to the other. It also required a fair amount of hard work. With saws, hammers, non-copper nails so the trees would not die, and a ladder, we soon had three sides walled in, those boards being on the insides and outsides of the trees. We filled in the five- or six-inch space between them with compacted pine straw and leaves to reduce the wind and laid boards across the top. We were concerned about what might find refuge under boards if we put in flooring. Having left the ground unimproved inside the clubhouse, if we were going to spend considerable time in it, we would cover it with a canvas. Light from the open side was strong enough for our limited needs. In the spring, these woods had many dogwoods and redbuds, as well as daffodils and irises, and I would wonder who from what past had planted the bulbs. Like much in springtime, their blossoming united notions of death and renewed life, and I sensed that even in childhood.

Our platoons consisted of neighborhood boys and other friends from school. What follows may frighten a parent, maybe others too, in that we were eleven or twelve years of age. Our BB guns, our Boy Scouts–acquired hunting knives, our trench shovels, and other paraphernalia were not enough to reenact the breaking of the siege of Bastogne or thwarting a German counterattack with as much authenticity as we required of ourselves. So, we made our own hand grenades. Ours required a glass, never plastic, pill bottle with a mouth large enough that a cherry bomb would fit into it. We would pack BBs and our homemade gunpowder tightly around the cherry bomb with its fuse upright. That fuse would fit through the hole in the bottle's screw cap. Tighten the cap. When appropriate, which was always soon, someone would scream, "Where's the dog?" to assure a dog was or the dogs were safe, never mind ourselves, another would light the fuse and heave it as far as possible, and shattered glass and BBs would explode in every direction. We'd hear the BBs and shards of glass hitting rocks and leaves and zinging over our crouched heads.

We would spend hours gluing together a battleship or an aircraft carrier from a Chapel Hill hobby shop's Revell collection, adding decals and signal flags to assure authentic appearances. That accomplished, we would gather and launch it with great fanfare into a stream or pond with lighted cherry bombs or three-inch firecrackers, whereupon it was blown to smithereens. There were no flying BBs or shards of glass in this naval warfare, only flying hard plastic. Amazingly, none of us was injured in these reenactments! As amazingly, not a single druggist ever asked why we were buying sulfur and saltpeter on a fairly routine basis. Even though it consisted of only two lines, "Sulfur" and "Saltpeter," we acted as if we were on an errand for an adult, presumed to be a parent or other relative or maybe an older brother in a high school chemistry class. Consistent with that strategy, we never went as a group on these purchasing missions. One went alone. The charcoal for this gunpowder came from pulverizing into a fine powder charcoal available on nearly every back porch, deck, or patio grill in that pre-propane era. Lastly, since no one wanted to be on either the German or Japanese side of these reenactments, we had to have fictitious countries for when we were at mock war with one another. Mine was Randal Land. What else? Perhaps it was an early sign of egomaniacal ambition.

Boy Scouts

In addition to war games, thankfully there were influences toward peace between peoples and nations.

I joined on October 30, 1955, at age eleven, a local Boy Scouts troop, and it was an early introduction to the concept of community service. Our Troop 826 was part of the Occoneechee Council, the named being that of a Native American tribe along the Eno River at the time of its earliest exploration by Europeans settlers. I have in my scrapbooks a cloth badge attesting to having attended its 1957 Campfire, and I recall having done a summer encampment on the US Army base at Fort Bragg near Fayetteville, NC. They may have been the same event. I have a wallet-sized card dated March 18, 1957, attesting to having completed one hundred hours of civic service. I have the original Application for Registration Transfer, which gives evidence of having completed Tenderfoot and Second Class requirements toward which I was working for First Class. It also indicates under Offices Held and Other Honors Secured that I was an Assistant Patrol Leader.

The reason I still have this application is I never connected with the Boy Scouts when we moved to St. Petersburg. Neither my middle school nor our church had a troop to which I could have presented it. This I regret, for I would have liked very much, especially now with sixty years of hindsight as to its value, to have worked my way through the remainder of First Class, as well as Star and Life ranks to Eagle. I do not know what happened to my BSA uniform or my sash and its accumulated merit badges, but I assume they did not survive Mother's move from our Thirty-Seventh Avenue North home to her last residence. Other treasured childhood possessions did not survive that move: my two cigar boxes of fossilized sharks' teeth collected over years on Manasota beaches south of Sarasota, Dad's father's double-barreled shotgun, my red-glassed solar box for viewing the sun, my baseball and other sports cards, an oil painting of a tropical beach that I had purchased from the high school friend who painted it, my and Roy's comic books, and his silver dollars. Only our model trains made the journey of several miles.

Cotillion

A Chapel Hill influence toward a peaceful, perhaps even cultured, existence was Mrs. English Bagby's Social Dance class, also known as Cotillion. It was undertaken on Friday evenings at Chapel Hill Country Club. There we had lessons in the "always-good-to-know" fox trot, "better-learn-this-one" basic waltz, "never-in-your-life" Oxford minuet, "I-don't-speak-the-language" Spanish waltz, "how-can-eight-people-do-this-right?" country square dance, "Isn't-World-War-II-over?" jitterbug, "Isn't-that-a-cheese?" Veleta waltz, "but-I-am-not-Polish!"

polka, "you've-gotta-be-kidding-me" Mexican shuffle, "what-in-the-world is a" trilby, and, of course, the always confusing grand march. The latter was greeted with disappointment by Mrs. Bagby but with humor by those with uncooperating senses of direction and feet. I had not yet turned twelve when this civilizing idea was thrust upon me, and while I dreaded anticipation of those Fridays, I enjoyed its social interaction once there. My dance cards were five-sixths completed most nights, instructor compulsion being the remaining remedy. At that age, a boy does begin focusing on girls, and her name was Carol.

Sports

Our Chapel Hill years encompassed those in which my bronchial asthma was addressed effectively. A back scratch test at Duke Hospital had shown me allergic to about everything in my daily life, from household dust to dog hair, pork, bananas, and many other whatevers. In that some of these could not be easily avoided, I began a series of shots over a year or more, first at several each week, then once a week, and at long last zero. My battle to breathe was won with those shots, or by the onset of puberty, or both, but it or they changed my life in positive ways. This new freedom permitted me to engage in athletic activities. This did not, however, give me an instant catch-up in the athletic skills I had not acquired alongside school mates and other friends. Authentication of that conclusion was my being cut on the first day from the 120 that reported in early May 1955 for Little League baseball tryouts. It was a disappointment, but the hours of practice and game times it freed up were eventually appreciated through other activities. Although cut by noon, I did make it into the Chapel Hill newspaper's photograph taken of all of us with the coaches in the morning. Adults asked me for months, "How's the baseball season going?" to which I would auto-respond, "Pretty much as expected!" in that I had not the slightest idea how it was going, the early lawyer in me showing how to avoid a direct answer.

Another health scare emerged during this period. I had no prior knowledge of it, nor was I brought into parent and doctor discussions concerning it, but a growth had been identified near where the throat becomes the esophagus. It was in an inoperable location for surgical removal. To reduce the odds of it being or becoming malignant, I undertook radiation therapy at Duke Hospital for a number of sessions. I remember vividly my head in a device to avoid movement during the procedure and a large ray-gun pointed at the internal growth. I believe each treatment was five or more minutes. That was apparently the end of the matter, but it wasn't. When I was in my midsixties, I had several bleeding stomach ulcers from taking too much acetylsalicylic acid in advance of unavoidable knee replacement surgery. When the gastroenterologist ascertained the reasons for vomiting and otherwise discharging blood, the immediate decision was made to cauterize the stomach ulcers. I went under, it was performed, and I returned home and to work with several strict requirements as to medicines and foods. At the follow-on appointment, the doctor informed me and showed me photographs of a growth in what may be the same location of the childhood growth. Could this be the same growth, one that never abated or one that later returned? Wisely, because she had had no discussion with me as to my Chapel Hill incident, she had ordered a biopsy, and it was benign.

UNC's sports were far better than mine. Before we left Chapel Hill in 1957 for St. Petersburg, the UNC men's Lennie Rosenbluth–led basketball team had a perfect 32–0 regular season record and defeated the University of Kansas's Wilt Chamberlain–led team by 54–53 in triple overtime for their first NCAA national championship. Our entire family joined in the Franklin Street celebration. UNC had defeated Michigan State 74–70 the previous night, for there was no day in between in those years, and also in triple overtime.

Several Other Thoughts

Occasionally but almost always on Sunday afternoons, Dad's parents would drive to Chapel Hill to see us. I looked forward to those afternoons and regretted fairly deeply when I had an expectation that they would drive over and they did not.

A different type of sadness came to me after we had moved to Florida. Our Chapel Hill dog was Peewee, an *Americanus muttus* but one who joyed seeing any of us return home. I sensed that he was becoming less a family member when my mother required him to be moved from being a house dog to one in our partially enclosed basement garage. That gave him in those pre-leash law years an independence he had not enjoyed when confined to the house. He took advantage of this new freedom by roaming increasingly wider arcs. As we were preparing to move, I became aware that Peewee was not going to make the journey with us. Mother did not want a dog complicating our lives in an unknown new location. An initially reluctant neighbor agreed to take Peewee for his children's enjoyment. Later we learned that Peewee had been shot by a farmer about a quarter of a mile from where we had lived because Peewee was "upsetting" his livestock, when he may have been just trying to get them to play with him in our absence. It was an unnecessary outcome. A Chapel Hill Community Center and Park now occupies what was that small farm. Our first dog in St. Petersburg was a boxer named Duke, who was shorter lived than the car that struck him, and Pal, a mostly springer spaniel who loved cooked vegetables, especially string beans, and miraculously made the move with mother to Fifty-Second Street North and lived a long life.

My brother Roy Jr., then known as Merle, graduated from Chapel Hill High School right before we moved to St. Petersburg in June 1957. He had acquired a few years earlier a 1948 Chevy black coupe. He was later stricken with a painful bout of kidney stones but was skillful enough to have an attractive girlfriend, all of which I remember but not as well as he does.

15

Escapes and Vacations

I N ADDITION TO AUGUST VACATIONS, DAD DESIGNED
shorter escapes for us. They balanced interests in roaming with the
consequence of limited funds. Some were brief, others were of more
traditional length. All qualified for praise if they got the four of us out
of our duplex apartment.

The most frequent and shortest were jaunts to places or events
within a day's round-trip driving distance. If the weather was bad,
defined almost exclusively as not golf-able, most or all of a day might
be available. Overnights were most often out of the question because
accommodations and additional meals meant additional costs. Most
in warmer months ended with a visit to Durham Dairy's ice cream
parlor where I would usually order butter pecan or lime sherbet. In
reviewing Durham Dairy's history on the worldwide web, I noted that
other families routinely also took these one-day excursions. One was an
African American's memory of going to Durham Dairy as a child but
not being able to eat her ice cream on premises because of their race;
they ate it in their car as they too drove around Durham. Even if more
than half a century later, I am glad I am now aware of that.

We went to historic sites throughout the Piedmont. The nearest was the Bennett Place less than four miles from Eighth Street or to nearby Hillsborough that intersected with the Daniel Boone Trail. We drove past the dilapidated remains of the World War II German POW site at Camp Butner. We went to rivers and reservoirs with Dad's fishing gear in hand. I wonder if he ever had a fishing license; perhaps none was required in those years. We went to the North Carolina State Fair in Raleigh in the fall in almost every year, the Ringling Brothers Barnum & Bailey circus in Durham in late fall, and occasionally the Ice Capades in Raleigh. A longer trip would be the Battle of Guilford Courthouse in Greensboro for its Revolutionary War relevance. If Dad drove between Durham and Chapel Hill on Cornwallis Road, instead of on paralleling US 15-501, we were proximate to but not quite on the route that Gen. Charles Cornwallis and his British troops rode and marched from their 1781 victory at Guilford Courthouse to their 1781 surrender to the French-reinforced American forces at Yorktown, Virginia.

It could be to an infrastructure of note, such as to the John H. Kerr Dam and Reservoir on the North Carolina-Virginia border, a sizeable lake-creating dam whose turbines were generating Duke Power electricity, in the outflow from which I recall us fishing after he returned from North Africa. Or to the Raleigh-Durham airport simply to see the planes arriving and departing at a facility that was then little more than an elongated building through which persons could just walk out to the arriving and departing airplanes. It was frequently to museums and other attractions in Raleigh.

For trips of intermediate length, I recall Cherokee on the North Carolina border with Tennessee, a mountainous headquarters village of the Eastern Band of the Cherokee Nation. It is the seat of the reservation's governance but is also a tourist destination and, as such, an income producer for it. Cherokee is located at an entrance to the Great Smoky Mountains National Park and not too far from the southern terminus of the National Park Service's Blue Ridge Parkway. It stretches along the Oconaluftee River and offers youngsters real and false images of Native American life as well as all sorts of goodies in tourist traps lining its main street. It is also the site of Chapel Hill playwright Paul Green's epic historical play *Unto These Hills*, the script for which was rewritten in recent years to be more historically accurate and more politically correct, which are not always the same.

My nose's memory recalls smelling tasseling corn and tobacco curing. I always regretted arriving back at Eighth Street.

Florida

As to actual vacations, we went to a Miami different in nearly every way from what it is now as one of our country's major gateway cities to and from Latin America. It was a much smaller city then, originally the southern terminus of oilman Henry M. Flagler's Florida East Coast Railway, which had reached it in September 1896. That was the year that "400 men" supposedly voted for its incorporation as a city but whose first census thereafter indicated only three hundred total inhabitants. Originally the site of a short-lived Fort Dallas, Miami was named for the Miami River, whose spelling as such was phonetically derived from Mayaimi, the Seminole noun for Lake Okeechobee. It is today a metropolitan area encompassing nearly six million persons. If you wish to see a reconstructed depiction of Miami not long after its founding, find the movie *Wind Across the Everglades* with Christopher Plummer, Burl Ives, Gypsy Rose Lee, and Emmett Kelly on a motion picture server. If you wish to see Miami today, just change your channel to nearly any of television's many crime and criminal investigation offerings.

I do not know how many days it took in my childhood to reach Miami from Durham by automobile, but I do recall visiting along our way the nation's oldest city, St. Augustine, founded in 1565, and Marineland of Florida near it. I recall an animated conversation Dad had with a vendor off Highway US A-1-A as to the disputed definition of "All You Can Drink!" orange juice for an advertised fixed price. Maybe that argument nurtured an early interest in law, for it was a dispute over definition. The Kennedy Space Center at Cape Canaveral further south was not yet even a gleam in a future astronaut's eye. I believe but am not totally sure my first pony ride was in Miami. If not my first, I have our oldest surviving photograph of such a ride, my brother being mounted on it, and also showing Miami's palm and citrus trees appearing to be near fabled Hialeah Race Track. I recall Cypress Gardens' botanical gardens, which survive, and skiing-focused theme park, which does not, near Winter Park.

Carolina Beach

Our traditional weeklong summer vacation was to Carolina Beach south of Wilmington and north of the Civil War's Fort Fisher. I wonder when Carolina Beach became the family's preferred vacation site, for in photographs from preceding summers, the family seemed to have gone to Virginia Beach not many miles above the North Carolina border.

August vacations at these beaches were for the extended Teague family, though the younger persons attending in a particular August would vary, especially as teenagers obtained summer jobs and some high school graduates had summer jobs, military service obligations, or were into college preparatory work preceding the new term. Carolina Beach was a four-hour drive from Durham or Chapel Hill in those pre-interstate highway years. My brother and I would compete for who would first spot white sand along the right-of-way or in the passing fields as Dad drove through the sandhills region. Today, it is about a two-and-a-half-hour drive via Interstate 40. Dad and his sisters would rent the same cottage each year. It was less than a block from the beach and within walking distance northward to its boardwalk. The smell of breakfast in its kitchen would awaken my brother, me, and our cousins, but we would seldom return during daylight hours to the cottage, except to grab a fast, cheap lunch or change into dry clothes for an evening on the boardwalk. I was told several years ago by my cousin Richard Tucker that "the cottage still stands," though that was hard for me to believe in that its survivability was questionable before hurricanes in 1954 and later years damaged housing along the beach front. In the spring of

2016, Darlene McKinnon and I checked it out, and that cottage at 200 Carolina Beach Avenue South was still there but looking far worse than it was when I had last seen it in the 1950s. It is dilapidated for sure and the only surviving cottage of similar build on that block.

Near our cottage and along the Intracoastal Waterway, I had my first saltwater fishing outing. Five-years-older cousins Richard and Robert Tucker and my brother went fishing without me for their obvious, but not acceptable to me, reasons. I managed to persuade Granddad Teague to take me "phishing" along the waterway's bulkheads with now unrecalled success or failure. It is recollected by others that I could not yet pronounce the word "fishing." Did that "phishing" outcome really matter to me? It probably did, even then.

16

Florida, Here We Come!

IN JUNE 1957, OUR HOUSEHOLD EFFECTS WERE SENT southward by moving van from Chapel Hill. We followed the next day by way of Durham. Following a Teague, Tucker, and O'Briant families' sendoff in the nature of an extended family picnic near Duke's West Campus, we began the two-day drive to 2829 Thirty-Seventh Avenue North in St. Petersburg. Dad had been working in his new job in Florida for some months and had traveled north to drive us to Florida's west coast. During the preceding period of Dad in St. Petersburg and Mom in Chapel Hill, we had driven during spring break with Dad's parents and a sister to experience St. Petersburg. We rented rooms at a Ninth Street family-friendly motel. We had traveled previously as a three-generation family along Florida's east coast, but this was our first trip to its west coast.

We moved that summer into a house larger than the one we had left. The white stucco rambler was highlighted with a two-foot band of orange, yellow, and brown faux stones. It divided comfortably sized front and backyards in a neighborhood of similar designs. The front yard was well tended with flowering shrubbery, palm and pine trees, and squishy St. Augustine grass. It balanced with the backyard's orange and tangerine citrus and Florida holly trees separated from the service alley by a thick shrubbery line. Some neighbors had banana trees, but we did not. Its kitchen was larger than the one we left, and an all-weather sitting room between it and the carport gradually became mine for school work, collections, saltwater aquariums, and household plants. Alas, there were several negative aspects to this house. It was not air-conditioned against Florida's annual eight or more months of stifling heat and humidity. We circulated sweltering air with floor fans, we accustomed ourselves to sleeping between or on top of sheets wet with our own perspiration, and we prayed endlessly for cooler weather. In the hottest months, its grass had to be mowed twice a week, and shrubs grew as if in a greenhouse. Actually, they were; it was and is called Florida. As my marine biology interests grew, our blisteringly hot roof dried starfish, urchins, seashells, sponges, and other specimens. The poinsettia bushes were taller by a yardstick than I was. That Florida holly was not a true holly. It was a Brazilian pepper whose hardiness, red berries near the winter solstice, and varying sizes made it popular for landscaping. It was quite popular with red-breasted robins in that consuming its overripe berries caused them to become quite drunk.

As summer neared its end, my brother departed for Stetson College in Deland, a smaller community not too far inland from Daytona Beach on the state's Atlantic coast side. He transferred after his freshman year to the University of North Carolina in Chapel Hill and then into the US Army. Dad's departure and life elsewhere and my science emersion and political adventures in high school were to follow, and as passing seasons became years, my departure for Washington became a closer reality. Our family of four became three and then two, my Mom and me.

St. Petersburg

It did not take long for me to become accustomed to varieties of citrus trees waving palm fronds, bananas growing in backyards, and afternoon storms as regular as clockwork. Severe winters up north were just a cooler set of morning breezes in St. Petersburg. I tried hard to make the best of Florida.

Despite it being one of the nation's most widely recognized retirement communities, one known with mixed intent as "the home of the newlyweds and the nearly deads," St. Petersburg was a city of spacious parks with Spanish-moss-laced oaks and breezy palm trees. More importantly for me, it was a city surrounded on three sides by subtropical waters. Named in 1892 after St. Petersburg, Russia, where one of its founders had lived half of his life, it had been the southern terminus of a railroad opening Florida's west coast. It had the nation's first open-air US post office from 1916 and its famous Million Dollar Pier from 1926. Its municipal Albert Whitted Airport was next to the central yacht basin from which airport the first scheduled passenger flight occurred on January 1, 1914, bound for Tampa on the other side of the bay, the float plane's sole passenger being a former St. Petersburg mayor, A. C. Phiel. That airfield became personal "firsts" for both Granddad and me when in the late 1950s, neither one of us having taken a plane flight, we flew on a single engine "Fly around the Bay" excursion for an unrecalled-number-of-dollars' flight of about twenty minutes. My adult life's flights would average between eighty and 120 each year, meaning thousands over my career, yet then as now, I always felt safer on the ground.

Nine and ten city blocks away from the Bayfront was patent medicine man James Earl "Doc" Webb's Webb's City, founded in and grown steadily since 1925 and billed by him as the "World's Most Unusual Drug Store." It occupied four or more city blocks and housed about everything known to be sellable. We had no way to know that it was a forerunner in marketing concept to the far more successful and later Walmart. It was a tourist attraction in Florida's number one tourist city, a distinction soon and long lost. St. Petersburg had its famous green benches on which its retired residents sat and chatted when they were not playing iconic shuffleboard matches or watching a spring training baseball game. Neither we nor St. Petersburg's city fathers knew it at the time, but the city was in the early years of a long economic decline.

Disney World and other attractions in Orlando, Busch Gardens in Tampa, Miami as the gateway to and from Latin America and the Caribbean, Cape Canaveral as the gateway to outer space, and growth in the Bradenton-to-Naples corridor south of Tampa Bay were realities soon to draw vacationers and residents to other opportunities. The opening of Florida by family-affordable air transportation and the construction of interstate highways for fast-moving vehicles and long bridges where only ferries has existed more widely opened the state. Did anyone mention the consequences of college students' spring breaks early in Fort Lauderdale and later in the Panhandle? The pre– and early post–World War II Florida was soon to become only a set of memories.

Some retired persons lived in exquisite residential areas with screen-enclosed patios and pools, known as lanais from the Hawaiian word for such an enclosure, along the area's extensive natural and engineered waterfronts. Others among the retired lived in shared housing and trailer parks, with men and women cohabitating but not marrying because that would have reduced Social Security checks. Yes, they were "living in sin" at ages when Judgment Day was right around the corner, but they were compelling arrangements for financial survival. We heard accounts of some aged so poor that they would take ketchup, salt, and pepper packets from café countertops and ask for hot water to make their own weak tomato soup. We heard accounts of elderly so ignored by their families that survivors could not be located upon their deaths. They were interred at public expense. Of course, the city had many hundreds of city blocks of comfortable and well-manicured middle-class housing too. In discussing these economic disparities with my parents, each would remind me that income and asset inequality had existed since one cave man captured a feral goat or boar and another had not. It was the human condition, and no politician, economist, or government administrator would ever change that reality except at the margin, all the experiments to do so having failed or shown signs of eventual failure.

We observed St. Petersburg's bars along Central Avenue and elsewhere busy as retirement alcoholism became personal, family, and community ills. The evening cocktail to aid sleeping grew into the earlier five o'clock highball, which became one or two at lunch with the guys at the golf course or the girls at bridge, which became the screwdriver or Bloody Mary to start the day.

Major League Baseball's Spring Training

Major League Baseball's spring training was important to my early years in St. Petersburg. The American League's New York Yankees trained at Miller Huggins Field by Crescent Lake Park not too far from Dad's restaurant on Ninth Street. It is now Huggins-Stengel Baseball Complex. The National League's St. Louis Cardinals trained at Al Lang Field downtown. It became Al Lang Field at Progress Energy Park and is now the reconfigured stadium of the Tampa Bay Rowdies professional soccer team.

The city and its climate had a long and beneficial relationship with professional baseball. It had come to the city in 1908 when the then-independent St. Paul Saints played an exhibition game against the National League's Cincinnati Reds. In 1914, businessman and future mayor, the referenced Al Lang, convinced the St. Louis Browns to come to the city for spring training at Sunshine Park near the city's Coffee Pot Bayou, but the Browns must not have liked the location or the city or its weather. Maybe it rained too much that spring. From 1915 through 1918, the Philadelphia Phillies trained at that park, but they and their Connie Mack legends moved south to the Sarasota area.

It was a very different era in Major League Baseball's spring training in my spring of 1958 and those that followed than it is in today's Major League Baseball. I was more familiar with the Yankees' Miller Huggins Field because I could reach it fairly easily on my bike, whereas the Cardinals' Al Lang Field was about twice the distance and effort. That was not the only reason I preferred the Yankees, for I had made a decision while watching in the old Hillandale Golf Course clubhouse either a 1952 or 1953 Yankees versus the then Brooklyn Dodgers World Series game that I was a Yankees fan. I discovered quickly and especially in the schoolyard that it was not going to be easy to be a fan of anything known as the Yankees. The Yankees were an American League team, and at that time in life, I had no need for the National League except to provide a team to be defeated by the American League team in the World Series. This attitude would not change until the National League's Montreal Expos became the Washington Nationals in 2005, albeit that it took me several years to become a Nationals fan. In my 1957 mind, moving to St. Petersburg where the Yankees had spring training was second best to living in New York City during baseball season.

Some words are in order about the Yankees spring training and history. They began in St. Petersburg in 1924, encompassing their 1927, 1932, 1936, 1937, 1938, 1939, and 1941 World Champions seasons and the careers of Babe Ruth, Lou Gehrig, and other legends, and continued there until 1942. During the war years of government-mandated gasoline rationing, they trained in Ashbury Park and Atlantic City, New Jersey, returning to St. Petersburg in 1946 only to leave again after their 1950 season, during which years they were World Champions in 1947, 1949, and 1950. They tried out Phoenix in 1951, after which they were that year's World Champion, returned to St. Petersburg the next year and stayed until 1961, encompassing my 1958–1961 springs and becoming World Champions in 1952, 1953, 1956, 1958, 1959, and 1961. But, they left again for Ft. Lauderdale on Florida's Atlantic coast, earning World Champions titles in 1962 with an uncharacteristically long stretch to 1977 and 1978. Their springtime wandering ended in 1996 at George Steinbrenner Stadium across the bay, for Tampa's city fathers were no dummies and knew how to land the Yankees. Build a first-class facility and name it George Steinbrenner Stadium, and he and his Yankees will come. It did not take Carl Jung to articulate or *Field of Dreams* to depict that strategy.

My spring afternoons at Miller Huggins Field witnessed Mickey Mantle, Yogi Berra, Whitey Ford, Hank Bauer, Tony Kubek, Elston Howard, and Enos Slaughter getting ready for another season. So was their manager, the legendary Charles Dillon "Casey" Stengel, who returned to this field in 1962 as the New York Mets manager. In 1963, the field was renamed Huggins-Stengel Field and is today the Huggins-Stengel Baseball Complex with the Yankees' Building #4 concrete block clubhouse of decades ago still intact. The '58 Yankees had a 92–62 regular season, the best in the American League, and won the World Series. The '59 Yankees had a poor third-place 79–75 season but managed to win the World Series nonetheless. The '60 Yankees bounced back into first place with a 92–62 regular season but failed to become World Champions. The players during these spring trainings were accessible to any kid who wanted a baseball autographed, with no agents insisting only on their commercial sale and their percentages from the income stream, and no security guards to impede your access to the players. The only security was provided each afternoon by a few St. Petersburg uniformed policemen on or off duty. I do not have a single one of those baseballs, and I suspect they were victims of my mother's move from Thirty-Seventh Avenue. As to St. Petersburg's St. Louis Cardinals, they now spring train in Jupiter on Florida's east coast.

St. Petersburg's location, occupying most of a peninsula with Tampa Bay on its eastern and southern sides and the Gulf of Mexico and adjacent bays to its west, added to my excitement of living in St. Petersburg. Over the next six-plus years, it narrowly and Florida broadly became liberating opportunities, and I took them. They opened doors to immediate and lifelong interests in marine biology generally and marine botany particularly. They opened doors through student politics to real politics. They opened doors to law and charitable organizations and long careers in both. No one would have expected that from my starting blocks.

My first St. Petersburg school was an initial disappointment. I attended Lealman Junior High on St. Petersburg's northwest side for my eighth and ninth grades. Lealman served a predominantly middle class set of neighborhoods, unlike Mirror Lake Junior High, which served more affluent areas on St. Petersburg's east side. Courses seemed conventional and instruction rote. After my years there, Lealman Junior High became Lealman Middle School, was closed as a school in order to become Pinellas County school system's administrative offices, then reconstituted blocks away as Lealman Innovation Academy as the county's "student-centered culture that connects the unique talents, skills, passions, attributes and needs of learners to personalized learning opportunities so they are engaged and invested in their own journey towards mastery" for grades six through twelve. If the new Lealman lives up to that mission, it will provide welcomed experiences for its students and their families and communities.

My eighth-grade curriculum embodied a risk of disappointment. Yet two teachers, Helen Faulkner in science and William Dunlop in English, as well as the happenstance of the United States' reactions to the Soviet Union's launch of the first orbiting unmanned spacecraft *Sputnik*, saved the day for me and for others. The American educational system was threatened by the seeming superiority of our Cold War adversary and its presumed superior educational system. President Dwight Eisenhower's call for immediate American advancements in science and related fields brought forth from Congress the National Defense Education Act of 1958. The distance in time between *Sputnik* and early reactions to its implications and the United States regaining of the lead in the space race were not immediate.

Motivated by Stella Ruth Carter in algebra and another teacher as I was, neither my eighth- nor my ninth-grade performances were stellar. While the lesson learned was that I would achieve only after I determined to do so, this recognition was unacceptable as an excuse for not already having done so.

17

The Note

I DO NOT REMEMBER THE DATE, BUT THE DAY WAS FRIDAY. Its images are seared into my memory. It redefined emotional pain, although the passage of decades mitigated it.

What happened? I came home from school much as I did any afternoon. I was usually the first to arrive because Mother was working. I unlocked the front door and noticed something white on the dark green, scratchy fabric of the living room couch facing me. With a few steps, I recognized it as a folded note held to it by a sewing pin. Unsuspectingly, I pulled the pin and unfolded it. It was a note from my father, and it informed my mother and me that he had moved out and would be in touch. I sat down, read it again, got up, and walked back to my parents' bedroom. I opened the closet door, and, sure enough, his clothes, shoes, and most else were gone. I sat, thought for a moment, and walked next door to ask our neighbors, the Herrs, if they had seen him loading his Oldsmobile, and they had. I returned to our house, sat down on that couch, and awaited Mumsie's arrival, for by then my brother and I had renamed her. It was a bad afternoon, bad evening, bad weekend, and the onset of a bad year. I have no recall of whether the note was addressed to either or both of us or to neither, or of what happened to it among her papers.

Mumsie undertook informing my brother, who was in advanced infantry training at Fort Jackson near Columbia, South Carolina. How she informed others by telephone or letter and over what length of time is unknown to me, but it probably followed a disclosure strategy of need to know. It could tell me much about her state of mind to know now when concealment moved to disclosure. My brother's fellow soldiers talked him out of going AWOL to be with us. Mother, who had cut out a poem in what appears to be newspaper print to paste it into her high school scrapbook, within which poem was "The greatest word is love," most certainly felt betrayed. As soon as we knew his new address, I vented my anger by writing Dad a letter, the tone and language of which I later regretted, but I felt its points needed to be set out. Even though Dad and I would over years build a different relationship, it took distances of time to mature cautious prospects for its success. Nearly six decades later, when I run my hand across scratchy fabric textures, I think of that couch and the note pinned to it. The note on the couch had been years in the coming. Its shock was in its finality and manner of delivery.

An immediate consequence was that it left Mumsie and me in St. Petersburg, some seven hundred miles from our extended families in Durham. That reality generated a question for which we had no answer. After his return from overseas, he had had five years to come to conclusions about his marriage. If he knew it was over, why move us to Florida? He could have gone for its career opportunity by himself. To isolate Mom from his parents and his sisters' families and her own family? Even under the circumstances, that seemed out of character, and Mother was too close to Dad's sisters for such a strategy to have worked. An obvious second question is, why did she not return to Durham? How could I have not asked her this? After her 2000 death, my brother and I discussed it at length but without any certainty of answer. She probably did not have the cash to cover the costs of moving, but that was a manageable detail within her larger family. Moving back would have been to an unknown income stream to maintain in part her household. Under the circumstances, moving back was probably seen by her as humiliating at worst and embarrassing at least within family and friendship circles. My brother and I concluded this perceived humiliation or embarrassment was probably 95 percent or more of her reasoning.

My Brother

Roy finished his freshman year at Stetson University in DeLand and transferred to UNC to continue his education. Mumsie paid for his tuition and related expenses at Stetson and UNC, but neither he nor I knew then or know now if she was doing so from her and Dad's funds or solely from her own.

His UNC experience redirected his life's trajectory. He enlisted in the army in order to avoid the near certainty of being drafted. In doing that, he chose three years instead of two but avoided having to remain in active reserve status for additional years. Those years gave him opportunities to see more of America and the world as his training, orders, and leaves dictated or permitted. The avoidance of active reserve duty was a good decision because both the Cuban missile crisis's emergency mobilization and the sustained call-ups of reserves during the war in Vietnam followed his discharge. He did his basic and advanced infantry training at Fort Jackson. He then served with the Second Armored Rifle Battalion of the Forty-Eighth Infantry, a mechanized unit of the Third Armored Division, in Gelnhausen, West Germany. Our troops had Americanized the city's name for easier-on-the-tongue references to "Glen Haven." By any name or mispronunciation, it sits along the Kinzig River in Germany's Fulda Gap, the focal point of what was expected by NATO strategists to be the Soviet Army's intended avenue of attack if the US-dominated NATO and the Soviet Eighth Guards Army, its vanguard of Red Army forces, engaging one another in combat. Gelnhausen is about twenty-five miles east of Frankfurt. The platoon leader of forty men in the battalion's Company B, Bravo

Company, was newly pinned Second Lt. Colin Powell, fresh from having finished his first round of officer schooling at Fort Benning, Georgia. The company's heaviest armor was a 280-mm atomic cannon, a monster-sized artillery piece with a tactical nuclear shell. I have seen the former sixty-fifth secretary of state, former twelfth chairman of the joint chiefs of staff, and former White House national security advisor on occasions in Washington and Mclean, but I have never asked him to recall his service at Gelnhausen in this or any other context.

Roy's marksmanship skills with the Browning Automatic Rifle, a .30-caliber light machine gun, meant he and his BAR team were frequently in competitions. BARs had seen heavy action during World War II and the Korean War. Roy visited Paris, where his uncle-in-law US Army Col. Earle J. Shear was stationed in the US Army's Quartermaster Corps, with his wife, who was my mother's sister Fran, and their children. Roy's active duty ended through Fort Lewis, a few miles southwest of Tacoma, Washington, from which he returned to St. Petersburg to resume both education and career.

Survival Strategies

After Dad's departure, Mumsie worked in several positions. She responded to the suggestion of a fellow worker that she seek one at TRW, Inc. Among other lines of business, it was an aerospace company. Its devices manufactured in St. Petersburg were potentiometers made for other TRW products, they being intercontinental ballistic missiles, ICBMs for short. A company acquired by TRW already had the contract for the Falcon radar-guided missile and the scientific spacecraft *Pioneer 1*. After the Soviet Union's successful 1957 launch of *Sputnik*, the United States' Atlas ICBM production line was altered to enable it to produce Atlas D rockets for our 1958–1963 manned space exploration program. It was this Project Mercury program for which Alan Shepard, Gus Grissom, John Glenn, Scott Carpenter, Wally Schirra, and Gordon Cooper were our earliest astronauts. What is a potentiometer, commonly referred to as a "pot"? It is an adjustable resistor with a sliding or rotating contact that increases or decreases current in the circuit to its intended use when the voltage level required at the receiving end of that circuit must not vary. In short, it evens the flow of electrical current. Mumsie had pride in her work on this one part, among hundreds, in these guided missiles, and so did I in her. Nearly each time a rocket would roar from Cape Canaveral, later named the Kennedy Manned Space Flight Center, Mother would exclaim with excitement that her pots were taking the ride. I wonder these many years later if what she and her fellow workers were doing was classified work. In any event, physics was one of Mother's two most favorite subjects in school, so this job tied well into that subject's roles in our country's civilian and military moves into inner and outer space.

Mom and Earl

Mother lived for years by herself in the Thirty-Seventh Avenue North house to which she had moved from Chapel Hill. Perhaps it was because she could best remember when Dad was there. There came a time to move for whatever combination of reasons, so she bought a house on St. Petersburg's Fifty-Second Street North. Years later, the wife next door died, leaving her husband a widower.

Earl Ralston was born in 1924, meaning he was eight years younger than Mom, and was raised in the Buffalo-Niagara Falls area of western New York, one can more accurately say its gateway to the Midwest. He was an army veteran of World War II's European theater of operations, and some of his basic training had been at Fort Belvoir, immediately south of our Alexandria, Virginia. Earl was semiretired when they met. After many hours of coffee and more of watching evening television together, Earl proposed marriage, and Mumsie said yes. She must have felt honored by the proposal, and they were married in St. Petersburg on November 16, 1978, and honeymooned in New England. Earl soon sold his house, moved into Mom's, and their marriage continued. She had a son and his family living near, as did he.

Years later, Earl had a stroke that left him nearly totally paralyzed and under twenty-four-hour care at the since-renamed C.W. Bill Young Veterans Administration Medical Center at Bay Pines. This beautifully architected center, built in the aftermath of World War I, is located along the shoreline of Boca Ciega Bay between the neighborhoods of St. Petersburg and its barrier island communities along the Gulf of Mexico. Bill Young had been Congressman William C. Cramer's district representative in the years prior to Young's election to the Florida Senate and prior to me joining Cramer's Washington staff in 1964. Young succeeded Cramer in Congress upon the latter's decision not to seek reelection in order to run in 1970 for election to the US Senate. The well-being of veterans was a major focus of Cramer and Young.

Earl's exit from this earth was slow, yet Mom would visit the center and sit with him nearly every day. My growing family was in St. Petersburg in the spring of 1992, visiting Mother and my brother and his family, as well as my wife Jessica Townsend's, family on Siesta Key in Sarasota. We visited Earl at the Bay Pines facility, and it was not an easy visit for us. Even in the debilitated medical condition in which the prospects of recovery would require heavenly intervention, Earl was not letting go of his last hold on this life. It was in that context that Jessie, out of earshot of at least me, shared with him in an assuring manner that it was all right to let go of the bonds of earth. A different type of heavenly vision, that of the peace of earthly death, occurred shortly thereafter on May 9. Mom and Earl had been married twelve years. Earl was interred in Section 19 of Bay Pines National Cemetery among comrades in arms from our nation's wars.

Mumsie's Passing

In late June 2000, I was finishing the business component of a trip to Tunis, the seaside capital of Tunisia, on behalf of the Fund for American Studies and its International Institute for Political and Economic Studies in Greece. I was undertaking groundwork for Tunisian university students to attend both. As I was leaving to be a tourist at the nearby site of ancient Carthage, Rome's enemy during its long Punic Wars and one of the most famous sites of its empire, a telephone call was received by the hotel's concierge desk. It was from my brother's wife, Barbara, and informed me that Mumsie had died from a blood clot following surgery she did not really need for a relatively minor condition. Living alone, she was sometimes bored and, well, just "down," for she would seldom acknowledge being depressed, and the proposed surgery was probably seen by her as something to do in the week ahead. It was a bad decision, and I wondered later whether she had any premonitions about it, because when she asked over the telephone before I left how long I was going to be in Europe and North Africa, she remarked that it seemed like "a long time." It was our last conversation, but there is more to this story.

The night she died but I did not yet know that, I had dinner alone on the hotel terrace looking out toward the Mediterranean. It was that time of the evening when in North Africa the setting sun makes the white buildings appear pink, lavender, and then purple as night creeps toward them. It is a beautiful, if not breathtaking, sequence of moments. The outdoor serving area on the terrace had a sound system, and the musical score of the Spanish composer Joaquin Rodrigo's *Concierto de Aranjuez* became part of the background music for that evening's setting sun. Named for the gardens at the Royal Palace in Aranjuez, Spain, built by Philip II in the late sixteenth century and rebuilt in the middle of the eighteenth by Ferdinand VI, Rodrigo's musical work is high drama in itself. After its original composition, the French composer Guy Alfred Bontempelli added what I feel are romantic yet quite melancholic lyrics ("En Aranjuez con tu Amor"), performances of which are available from iTunes, Spotify, and other sites and for viewing on YouTube, those of Andrea Bocelli, Jose Carreras, and Placido Domingo being highly moving.

I was quite taken by the orchestral piece because of its dramatic notes, its evocation of this region, and it being one of Dad's two most favorite musical pieces. It took on a far deeper significance when I was informed of her death. Its timing connected in my mind the two of them, divorced decades before but now perhaps reunited in their deaths. It was hard for me to imagine the next morning that it was only a coincidence. Dad's other most favorite musical piece was classical harpist Robert Maxwell's *Ebb Tide*, written after Dad had returned from North Africa and recorded in 1953 by Frank Chacksfield without later added lyrics.

Roy and I were now truly adults because neither of us was any longer anyone else's child.

Mumsie had returned to Durham for vacations and other family events, but she did not return to Durham otherwise until my brother and I had her body transported to it in early July 2000 for interment at Rose of Sharon Baptist Church, nearly within walking distance of where she had been born, to bury her next to her parents and to await the eventual burial of two of her four sisters. The name of this and other churches similarly named is the term to which Jesus referred to Himself from Song of Solomon 2:1, in which we find "I am the rose of Sharon, and the lily of the valleys."

Picking up the Pieces

Returning now to our Thirty-Seventh Avenue North circumstance without Dad, and though I did not recognize it at the time for what it was, several families in our neighborhood gave focused attention to me for that fact. Even though I was at the beginning of my teenage years, I was the second youngest person in our immediate neighborhood. Remember, St. Petersburg was a retirement community.

Our next-door neighbors, the Herr family, brought me into their lives and activities in transformative ways. More on that later.

The widow living on the other side taught me how to play the card game canasta to the extent I felt like I was getting to be world class at it.

A gentleman across the street and a friend of his began taking me on their weekend fishing day trips. He was an insurance agent, although I do not know details of his affiliations or what types of insurance. He had been in the navy in the Pacific during World War II and among the first Americans to enter Hiroshima or Nagasaki after the Japanese surrender in 1945. That soon after the dawn of the atomic age, there was little knowledge about the dangers of radiation from nuclear blasts. Consequently, his hands, arms, and face were discolored from his handling of debris from them. The three of us would go fishing to areas around St. Petersburg's piers and bridges. We would go to flats along the Sunshine Skyway Bridge and connecting isles, about twelve miles in length. Sometimes we would fish from the fishing walkways along that bridge. We'd go to areas along the Gulf of Mexico north of the sponge-harvesting Greek community of Tarpon Springs. They would rent a boat and motor up brackish Long Bayou, the outlet from freshwater Lake Seminole into the sea water of Boca Ciega, in English "blind mouth" as in the blind mouth of the bay, northeast of Bay Pines veterans' hospital grounds. The bayou was lined with mangroves whose limbs hung over the water. My task was to stand on the boat's bow with an oar in hands to knock water moccasins sunning themselves on those limbs into the water and not into the boat. Take my word for it, you do not want to be in a small craft with a moccasin. There were alligators in waters around St. Petersburg, even in ponds and lakes within the city, for they traveled into them through drainage pipes in order to seize unwary ducks, other birds, or an occasional pet. That we never encountered them in any of these fishing trips is surprising and appreciated.

18

The Wider Door of High School

MY FIRST DAY OF HIGH SCHOOL WAS FRIGHTENING, BUT whose first day of high school is not? The first week was not much less jittering. By the end of the first month, my nerves were settling down, and by the end of the first semester, I had an increasingly tight handle on my and others' patterns of expectations.

I attended Northeast High School at the intersection of Sixteenth Street and Fifty-Fourth Avenue North for my tenth through twelfth grades. It was referred to simply as NEHI, and I never saw that acronym not fully capitalized. We were the Vikings. My interests became more focused, and Dad's observations about rewards from hard work began to occur. Life became divided between my classes, what became my marine sciences focus, and my emergence in the political arenas of student government and the youth politics within it, pretty much in that order.

NEHI's principal feeder schools were Lealman and Mirror Lake Junior Highs, and the economic and social divides between them were readily observable from the cars students drove to the clothes they wore. Mirror Lake alumni's parents had higher educations and refined senses of how to guide their children. They also had more available funds to support their teenagers in and out of school. That and not having to work after school or on weekends, as many Lealman students had to do, was another plus for those from Mirror Lake. They occupied most of class and club officerships. It seemed that most teachers comported themselves with such recognitions. Mirror Lake cliques transported themselves into nearly identical NEHI cliques. Some students from Lealman just brushed off these points as facts of life, and some students from Mirror Lake did not try to take unfair advantage of their opportunities. As the question, "Is it better to graduate at the bottom of your class from Harvard than at the top of your class from Nowhere University?" focuses on comparative opportunities, achievements, rewards, and public perceptions, each feeder school had its best students and its worst students. In these ways, Northeast was a mosaic and a place to grow for any student intending to do so.

I have a one-page sheet of four charts indicating by footnote that a minimum of twenty credits were necessary for a diploma, with each academic year having boxes to be completed as to course name, teacher, room, and credit. My ninth-grade classes taken at Lealman included algebra 1, biology, civic, and English 1, and my tenth-grade classes at NEHI included algebra 2, world history, physics, and English 2. Eleventh grade was Latin, plain geometry, which I aced with the highest average my teacher, Ms. Helen Stamper, said she had given "in years," American history with perspectives-sharing Daniel Crum, chemistry, and English 3. My senior year classes included a combined economics and psychology, and whoever cobbled together that curriculum for a high-school-level class deserved a Nobel Prize in economics for having unknowingly invented behavioral economics decades before that prize was awarded in 2002 to Daniel Kahneman for doing exactly that. It also included physics, English IV, and senior math. We were so advanced in theory but unadvanced in reality that the highest semester grade was a failing fifty-seven. As a consequence of it being such a difficult theory and application class to comprehend and regurgitate in examinations, our class's grades were bell-curved for a far better result for most. To the best of my knowledge, because some in our class had younger siblings still working their way through Northeast, that particularly designed senior math curriculum was never again offered.

My senior placement test and ranking results were taken by and for Randolph C. Teague, so maybe they were not mine. Of course, they were, and I scored 98 percentile in psychology, 97 in mathematics and science, 96 in natural science, 88 in social science, but only 81 in English. Readers can now be the judges of that last score. Both my SAT scores and my class standing were strong but not at the top of either. Allan Gaither was to give the valedictorian address, and I was to give the president of the student council's address at our June 3, 1962, baccalaureate. I thumbed through an anthology of speeches and decided on the title for mine: simply Farewell Address. It had worked for George Washington! In recently reviewing the event's printed program, I noted that public schools had not yet been proscribed by courts from such religiously based bookends as invocations and benedictions.

Marine Sciences Emerge

My high school years encompassed classroom and extracurricular activities within a four-sided frame of concentration on grades, ambition defined in the short term as university admission, social interactions, and a set of extracurricular activities beyond the customary. The latter was a deep emersion at the Science Center of St. Petersburg in marine biology generally and marine botany specifically. It would pay measurable dividends.

I had been captivated with the sea since the 1952–1953 broadcasts of NBC's twenty-six half-hour segments of the television documentary *Victory at Sea*, those dates indicating that I was eight to nine years old. Later reading John Steinbeck and Edward F. Rickett's *Sea of Cortez* and Professor J. L. B. Smith's *The Search Beneath the Sea*, his account of his successful west Indian Ocean search for a fish thought to be extinct, the coelacanth, reinforced my captivation with what lived in salty realms. So too did Rachel Carson's *The Sea Around Us, The Edge of the Sea*, and

Under the Sea Wind and A. C. Spectorsky's *The Book of the Sea*. That captivation would almost certainly have gone nowhere had we remained in Chapel Hill. The move to St. Petersburg opened doors in ways not imaginable until that move. We will come back to them.

Student Council

An ambition came together in a spirited and successful campaign for student council president. The race arose from a handful of considerations. Mirror Lake students had dominated sophomore and junior classes' offices, as well as student council offices, and appeared destined to do so in our senior year. Resentment was running against them and not limited to students, yet there was no candidate willing to step forward and challenge Robert Amley, who had been the council's treasurer in his sophomore year and its vice president in his junior year. Almost no one in our class had been born in Florida, much less in St. Petersburg. His father was a respected dentist, and Rob expected to join him in dental practice. He was a member of a half-dozen intramural clubs, a host for homecoming, on the basketball team, and a really nice guy. He had only one political flaw, and it was a potentially fatal one to his reelection campaign: he came to Northeast from Mirror Lake. Seen more analytically, he might not have enough votes in a Lealman versus Mirror Lake dustup.

I had achieved a fair amount of visibility at and for the school through my activities, which included the debate club and its local and regional competitions, the Latin Club and its toga parties of endlessly sniveling inquiries, and the junior class's Ways & Means Committee. The latter was the key, for it was struggling together with angry students and a frustrated school administration with a nearly out-of-control parking lot situation. The near crisis was easy to define: too many vehicles for too few spaces. Furthermore, there was a credible suspicion, inasmuch as NEHI was on a municipal bus line into and out of the city, that non-students were filling our unguarded free parking spaces and taking public transportation into and out of the heart of the city. It was the opening of a campaign issue that would get wider. There was also my visibility, not only on its grounds but also in the city, from my experiences at and with the city's Science Center. We will return to its consequences for my student council presidency race following this next section, one encompassing my life at about the same time as my student government interests.

19

The Science Center of St. Petersburg

THE SCIENCE CENTER WAS A NONPROFIT EDUCATIONAL organization created for public purpose and access. It emerged from the interests, commitments, skills, and hard work of a handful of persons intended on giving students access to science education not being offered sufficiently in area schools. It was to pick up where the schools had left off but do so through a one-on-one "learning by doing." None of these objectives were met immediately, for the Center's gestation period was nearly a decade.

The Center was founded in 1952 by William Guild, known widely as simply Uncle Bill, but its facility at Eleventh Street and Arlington Avenue North did not come into its possession until October 1959 when a vacated Jewish synagogue became available through the auspices of the city government. The advantage of that location was that it was near the center of the city. Later described as "a mysterious Pied Piper of science," Guild put advertisements in area newspapers as early as 1951 in a sustained effort to find educators and others interested in starting a science club for youngsters. He hoped to find a "spark of scientist" in as many students as would show both interest and capability. The Science Center's 1959 letterhead declared it to be "a non-profit educational program dedicated since 1952 to conservation of natural and human resources" as well as a national sponsor of "previews for teachers," "science centers," and "junior research laboratories."

The Center gradually acquired reinforcing organizational support as well as local, state, and national visibilities. It became an institutional member of the American Association for the Advancement of Science, American Institute of Physics, National Science Teachers Association, National Association for Gifted Children, and Florida Foundation for Future Scientists. The Center was about 160 miles from Cape Canaveral and its Cape Kennedy National Aeronautical and Space Administration (NASA) launch facilities. You could hear on our Florida west coast an *Apollo* launch on the east coast. If unobstructed by buildings and trees, as in looking across Tampa Bay, one could see the contrail from *Apollo* engines' exhausts as it rose and turned down or up range to gain the 17,000+ mph required speed to punch out of Earth's gravitational field. *Apollo* main booster rockets created the second loudest noise made by humankind's inventions, the first being an atomic explosion. The returning *Apollo 10* reached a speed between the moon and Earth of 24,791 mph, which is almost seven miles per second or about 420 miles per minute. But, back on Earth, something was lacking at the Center.

The core problem in 1960 was that Guild's management skills were more limited than his vision and energy, and it needed those two characteristics but also others' vision, abilities, and energies. The county's public, nonprofit, and for-profit financial resources were needed to assure the Center's success. Guild saw it primarily as a hands-on museum for children, but there were already "a lot of those across the country." To some degree, it may have been a generational issue, and certainly the October 4, 1957, Russian launch of *Sputnik* added to the national urgency of an organization with the Center's mission and potential. As described in a later newspaper column on the Center's history, "Somehow Guild's idea of what was needed, and the ideas of the city's fathers and the center's backers, did not agree. There were personality conflicts and the museum idea died in May 1960. But there were too many enthusiastic students, too many interested people and too much obvious need to let the idea of a place for scientific studies die. Bill Guild's board still existed, had gotten itself chartered by the state as a board of governors, and was determined in its efforts." Guild's founding role should not be challenged, but it was in hindsight confined to the Center's prenatal days. The Science Center of St. Petersburg was about to become the Science Center of Pinellas County and its place as "the very first science center of its kind in the world" assured.

Nell Rodgers Croley

There entered Nell Rodgers Croley into the Center's maturing leadership scene. Originally from Alabama, she was an area teacher who had worked within the Center's leadership long enough to have overlapped with Guild, and those experiences helped assure a stabilizing continuity among its growing supporters. She had been a college-level microbiology instructor and a science teacher on both elementary and high school levels. She was described by her principal in a "Wonders of Science Are Hers" newspaper column as "the best teacher in the state." She held advanced degrees in bacteriology and science education and was committed to the idea that young students could conduct original research utilizing the scientific method. It was a logical choice for the county to make, but it did not happen instantly. Her role could have ended, but thankfully it did not.

While Croley was in Alabama on summer vacation, William Beggs and Dr. Allyn Giffin on behalf of the Pinellas County Board of Education telephoned her and offered the position of Science Center director "guaranteed" for "some kind of pay" to be determined subsequently. She accepted and undertook the daunting assignment to take the steps required for it to achieve its mission.

According to her daughter Carol, Oliver J. Olsen, the head of

Florida Steel, became involved in the Center's life and among other things flew Ms. Croley and Center students on field trips from Crystal River quarries north of St. Petersburg to Naples fossil sites south of it. In time aloft and otherwise, he suggested to her that he could be active in the building of a large, modern facility to house the Center's expanded mission and contemplated programs and that he knew of others who could be. As a consequence, the area's for-profit sector stepped forward with his Florida Steel, now Gerdau AmeriSteel, E.C.I., an electronics components manufacturer, General Electric, Honeywell, and other corporations donating not only funds and equipment but also equally sought and needed management and technical expertise through their giving of valuable time. With those local government and for-profit components in place, the area's nonprofit sector stepped forward, and the Junior League of St. Petersburg led the way by supplying "the center with money over the years and people power beyond measuring" and became the nucleus of the Center's Guild, its principal fundraising arm.

County, corporate, and nonprofit influences and funds were thus secured to build a facility on Twenty-Second Avenue North in northwest St. Petersburg, making it more accessible to students in Pinellas Park, Largo, Clearwater, Tarpon Springs, and other localities north of St. Petersburg, which is the southernmost city in the county, and to staff, maintain, and sustain it. As time passed, college graduate students in marine science, botany, zoology, and more were hired to assist young students in developing their research projects.

I served the Center as student president in 1960–1961 as its second in that position after its first, the now-renowned entomologist, that's a specialist in insects, Dr. Robert Blumberg, surrendered the position to give himself more time to prepare for his college entry.

This place in the narrative suggests I further introduce Ms. Croley's daughter, now Frances Carol Croley Aregood (now known as Carol Aregood), an early and major worker bee on the Center's behalf and a valued partner in our related marine biological endeavors.

Carol was a student at Dixie Hollins High School northwest of

St. Petersburg when we met. She was active in the Center when I was, perhaps also before me and after me, and we explored many a bay, cove, and beach on Florida's west coast in search for and collection of marine mollusks, that is shells, specimens for her and marine algae, that is seaweed, specimens for me. More importantly, she and her future husband, Charles Aregood, assembled the materials necessary for the Center's 150-plus-page grant proposal to the US government for the Title III funds necessary to bolster the Center's effectiveness through acquisitions of laboratory equipment and the covering of other expenses.

Our Thirty-Seventh Avenue North neighbors, R. T. "Tex" Herr, his wife, Evelyn, and their daughter, Judith, had introduced me to the Science Center by informing me of its mission and taking me to it. Mr. Herr was a retired executive with IBM, lastly in its Chicago sales district. He had experienced a heart attack and protracted recovery, which had the family living in our neighborhood in order to stretch his retirement dollars. The Herrs were generous to and patient with me beyond any measure of my expressed thanks to them for their generosities of advice and guidance as to education, career, and life. I spent more evenings with them than I did with my mother during those years. I should have told Judith and her parents how much they each meant to me, and I regret my failures to do that. Their help to the two guys living next door was not limited to me, for Mr. Herr was the person who helped align my brother, having returned from military service in Europe, with a career-long position in customer relations with Florida Power Corporation, the region's electrical power utility now owned by Duke Energy.

The Center moved to its more centralized location and was renamed the Science Center of Pinellas County at which it housed the Science and Technology Education Innovation Center. Its website reported in 2015 that it was "the first science education facility of its type in the United States." Who could know then or even now what may have existed in the Soviet Union's educational system before or after October 4, 1957? It has been described also as "one of Pinellas County's noblest achievements." Much had happened between 1952 and the early 1960s to assure the sustainability of the Science Center's undertaking.

Science Fairs

When they worked together, Guild's aspirations for youngsters and Croley's knowledge as a teaching scientist combined to help each student undertake serious research as well as build resumes for college applications.

Before I had won first place in zoology at the 1960 Eighth Annual Pinellas County Science Fair for research leading to and reported through my "Research in the Zoological Employment of Marine Algal Products" exhibit, Guild had sought my admission to the Phillips Exeter Academy in New Hampshire, for which I took the written examination on December 12, 1959. The result of this "bridge too far" was that my mother working at TRW for customary wage could not match the generous 50 percent scholarship offered, much less the travel and related expenses of a prestigious preparatory school. We swallowed hard, for we both regretted that concession to the realities of life, time, and place, but I continued to move forward.

My 1960 science fair project's win was an effective recovery for my battered emotions on Dad's departure, as was its nomination to and exhibition at the Florida State Science Fair. Somehow, Guild had secured for me a "Judge" badge for the fair in which I was competing, and he even managed to gain us access to the March 11 attempted launch at the Cape of an Atlas ICBM suborbital test. That test failed as it exploded on the launch pad at thirty-six minutes past midnight. The resulting fireball lit the night sky, sea, and land around us as brightly as daylight, except that all were the deep color of a Florida orange. It was an experience never to be forgotten, and I recalled it when I was at the renamed Cape Kennedy for several later and successful *Apollo* launches.

One of the seniors when I was a junior at Northeast High, James Blair White, was a brother of Edward H. White Jr., the third astronaut with Virgil "Gus" Grissom and Roger Chaffee to die on January 27, 1967, when their capsule caught fire during a prelaunch test for the *Apollo 1* mission. Their father was an air force major general, and that elder son had been the first American to walk in space. Our Northeast High's younger and by then Major James B. White was an air force pilot whose fighter went down over Laos on November 11, 1969, during the Vietnam War. To the best of my knowledge, he is still officially listed as missing in action.

Yet there was something much bigger, far more dramatic, after that Phillips Exeter disappointment. It happened nearly immediately.

20

Distant Seas

A T BILL GUILD'S ENCOURAGEMENT, I HAD POSTED A letter to Dr. John Dyas Parker at the Academy of Natural Sciences of Philadelphia expressing my interest in joining its expedition in formation for specimen collecting in the Indian Ocean and the western South Pacific. I informed him unabashedly that I had knowledge of marine biology generally, marine botany particularly, as well as youthful enthusiasm and rising abilities. In his reply, Dr. Parker set forth the expedition's intended itinerary as Madagascar, the Seychelles, Diego Suarez, the Andaman Islands, New Ireland, Rarotonga in the Cook Islands and "the dangerous islands," without giving that description a definition, as well as Indonesia, Portuguese Timor, Borneo, and various areas in the Persian Gulf and the Red Sea. The academy described itself in 2015 as "the oldest natural science research institution and museum in the New World" and now within Drexel University.

Over the following weeks, Dr. Parker informed me that it had been his idea to find a young member for the crew with his hope that such person would be stimulated by the expedition to study further within the academy's fields of marine sciences, a search process he described to me as "Catch'em young and train'em right." He made no attempt to disguise the fact that manpower within the crew was as important as its dredges and other equipment, its financing, or its eventual publications. I was to understand that each of those three touchstones were over a common denominator of fieldwork being done properly. These were the thoughts he had in mind when he suggested to Guild that he keep his eyes open for a candidate and find funding for that candidate.

What a candidate would have to do was Dr. Parker's continued guidance to me. I would have to cover my costs, as to which Guild indicated to Parker he "might be able to help there." With that funding credibly expected, I would become part of the expedition. Underway, I'd be required to get along with crew members, a process he described as "harder than you think" because it meant shouldering certain and uncertain burdens in widely varying circumstances, ranging from safe ports of call to islands with known cannibal populations. He made it clear that this would be difficult. Throughout these tasks were problems arising from continuous hard work undertaken under time pressures within which every minute had to be utilized effectively, typically requiring hard physical labor twelve to fourteen hours each day and seven days a week. He gave warning of the less-than-desirable food we would be expected to eat to maintain our energy, and there would be little or no time for diversions or relaxation. His warnings continued, making it clear to me that the expedition was going for shells, shells, and shells, yet it would not "look askance" at my scientific paper on the algae of, he wrote specifically Madagascar for reasons unknown to me, provided that the expedition's work on shells had come first. He ended this round of getting to know one another and the expedition's contexts by enquiring whether I still had an interest and, if so, to let him know and do so promptly.

I responded thoughtfully as to the points he had raised. In his reply to that response, he explained how active the intervening period had been, including news of an unfortunate setback in that one of the expedition backers, deemed by the academy to be "scientifically incompetent," had withdrawn his financial patronage, a consequence of which was an expectation of delay until that autumn. Dr. Parker advised that the expedition would occur, so I should "hold on" to my dreams for it, explaining that pure science at that point was dependent on its sponsorship, which required being accustomed to these types of disappointments. Perhaps to move beyond this disappointment, he said both he and fabled R. Tucker Abbott had wondered how I had become interested in algae. Wondering if they were beginning to second-guess Parker's intention to have a young person on the expedition or about me, I made it clear that I had come to be interested in algae because different species were ever present in the Center's marine specimen collecting, and there was under way an expansion of the commercial applications of by-products from algae that could be a career long focus. Respectfully, I made it clear that I was a serious student of marine algae, had read widely including any book from field guide to scientific treatise on algae that I could locate, borrow, or buy in those pre-Amazon.com and pre-eBay years, had undertaken field collecting and laboratory identifications of subtropical species, and had done so with persons more knowledgeable than me for its learning value. Books on algae were available at area bookstores, especially at St. Petersburg's Haslam's Book Store, even if they were next to books on space aliens, perhaps because "algae" and "aliens" were in alphabetical order. I assumed he was satisfied with my defense, but he pointed out that the academy's library was the oldest scientific library in North America with about six million titles.

In these respects, seaweed snacks were not yet sitting next to cash registers of sandwich shops as they would decades later, but seaweed by-products' commercial uses already included values; for example, a kelp by-product made ice cream smoother and cosmetics adhere to tissue, algar media was essential for biological laboratory research, and so on. As additional research and development continued, their uses would bring them into broader public awareness.

Was I willing to defer graduating from high school for a year because of the expedition's length? You better believe I was. Why did it mean so much to me? There were at least four reasons: advancement of life and career-tied focuses; scientific, organizational, cultural, and foreign language learning; prospects for scholarships for university studies; and sheer excitement. How could someone not yet seventeen years of age turn down such expanded opportunity?

The mounting of the expedition was exciting. My angst over how I would fit in and my collecting objectives and equipment requirements personalized it. Not a mistake could be made by me, for failing to bring a single item needed would be counterproductive and embarrassing, not to mention unavailable in Zanzibar, Mombasa, or any other port. I wondered about what personal needs from attire to toothpaste to bring with me but assumed a list from decades of their experience from expeditions would be forthcoming.

The scholarship potential merits further discussion. Expedition experience could assure application reviewers of the surety of their financial investment in me. It was what I had to have in order to attend a university with a leading marine biology program of instruction and field experience. The University of Miami in Coral Gables was my first choice. It was founded around the aspirations and knowledge of Dr. F. G. Walton Smith, a British marine scientist who came over to the US mainland from Nassau in 1940 at the age of thirty-one. He founded the International Oceanographic Foundation and became as renowned in marine science fields as Tucker Abbott, Eugenie Clark, and others. Miami was my principal target for admission because its focuses were on tropical and subtropical marine sciences, which fit tightly with experiences I had and hoped to obtain. The reputation of the Marine Biological Laboratory and Oceanographic Institution at Woods Hole, Massachusetts, was known, but its focuses were primarily on the ocean waters of the Northeast, the Canadian maritime, and the North Atlantic. It was from Woods Hole that the oceanographer Dr. Robert Ballard discovered in 1985 the sunken RMS *Titanic* 12,000 feet below the Atlantic surface. Duke University's academic program and Beaufort-based marine laboratory were not known to me. William & Mary's Virginia Institute of Marine Sciences at Gloucester Pointe was not known to me until nearly half a century later. A sixteen-year-old among the working staff of this substantial expedition ought, I reasoned, move my admissions applications to the top or close to the top of the proverbial application stack.

This expedition was to be led by Dr. R. Tucker Abbott, whose reputation as a malacologist was without parallel. Beyond that of his fellow scientists, he was known in the popular press as Mr. Seashell. Malacologists study mollusks, which are invertebrate animals whose most widely and popularly known members are clams, oysters, and whose surviving external skeletons we find on beach walks—shells! Molluscs, as they are known in science, are the largest marine phylum with about 100,000 known species, comprising nearly a quarter of all named marine organisms. After months of planning and heightened expectations, the expedition failed to garner the required funding. To the best of my knowledge, it never happened in the shape or timeline planned by Parker, Abbott, and others. I explained its demise as best I could to those who asked about its status. More probably wondered but did not ask, but I continued my high school education. What else could I do?

To close this discussion, after scholarly research at the Smithsonian Institution, the Academy of Sciences in Philadelphia, and the Delaware Museum of Natural History, the Harvard-educated Dr. Abbott died at the age of seventy-seven on November 1995 at Sanibel Island, Florida, one of the "shell capitals" of the world. He had traveled the world's seas, sea beds, and shorelines, discovered a thousand new species of mollusks, which is about 1 percent of all of them, authored thirty books, and opened his own Bailey-Matthews Shell Museum at Sanibel. He is buried at Arlington National Cemetery across the Potomac River from Washington and several hundred yards from the Tomb of the Unknown Soldier. My significant other, Darlene McKinnon, and I paid our respects to him at his headstone on a beautiful autumn Sunday afternoon in 2016. I had driven past this cemetery on the way to work and on the way home nearly each day for decades without knowing that I was passing his final resting place each time. Dr. Parker died earlier, in 1977, and is buried in Northport on the north shore of New York's Long Island, about a two-hour drive from Montauk on its easternmost point where the movie *Jaws* was set and filmed for its 1975 release.

The woman who would become Abbott's equal in reputation was Dr. Eugenie Clark, an ichthyologist, that's the study of fish, and oceanographer, that's the study of oceans, known globally for her revolutionizing and popularly published shark studies, *Lady With a Spear* and the later *The Lady and the Shark*s. I had met her on a Science Center field trip to her Cape Haze Marine Laboratory and its "little wooden building, 20 x 40 ft." research site about forty-five miles south of Sarasota. That almost primitive facility would be succeeded by Mote Marine Laboratory in Sarasota as a consequence of its substantial financial support for her and others' work in marine sciences from William R. Mote, a wealthy New York businessman who had been born in the Tampa Bay area and never lost his love of "getting his toes wet" in it. It is a point of pride for me to have met her.

Carol Croley

Were there changes ahead in our focuses on distinctly different areas of marine biology? Yes, and more than one.

I was studying marine algae, which are a lower, more primitive botanical class than more well-known sea plants, for example, turtle grass. Carol was studying marine mollusks and already an emerging malacologist of demonstrated ability. Her area of science meant shells and what lives within them. Carol and I worked collaboratively in the broader field of marine biology, but we worked separately on our science fair projects because the fairs embodied competition among exhibitor's researches, writings, and displays.

As a budding malacologist, why was she not identified by Bill Guild for proposed selection by the academy for an expedition focused on shells? I assumed that Guild discussed the matter with her mother, probably even before he made me aware of it, but I was never informed by anyone of such a discussion. I believe by the process of logic that it was because it was to be an *all-male* expedition, common at that time, for reasons that may be deduced from Dr. Parker's letter reciting the risks at sea and port, inferred as risks of persons living and working closely being a risk of living too closely, especially with someone under the age of majority. Again, I am guessing at that, for I cannot surmise any other reason. Remember, these decisions were made by others near the turn of the 1950s into the 1960s, not in today's searches for gender neutrality in scientific disciplines.

Her career shift in marine biological studies at university from her focus on mollusks to a focus on algae was a startling surprise to me when she shared it half a century later. Let's let her speak for herself in regard to how her career developed after our years at the Science Center, a voice set out in her June 24, 2015, letter to me in her effort to assure the credibility of the detail of these matters.

> I did grow up to be a phycologist, [my] studies beginning at USF [University of South Florida]. My research at Content Key (mouth of Florida Bay) on offshore benthic [the lowest level of water above the ocean floor] flora of South Florida, and extensive works on species "new" to the Gulf of Mexico have appeared in various journals. In 1968, I spent the summer working at the Smithsonian's Department of Botany seeking type specimens for the newly reported algae. I traveled to Farlow [Herbarium] (Harvard), New York Botanical Garden (NYC) and other [collections]. Late in 1968, Max Hommersand (whose area of research was the morphology, systematics and biography of the marine algae, with emphasis on red algae, algae's highest class) appeared at the Smithsonian and offered me a graduate assistantship at UNC-Chapel Hill. I spent wonderful times ther researching a genus of tropical red algae, Dasya. Those were the days of descriptive phycology. Now, most studies discussing systematics of algae incorporate information gleaned

from DNA analysis. Anyway, I held teaching positions at Trenton State College, The College of the Virgin Islands (St. Thomas), sailed for the Oceanic Society as a marine biologist on the SS National Bowditch in the St. Francis Channel in and around the U.S. Virgin Islands and British Virgin Islands, and taught coral reef ecology on Glover's Reef off the coast of Belize for the American Universities for International Education. When I became pregnant with Jennifer Joy, my first child, I could not continue the summer of 1976 on that remote atoll, so I joined (husband) Charlie in Mississippi. *** I continued to publish from time to time and recently donated my huge library to the University of Louisiana at Lafayette for the use of a colleague and her students. Another phycologist friend donated his library at the same time and place! Once in a while I check my three names in the literature and have noticed more and more herbarium portals are appearing on line. Fun to see my old specimens appearing on line!!! Charlie was drafted for the Vietnam War, served his 2 years as a cryptographic specialist and left the Army to join me at Chapel Hill where he studied history.

Her explanation of her post–Science Center career is impressive. By contrast, my post–Science Center career took me to political science, public administration, and law. I stayed as much abreast of developments in marine biology generally and in marine algae specifically as I could under the circumstances of career, family, and income. My interests in these matters came nearly full circle in the spring of 2015 when I was invited to serve on a board of the Virginia Institute of Marine Sciences whose School of Marine Science is a graduate school of the College of William and Mary in Williamsburg. VIMS has a three-part mission: to conduct interdisciplinary research in coastal ocean and estuarine science, educate students and citizens, and provide advisory service to policy makers, industry, and the public. It provides those services in Virginia, the five-state Chesapeake Bay and its tributaries, the East Coast, the nation, and the world by "conducting research and providing sound scientific advice concerning the often-contentious issues surrounding the use and conservation of marine resources." Chartered in 1940 as was the University of Miami's marine sciences school, VIMS is among the largest marine research and education centers in the United States. It is located at Gloucester Point on the western side of the Chesapeake Bay and on the north shore of the York River across the bridge from Yorktown Battlefield, where on October 19, 1781, General Charles Lord Cornwallis surrendered to the allied American and French forces of General George Washington and the Marquis de Lafayette. There I go connecting dots again, but, regretfully, I resigned from VIMS's advisory body in late 2017 for lack of sufficient time and treasure to support its important work, voluntarily departing so someone with time and treasure could serve.

Spain and Portugal

In the *St. Petersburg Times* of March 20, 1962, an article entitled "Young Scientists Win Cash, Trips, Honors" reported that "top science fair prize winners" included Carol and me. Carol won its number one position, which qualified her for the National Science Fair in Seattle, Washington. I won the number two position for the exhibit, "The Influence of Hydronium Ion Concentrations upon the Metabolic Processes of *Gracilaria verrucosa*," which is to say on the adverse influences of polluted water runoff into coastal regions on the reproduction of a prevalent Florida west coast red algae. I was happy for her and myself. She was to head west to the National Science Fair in Seattle, and I was to head east to Europe. My award was an all-expenses-paid ten-day Young Columbus Expedition tour of Spain and Portugal via the Azores, the award dedicated to our science fair and paid for by the St. Petersburg Times Company.

Carol and I continued to work together at the Science Center and in its marine science fieldwork, and our third in much of this work was my next-door neighbor Judith Herr. I treasure to this day our three's work together, for it was full of learning experiences. We worked hard at it, we had fun at it, and that work gave rise to the separate aspirations that bolstered each of us. I regret not having stayed abreast of Carol's career as it was developing, but I am more than pleased that our reconnecting has made me aware of how her career developed and the contributions to marine sciences made by her. They also gave me a fuller appreciation of her mother's contributions to the Science Center. I have not been able to locate Judith Herr to express my thanks to her and her parents, so I do that here in case a reader knows of her present whereabouts.

As to my European trip, on May 3, 1962, I was airborne from Tampa's airport to New York City for a predeparture dinner with fellow Young Columbians and, can you believe, Zsa Zsa Gabor and the taking of a photograph that appeared during my absence in the *St. Petersburg Times*. On May 4, we lifted for the Azores and Madrid. My luggage arrived three days later, an auspicious beginning to a life and career of extensive international travel.

In Madrid, we walked its streets and mingled with the Madrilenos who seemingly defied any need for sleep. We toured the Palacio Real and the Puerta de Alcala arch and walked among the jumbled shops of the Carrera San Jeronimo. We gazed at the Goya, El Greco, and Velazquez paintings in the famous Prado Museum. The Hollywood actor, Cesar Romero, known as "The Latin from Manhattan" and a grandson of Cuban national hero José Marti, was there as simply a tourist, as were we. We explorers lit votive candles by cathedral altars adorned with gold and silver brought from the New World. Some of us ate our first paella while listening to the castanets and thundering boots of flamenco dancers. On a Sunday afternoon, we watched the contest between life and death in the Madrid bullring, made more famous in America in Ernest Hemingway's *Death in the Afternoon*. The individualized, meaning our own name on the poster given to us, bullfighting posters that the trip's organizers had arranged were welcomed souvenirs even if mine was misspelled "Randal Teaque," but it too disappeared in mother's move from Thirty-Seventh Avenue.

My hand-tooled fencing foil and nearly matching letter opener from Toledo have traveled with me to this day. We soaked up, like the young sponges we were, a Madrid not too distant in years from Hemingway's. Postcards and photographs were expected outcomes for those at home. Near Toledo, we toured General and Caudillo Francisco Franco's tribute to himself in the Valley of the Fallen in the Guardarrama Mountains, and the Royal Site of San Lorenzo de El Escorial about forty-five miles west of Madrid, the latter a historical residence of the kings of Spain as well as a privileged monastery and, in our time, the setting for much of Gary Grant, Frank Sinatra, and Sophia Loren's 1957 movie, *The Pride and the Passion.*

We flew the short hop to Lisbon and toured it and Portugal's Costa do Sol, Pena, Coimbra, including its university established in 1290, Oporto from whence come port wines, Figueira da Foz, Cabo da Roca, the latter being the eastern most point of continental Europe. I turned eighteen on this trip and in Lisbon.

When one night in Lisbon we found ourselves in the midst of another uprising against Portugal's Antonio de Oliveira Salazar, with sounds of gunfire and tanks rolling through the streets and thereby confining us to the hotel, it added to our excitement. When on takeoff of our TWA Boeing 707 flight bound for New York City, we had some of the ditching equipment drop from the cabin overhead from the severity of vibration from a too-soon liftoff and near stall because the tower had reported to the pilots that the plane may have been shot at by rebels, it added to that excitement. I have not sought to verify the details of this incident, but it was far too much excitement. An unavoidable consequence of this trip was, as the student council president whose attendance at it was deemed mandatory, I missed my senior year's prom. I had as council president elect missed the preceding year's prom because of my attendance at a Miami program.

Gulf Coast Marine Biology Company

I kept my shoulders to the wheels of my marine biology work. It was not easy. I kept my memberships in the International Oceanographic Foundation, Florida Foundation for Future Scientists, and Florida Junior Academy of Science. I kept a saltwater aquarium in our enclosed porch area, and its maintenance was more difficult than with a fresh water tank. Despite aeration, filters, and daily attention, its water had to be changed weekly, and the easiest place to obtain replacement water was near the north entrance to the Sunshine Skyway Bridge across the mouth of Tampa Bay. This task was not so much its distance but rather the collecting and weight of the water. While seawater is only marginally heavier than fresh water, a single ten-gallon tank required two five-gallon plastic containers to be filled, nearly forty pounds each. In addition, the new water had to rest on the porch until its temperature equalized with that in the tanks so as not to shock and thereby kill the fish, hermit crabs, and other life. Emptying each aquarium of the past week's water and cleaning it was an odiferous routine.

Knowing that my mother and I were going to have to meet at least out-of-pocket expenses at any university that admitted me, I created a for-profit enterprise and named it Gulf Coast Marine Biology Company even though we never incorporated it. Its one-line advertising slogan was "We specialize in marine biological specimens from the beautiful shores of the Gulf of Mexico." I marketed through correspondence, collected specimens to fill orders, and carefully packaged and shipped them to ordering laboratories. This venture did not generate much income, but it did cover the costs of materials and some scientific equipment.

Summer Work and Summer Fun

A consequence of my Science Center, science fair, and related marine sciences work and their visibilities was an invitation to work as a summer employee at the Coastal Research Laboratory of the Bureau of Sport and

Commercial Fisheries of the Department of Interior at St. Petersburg Beach. This facility was adjacent to the 1928-opened Don CeSar Hotel, in the 1960s a Veterans Administration office building, later reconverted to a resort of the original name. The adjacent laboratory facility is still there but as an art gallery.

I worked at this facility during the summer between my junior and senior high school years and again the next summer. I began as a GS-1 and was promoted to a GS-2 for the second summer. Based on that limited experience and knowledge of the federal workforce, I thought I had the system figured out; just do this for fifteen years and I would be a GS-15. Then I was informed of the multiple subgrades within each grade. I rush to add that this was not a factor, only background noise, in undertaking later public sector employment but coming at it from another direction, that of the executive office of the president of the United States.

Those summers in the lab and on its research vessel are among the most enjoyable of my early life. Time and work were divided between a professionally serious chemistry lab and professionally able data and specimen collecting "at sea," if I can refer to the Gulf of Mexico's 615,000 square miles and 660 quadrillion gallons of salt water as a sea. We worked in the Gulf on the RV *Kingfish*, a fifty-two-foot Chris-Craft cabin cruiser converted for collecting marine specimens and hydrological and other physical data. Fauna and flora collected mostly in nets and water samples taken at varying depths and collected in bottles closed by a series of dropped weights on a cable would be returned to shore for analyses on a number of matters relevant to the west coast of Florida. When we encountered summer storms and the boat was cutting through the waves with thunder and lightning and an occasional waterspout around us, I'd simply stand on deck beside the captain and hum the overture from the NBC documentary *Victory at Sea*. Oh, to be that unafraid again!

Among the more important public contexts for the lab's work was the occurrence of "red tide" associated with Tampa Bay's and other bodies of waters' tidal and storm-surged flows into the Gulf. Red tide is an algae bloom, first recorded in settled Florida in 1844, within which microscopic algae discharge toxins which paralyze the gills of fish, causing them to die in massive numbers, wash ashore, and cause the odor of tens of thousands of rotting fish. I write settled Florida because Spanish explorer Ponce de Leon encountered in 1513 a red tide outbreak so severe that he turned southward toward Cuba. It kills shore birds and even 800–1100-pound manatees and emits eye-burning ambient toxins to waif on air currents into shorelines communities. The organisms by the millions discolor the water, sometimes red, thus "red tide," but sometimes light or dark green, brown, or even clear. These blooms occur in the United States almost exclusively in the Gulf of Mexico, on Florida's east coast, and occasionally off of North Carolina. They can last days, weeks, or months but also change daily due to wind conditions and water salinity. None of this is good for shoreline beaches and resorts or recreational or commercial fishing.

Marine algae are among the oldest members of the plant kingdom, reaching back many hundreds of millions of years, for plants in the sea preceded those on land. Algae have little tissue differentiation, no true vascular tissue, no roots, no stems, no leaves, and no flowers. They range in size from microscopic individual cells to huge plants more than one hundred feet long. Kelp off the coast of California is the most common example of a large species. The brown algae, *Sargassum,* has bubble-like flotation capability and is common along the East Coast. It is so prolific in the mid-Atlantic Ocean that the area is known as the Sargasso Sea, and ancient sailors were afraid their sailing ships would become entangled in it and they would never escape it. A green algae along the Gulf and Atlantic coasts looks like but of course is not lettuce. *Ulva lactuca* is its scientific name, and sea lettuce is what it is usually called by beach combers and fishermen. Another green algae along these coasts looks like long green intestines and is many feet in length. *Enteromorpha intestinalis* is appropriately its scientific name, and gutweed or grass kelp is what it is sometimes called by boaters and harbor masters. The New England region's most prevalent alga, depicted in Rachel Carlson's *The Sea Around Us, The Edge of the Sea,* and *Under the Sea Wind,* is *Ascophyllum nodosum,* commonly known as rockweed, knotted wrack, or Norwegian kelp. Together, algae provide shelter and food for marine life. As already noted, some have commercial value for medicines, cosmetics, food, and fuels. Its by-products are found in ice cream, milkshakes, dressings, sauces, baked goods, toothpaste, and lipstick. More than any other function, algae at sea, including microscopic species, provide the bulk of Earth's oxygen supply through photosynthesis.

The lab's scientists knew of my research focuses, so they availed me of a second-floor corner room with excellent sunlight in which to set up an artificial environment for my experiments. I was on the taxpayers' payroll for the lab's work, not mine, so my own work was after hours so to speak. Instead of misusing government equipment, I purchased and brought with me what I needed at summer's onset. Besides, I needed it for the next science fair exhibit. Five aeration beakers would bubble twenty-four hours a day, each with a different base or acidic concentration with the same amounts of mature *Gracilaria verrucosa,* a red seaweed, in each. Cross sections of my *Gracilaria* tissue and microscopes for their examinations permitted me to determine how each cluster was reproducing and to record my findings.

In addition to the lab's red tide focus, I worked on a biological and economic study of squid in Tampa Bay, a project headed by Alexander Dragovich and John Kelly Jr., published in the November 1962 *Proceedings of the Gulf and Caribbean Fisheries Institute,* wherein I received an appreciated acknowledgment of technical assistance as Randall, that second *l* inescapable once again.

If working for this research station at its shoreline and spending several days each week on Tampa Bay and Gulf waters on its research vessel were not enough, a weekend could hold a different adventure on those waters. One of the lab's employees was John S. Thompson III, maybe four or five years older. I don't think I ever asked him or anyone else at the lab if John were a permanent or a temporary hire. Grandfather Thompson was a pianist, composer, and educator of major note, including his authoring of piano method books, *Modern Course for the Piano, Teaching Little Fingers to Play,* and *Easiest Piano.* Those books are published by the Willis Music Company and are available through Amazon.com, eBay, and other web services. In short, Grandfather John had earned well-deserved money from which Grandson John could enjoy life more fully.

Grandson John's principal contribution to my burgeoning marine sciences career was his ability to take the family's cabin cruiser into the Gulf. Their boat was about the length and beam of the RV *Kingfish* but a later model with more comfort and a more sophisticated electronic package. It had coolers for ingredients not allowed on US government craft, and it had a .30-.30 for safety as crime at sea was a reality in the Gulf and Caribbean long before recent years' drug running. For example, August Busch's *Eagle*'s crew, which docked for part of the year adjacent to the lab's *Kingfish*, had significant hardware to defend it against an attempted hostile boarding, and his well-trained crew knew how to use it. I suppose in earlier years in these waters, certainly including the Prohibition era, a crime was "rum running," as an expression of running any type of booze into the United States from the Bahamas, Cuba, Hispaniola, Mexico, or elsewhere.

John would steer the craft into the Gulf distant enough from land and its light to be in total darkness for stargazing on moonless nights. He'd anchor in locations off shipping lanes yet in water shallow enough for the anchor to hold the boat's position. A favored activity in such darkness was to cut all but the mandated green and red port and starboard lights and hang a battery-operated bright lantern on a line from the bridge to right above the water line to see what sea life would be attracted to that light. Most commonly, large cobia, known in some waters as black kingfish, would come to the surface. Cobia can grow to two meters in length, but I have never seen one of that length. They are good eating, but you do not capture them in this manner, so we did not. Other fish would surface. Occasionally there'd be a shark.

We motored to different locations during daylight. We'd troll in between positions, but we never caught an Ernest Hemingway–sized bill fish for the probable reason that they seldom exist that far north of the Straits of Florida between the Keys and Cuba. If life at the lab and on its vessel was work and fun, this was simply fun.

A competition among research station employees was who could get the "longest" suntan, defined as dark enough to last until Thanksgiving as the penultimate and Christmas as the ultimate challenges. Working shirtless on the boat two or three days a week and going back out on weekends, plus marine specimen collecting on other days, added to the darkness of my tan. Of course, now we know it added to the risks of skin cancer. My answer to the latter is going to my dermatologist at least every six months, for nearly 90 percent of melanomas are on backsides. I do not love his nitrogen spray gun, but I am grateful that it was invented.

A Shift in Focus

Were my intent and hard work in marine sciences enough to get me into the University of Miami? Yes, but prior to admission, I was offered a National Defense Education Act loan, not a scholarship, to cover tuition. If based on financial need alone, it was hard to imagine any applicant needed it more than me, but other applicants' academic strengths must have outshined mine. Nonetheless, I felt I could "convert" from a loan to a scholarship once on campus and after demonstrations of my interests and abilities in the marine biology curriculum, programs, and laboratories. Success at that would have meant some tuition covered by loans and consequential personal debt but other tuition covered by scholarships. Assuming adequate income, this strategy seemed manageable. Assuming more income in later years, I could have contributed some of it to the university to help provide scholarships for students in those years. Instead of accepting the loan, I shifted my career focus away from the seas.

Are there times now when I long for the sea? Of course there are and usually in the depths of Washington winters. I have filled some of the emotional void by staying abreast of marine biology matters. As a lawyer, I had clients who worked in these fields, from a sailboat charterer in Annapolis to a highly specialized deep-ocean technologies corporation headquartered in Norway. If and when my memories fade, I hope I can still recall the years that I gave to the sea. Looking back on them, when nothing was expected of me beyond getting through high school with grades strong enough for college admission, I know there was commendable output, recognizing that it was being matched, and often surpassed, by the output of others, many of whom were my classmates or other friends. The sea had a fascination for me that nothing else could match then and barely match now. It was a thrilling time to be engaged so fully. Sea water is in my blood, as it is in each reader's, but a great love and respect of the sea and life within it are thick in my veins.

The little income from my Gulf Coast Marine Biology Company and those two summers at the lab helped pay for some credits hours in my three semesters at St. Petersburg College, as I waited for the words from Washington that would move me there to a congressional staff position and to American University for a first degree and to George Washington University Law School for two law degrees. But I first had to complete high school.

My campaign for Northeast High School Student Council president and its yearlong incumbency is an integral part of that transition. It is that campaign and what followed from it that shifted me from marine biology to government and law and the politics that interlock them.

21

Campaign for Student Council President

D URING THE SPRING SEMESTER OF MY JUNIOR YEAR, I was encouraged by students to run for student council president. Some I knew, and others I did not. A few were former Mirror Lake students who had gone to school with my almost certain opponent, Rob Amley, which fact perked my interest. I remained undecided until an additional factor tipped the scales. I was asked by my American history teacher, Dan Crum, to meet with him. He informed me that my candidacy could have support from a number of teachers, indicating the student parking issue could become Amley's Achilles' heel in that he had served in student government positions as it worsened and did nothing or too little about it.

I entered the race. With the recent Kennedy-Nixon debates in mind, I challenged Amley to one in the auditorium during school hours, if both could be arranged, and, based on my discussion with Mr. Crum, I thought they could. To debate after the last period would advantage Amley because some of my supporters would not be able to attend and cheer me on because they had after-school jobs. Amley was reluctant to give me equal standing in students' eyes, so he delayed his response, and that was a bad indecision. Reluctantly, he agreed to the debate, and a date and time were set during school hours in the auditorium. Supporters set about making enough name-badge-sized stickers to inundate the school to give impressions of momentum. One with artwork of a blindfolded student read:

DON'T VOTE BLIND
ELECT TEAGUE
STUDENT COUNCIL PRESIDENT
FAIRNESS TO ALL STUDENTS

One with a student scratching the back of his head had the caption "Figure It Out For Yourself" and carried that same "Fairness To All Students." Another, again with that last line, featured a wide-eyed owl with the caption "Be Wise!" A fourth had a sitting student with a face buried in a book entitled *Facts* with the caption "Examine the Facts." One had an image of two students shaking hands with the caption "Join the League / Vote for Teague." A sixth had a cheerleader shouting "Shout Out The Good News" from the megaphone. A seventh had a Sherlock Holmes–capped student looking through an equally Sherlock Holmes–styled looking glass at the inscription "Why Search?" The last had an attempted image of me pointing in an Uncle-Sam-Needs-You pose and the caption:

Teague
Needs
YOU
Need
Teague

The repetitive text "Fairness To All Students" became my campaign theme, and it requires an explanation. It was not a version of today's income or asset inequality class warfare. I was not contesting earned wealth or inherited privilege or the right to have and enjoy them. I was

212

arguing for inclusion as a preference over exclusion. I did not want the former Mirror Lake students to leave all of their elected positions so that Lealman students could then occupy them. I felt one exclusion should not give way to another. I was contending the Lealman and Mirror Lake students should both serve in student government. This message that Teague wanted fairness through a more balanced representation was getting through. The campaign badges reinforced it, and students scrambled to get all eight, and several became posters. There was also no danger the parking lot issue would abate, for it was lived by students each morning in their scrambles for parking spaces.

I had concluded the contest's outcome would depend on the debate, and it did. I hit hard on the unfairness to the Lealman alumni of a student government dominated by students from only one of the two dominant feeder schools but sought to do so without angering Mirror Lake alumni. Losing votes while gaining votes seemed to me to be risky politicking. I focused also on my extracurricular activities in science because I had no sports prowess to claim. Even though the Indian Ocean expedition had not occurred, I spoke to it and my Science Center work. They created impressions of hard work and its rewards. Amley seemed floored by the debate's direction and momentum. He had been caught flat-footed, but there was no second debate through which to recover, another tactical design that worked on my behalf. Several of his friends came up to me as I was leaving the stage to tell me how unfair they felt my "fairness campaign" was, but others of his friends quietly told me they thought I was right. It was an early lesson for me on women's deeper senses of community.

I won the student council race, but Mirror Lake students won senior class races. The balance I was seeking played out in that way. The *St. Petersburg Times* and the *St. Petersburg Evening Independent* gave the race and its outcome good coverage, and the *St. Petersburg Times* gave me a "Youth Comments" column to discuss it. The hard work to end the parking lot crisis required a system of mandatory stickers on eligible vehicles and entrance and lot monitors. Its success overcame the broad administration, faculty, and student uneasiness that it might not. By the end of our senior year, our race's loser and winner, Amley and me, had both been chosen through the yearbook's popularity contest to be among the twenty-four "Top Seniors."

On June 8, 1962, 381 of our senior class graduated and headed our separate ways, many to never see each other again or ever return to the school's campus, a startling observation made then and as the years grew. Remarkably, our class made it through the Vietnam War without the heavy losses that hit NEHI's later classes. Alumni attending the fortieth reunion in 2002 were surprised as to how few had died. Those of us attending the fiftieth reunion in 2012 were surprised at how many had died during the intervening ten years. The number increased measurably by our fifty-fifth reunion in 2017. It's now a certainty, not merely a trend.

One of the student council members was June Alice Leonard. Moving forward several years, as I had gone to Washington to work for Congressman Cramer, she had gone to Washington to work for the Federal Bureau of Investigation in its Washington Field Office then located in the Old Post Office Pavilion, which now houses the Trump International Hotel four blocks from the White House. The congressman pointed out to each of us that the other was in Washington, we met, began dating, and were married by the chaplain of the Senate, the Rev. Frederick Brown Harris, with family and friends enjoying the moments. It was too soon for either of us to have made such a commitment, so the marriage came to an early and quiet end. We both learned from it, welcomed the continued friendship of over half a century, and shared not infrequently the latest in our lives. A graduate of the University of Florida and Florida State University's law school, she became a financial crimes prosecutor before Florida's state courts in Gainesville and surrounding counties for much of her career.

22

The Young Americans for Freedom

A T THE BEGINNING OF MY SENIOR YEAR AT NORTHEAST High, I was introduced by Dan Crum to a teacher new to our campus. He was David Richard Jones III and had come to Northeast from a high school in Clearwater, a Gulf shore city north of St. Petersburg. I was to learn quickly that David Jones as a determined young man was an understatement.

David Jones

David Jones was the second baby born in Buffalo on January 1, 1938, losing out by minutes to the first, but he was the first to have been born in one of its hospitals, as attested by a photograph of him and his parents and accompanying text in the *Buffalo Times* the next day. His father, obviously David R. Jones Jr. but also "Bus," was working part-time in a steel-manufacturing suburb. The steel industry had more jobs available there in the waning years of the Depression than it did in his hometown of Follansbee, West Virginia. Instead of a steel plant worker toiling eight hours a day and five days a week and others not working, a worker worked fewer hours during the week in order that other workers would also have jobs and incomes.

As a consequence of the Joneses moving back to Follansbee as steel production rose to meet prewar and World War II demands, the young Jones was to be raised there, a coal-fired steel town with less than five thousand people and sitting on the south shore of the Ohio River. Follansbee Steel Corp. had been founded in 1902 by brothers John and Robert Follansbee, a Chicago-based family of financial acumen and business achievements. Having nothing to do with Follansbee Steel Corp. or Follansbee, West Virginia, as either or both related to the Jones family, Follansbee family members were decades later donors to Young Americans for Freedom, which is the YAF of this chapter, and other David Jones–led national conservative educational and political action organizations.

Jones's father worked in its Koppers Chemical plant until he enlisted in the navy, although he had been classified as exempt from military service because of his marriage and children. On discharge, he returned to the Koppers plant for the remainder of his working life. As Lee Edwards set forth in a 1998 *David R. Jones* forty-three-page "Champions of Freedom's First Principles" publication of the Fund for American Studies, Bus Jones was "a very strong union man" and labor organizer at the Koppers plant, but "an old-fashioned union member - patriotic, church-going and highly skilled" who "got on well with management, especially the head of the Follansbee Steel mill, who happened to be his father-in-law, William Lake." Inside the organized labor movement, the Joneses supported George Meany's and later Lane Kirkland's anti-Communist side, which stood in contrast to Victor and Walter Reuther's hard-left side and Harry Bridges's Communists on the West Coast. Jones's brother, John Lake Jones, shared with me that the families had a deep sense that successfully climbing income ladders, in short getting ahead, was tied to an individual's freedom to do so.

Community pride is just that, and despite its small population, Follansbee and its nearby communities gave the nation the National Football League's coach Lou Holtz, born there in 1937 and raised in nearby East Liverpool, Ohio; Olympic hurdler, sprinter, and three-time gold medalist Glenn "Jeep" Davis, born in nearby Wellsburg, WV, in 1934, a professional football player with the Detroit Lions and then a teacher and coach in Barberton, Ohio; US concert pianist and Boston University pedagogue Anthony di Bonaventura, born in Follansbee in 1929; and, in my and others' opinion, David Jones, not born there but nurtured and educated there.

Jones was a summer counselor at the YMCA of West Virginia's Camp Horseshoe in the Monongahela National Forest during at least two of his high school years. He may have been a previous year's camper there.

Jones also played flute in the Follansbee High School band. I do not recall him ever sharing that with me. As a consequence of being on the football field only by being in the band, he tried out for the team and earned a place on it for his senior year. Not only did the team win its first state football championship in 1954, but Jones found himself shortly thereafter in a "Victory and Defeat"–captioned Harry Seawell photograph in the pages of *Look* magazine by the happenstance of being near the team's cocaptain and winning-margin scorer Richard Wilinski when the photograph was taken. Wilinski went on to college football prominence, Jones did not wish to try, but they both became prominent in their respective advocacies of voluntary service as did their families.

Jones's mother, Doris Lake Jones, attended West Liberty State College for one year, which permitted her in those difficult economic times in West Virginia public education to teach without a certificate. She stopped for a while in order to raise their three boys, later taking courses for certification at West Virginia University. David Jones attended George Williams College, now within Aurora University, in Chicago on an academic scholarship. There, he pledged Phi Zeta Tau fraternity, played basketball, and worked for the Salvation Army Settlement House. He switched to closer-to-Follansbee's West Liberty State College in nearby Wheeling and graduated in 1960. In between, he had attended for a short period Lincoln Memorial College, now Lincoln Memorial University, in Tennessee. His mother probably recommended to David that he secure his degree at West Liberty. More importantly, it seems to me, he met at West Liberty his future wife, Corinne Adele Watts of Dormont, a community near Pittsburgh. I rush to add that attending three schools for one diploma does not reflect adverse academic issues. Tuition costs were always an issue, and on at least one occasion, his mother, who by that time was managing the family's neighborhood store, Heights Confectionery, required surgery and a convalescence period, and it was Dave who returned home to manage it in her absence. Furthermore, David Jones was to earn a master's in higher education administration from Vanderbilt University's Peabody College, was a lecturer at Vanderbilt and its Peabody College, and became a vice chancellor at Vanderbilt. He had what it took.

Jones's mother's brother, his uncle, was John B. Lake, known widely as Jack. He rose in only eleven years from advertising director to publisher of the *St. Petersburg Times*, now the *Tampa Bay Times*. Lake was an avid baseball fan and years later received a 1 percent ownership interest in the St. Louis Cardinals as a perhaps revertible at death "gift" from its majority owner and professional and personal friend August (Gussie) Anheuser Busch III of Anheuser-Busch Brewing in St. Louis. Busch was the Cardinals' president from 1953 to 1989. The Cardinals' spring training was at then-named Al Lang Field on St. Petersburg's Tampa Bay waterfront. Thus, the *St. Petersburg Times* was the hometown newspaper of the Cardinals during spring training. Mr. Busch kept his professionally crewed yacht, *The Eagle*, moored at St. Petersburg Beach near the Bureau of Sport and Commercial Fisheries' RV *Kingfish*. While it was an indication of his wealth, that was only a coincidence of dock availabilities, but we were proud to dock the Bureau's *Kingfish* near it. I admired Mr. Busch's providential descent, his families' and his patriotism, his business acumen, his love of baseball, his commitment to St. Petersburg, and not least this floating toy.

Lake was later instrumental with area businessman Jim Healy in paving the way for the region's own Major League Baseball team, the 1998 expansion and originally named Tampa Bay Devil Rays, now playing without that Devil. He threw out the first pitch of their first home game. Fans had walked to the stadium down Jim Healy and Jack Lake Baseball Boulevard. All of that was in his future when nephew David Jones and his wife arrived in St. Petersburg. They had done so in a big Oldsmobile, but they quickly shifted to a more Florida-appropriate convertible sports car, which seemed to always have mechanical issues. By the time Jones reported to Northeast High, he had taught the preceding year in nearby Clearwater but was only six years older than most of those in his senior classes. Jack Lake's position in St. Petersburg may have had something to do with their decision to move to Florida, but it was just as likely they wished to escape the Rust Belt for the Sunshine State. It is possible also that the young Joneses came to Florida because David was attracted to the state's requirement that all high school students take a Problems of Communism course. It had been enacted by its legislature in the wake of Fidel Castro's Communist revolution in neighboring Cuba, only ninety miles from Florida's Key West. It was probably a combination of these considerations.

David and Corinne lived first in the apartment over the Lake's Snell Isle garage. He quickly moved into St. Petersburg's community life by becoming active in the St. Petersburg Junior Chamber of Commerce, the Jaycees, where he became its vice president and received its Man of the Year award and in the Tyrone Civic Association. Mindful that he was a teacher, he joined the Florida Education Association, the National Education Association, and the Florida Council of Social Studies. She continued for a while as a dental assistant, but when they moved in the mid-1970s from the Washington area to Nashville, she created for herself the position of director of development for the Tennessee Performing Arts Center, where she excelled in nonprofit fundraising and was recognized for that achievement.

The course caption under Jones's photograph in my senior yearbook, *Viking Log,* says American History, which is true, but it falls short of other descriptors. He won the Teacher of the Year award of the St. Petersburg Woman's Club for both the city and region and became one of fourteen finalists in the statewide competition, as well as the recipient of the Florida American Legion's teaching award for patriotism. At

Northeast, he had infused his American history course with appreciable levels of psychology, and students reported that dimension enlivened his classrooms. He was our debate team coach for the National Forensic League's local and state competitions.

Jones was to become my career navigator, a door-opening mentor, and a professional and personal friend. The two and sometimes the three of us became partners in all manner of undertakings. I followed him into organizations' director and officer positions and political campaigns. Not following but side by side, we entered into related jobs, including in the executive office of the president of the United States and on Capitol Hill as Jones became chief of staff to Senator James L. Buckley on the Senate side and I became chief of staff to Congressman Jack F. Kemp on its House side. I followed him to the Soviet Union and China and succeeded him as president of the American Council of Young Political Leaders (ACYPL), the bipartisan United States chapter of the Atlantic Council of Young Political Leaders (AAYPL), the young leaders' arm of the Atlantic Treaty Association (ATA). ACYPL continued after the Cold War and remains a vibrant organization involved in advocacies of democracy through exchanges with other countries' young political leaders. As Jones was chairman and president of the board of trustees of what over time became the Fund for American Studies, I succeeded him in that chairmanship upon his 1998 death. I had not succeeded him as president of the National Federation of Independent Business Foundation. I did offer eulogies at his April 1998 funeral service in Nashville, at a memorial service to him in Washington, and at two later testimonial dinners in those cities.

YAF

The earliest of our organizational adventures was Young Americans for Freedom. We were both at Northeast High when it emerged.

YAF was a philosophically oriented and politically active national youth organization. It had been founded in September 1960 in reaction to the perceived drift of the nation, its founders' perception of a Republican

Party equally at drift, and the need for a conservative national youth movement. That party had just nominated Richard Nixon and Henry Cabot Lodge as its ticket for the White House, which had disappointed those who became YAF's founders as well as others. Nixon was seen by them as having caved in to New York governor Nelson Rockefeller. President Dwight Eisenhower's ambassador to the United Nations, Henry Cabot Lodge of the Boston Cabots and Lodges who spoke only to God, had been forced onto the Nixon ticket. Yet, this YAF versus the Cabots and the Lodges was not a problem for me or the Cabots when I worked nearly twenty years later as division counsel in the family's Boston-headquartered Cabot Corporation.

YAF's founding was the idea of several score of college students, recent college graduates, and nationally prominent middle agers. Some had worked together in the Student Committee for the Loyalty Oath, an oath required by the National Defense Education Act, which would have been my loan source at the University of Miami. Others had been active in Youth for Goldwater for Vice President, which lost to the nonexistent youth of Lodge for Vice President.

YAF's founders were hosted in September 1960 at the Connecticut estate of William F. Buckley Jr.'s family, known as Great Elm in the village of Sharon. Buckley had burst onto the national scene in 1954 with his best-selling *God and Man at Yale* in which he analyzed and opposed the growing anti-Americanism and anti-faith instruction found in the faculty and intellectual community at Yale and on other campuses. A 1952 cofounder of today's Intercollegiate Studies Institute, originally named the Intercollegiate Society of Individualists, Buckley soon launched a journal of opinion, *National Review*, and thereafter the longest-running television show of public opinion, *Firing Line*.

Buckley's guests in Sharon deliberated several days. They adopted their organization's name because they were "young," "Americans," and for "freedom." It seemed a natural combination of the words and the realities underlying them. The acronym YAF emerged accordingly and immediately, as did its members being referred to as YAFers or YAF'ers. So did immediate attacks on them from the political left, from which they were hostilely referred to as Young American Fascists, never mind the fact that their core tenet was a belief in limited central government, an opposite belief of the big government and centralized control sought by fascists and the Communists identified in YAF's founding statement as the then single greatest threat to our freedom.

The nation's youngest editor of a major city newspaper, M. Stanton Evans of the *Indianapolis News*, age twenty-six, was chosen to script the first draft of what was to become the Sharon Statement because of his knowledge of issues and his writing skills. Revised and adopted, it stood in opposition to the Students for a Democratic Society's (SDS) Port Huron Statement. A generation of young conservatives had awakened to state their views of the nation's core challenges. The Sharon Statement stands as one of the most concise and rallying statements of conservative and libertarian principles written in our time. Evans would the next year author *Revolt on the Campus*, which prefigured the massive campus unrest of later in the 1960s, especially of the anti-Vietnam War demonstrations, and he outlined a thoughtful strategy for responding to it.

The Sharon Statement's principles are reflections on the issues not only of 1960 but of the anticipated future. It was offered to the ages, and its intellectual and political shelf lives remain. Dave Jones shared it with me, I read it, and I had trouble believing there were persons of importance, young and old, that could and would disagree with its principles. How naïve I must have been, because I failed to recognize that it embodied a debate as old as civilization: whether governments are created by the people and therefore subservient to them or the people's rights are derived from only what government grants to them. After I read *God and Man at Yale*, which I did soon after my discussions with Jones, I had a firmer grasp of that debate's dichotomy in nearly every facet of individual life and collective society. Here it is:

The Sharon Statement
Adopted in conference at Sharon, Connecticut,
9-11 September 1960.

IN THIS TIME of moral and political crises, it is the responsibility of the youth of America to affirm certain eternal truths.

WE, as young conservatives, believe:

THAT foremost among the transcendent values is the individual's use of his God-given free will, whence derives his right to be free from the restrictions of arbitrary force;

THAT liberty is indivisible, and that political freedom cannot long exist without economic freedom;

THAT the purpose of government is to protect those freedoms through the preservation of internal order, the provision of national defense, and the administration of justice;

THAT when government ventures beyond those rightful functions, it accumulates power, which tends to diminish order and liberty;

THAT the Constitution of the United States is the best arrangement yet devised for empowering government to fulfill its proper role, while restraining it from the concentration and abuse of power;

THAT the genius of the Constitution – the division of powers – is summed up in the clause that reserves primacy to the several states, or to the people, in those spheres not specifically delegated to the Federal government;

THAT the market economy, allocating resources by the free play of supply and demand, is the single economic system compatible with the requirements of personal freedom and constitutional government, and that it is at the same time the most productive supplier of human needs;

THAT when government interferes with the work of the market economy, it tends to reduce the moral and physical strength of the nation; that when it takes from one man to bestow on another, it diminishes the incentive of the first, the integrity of the second, and the moral autonomy of both;

THAT we will be free only so long as the national sovereignty of the United States is secure; that history shows periods of freedom are rare, and can exist only when free citizens concertedly defend their rights against all enemies;

THAT the forces of international Communism are, at present, the greatest single threat to these liberties;

THAT the United States should stress victory over, rather than co-existence with, this menace; and

THAT American foreign policy must be judged by this criterion: does it serve the just interests of the United States.

Those at Sharon identified themselves as conservatives, but roughly ten years later, there would emerge a deep divide between traditional conservatives and libertarians with *National Review* Senior Editor Frank Meyer–coined fusionists seeking to stress that in common. YAF's ranks excluded the John Birch Society, Liberty Lobby, and other Far Right organizations' leaders and known members. It was a firm precedent and became useful in 2016 and 2017 as these and other conservative, libertarian, and fusionist organizations excluded wackos, despite concentrated efforts by the political left and its aligned national new media to lump them together in descriptions.

When YAF celebrated its tenth anniversary at the Buckley estate in 1970, its participants dedicated a bronze plaque of considerable measurement and placement at the base of the elm for which the estate was named. Authored by Bill Buckley following an event-planning weekend that my wife, Mary Kathleen King Teague, and I had spent there with him, his siblings, and his elegant mother, Eloise, it read:

On this site, on September 9-11, 1960, young Americans gathered to found an organization through which they might more effectively show their devotion to the ideals that brought forth this country. They called themselves Young Americans for Freedom, they enumerated their common beliefs in The Sharon Statement, and they returned to the communities from whence they came, to work in behalf of the principles they understood it to be the great historical mission of America to serve. This memorial is to their faith. It is mounted here prayerfully, to begin our common hope that when time will have reduced these letters to dust, the freedom these young Americans strove for, will flourish in a peaceful world.

Inasmuch as Jones and I paralleled each other in YAF to such an extent that we became national executive directors in succession, I should know by whom he was introduced to YAF. I do not. I never asked him but will continue to ask others. At the time he introduced it to me, he was intent on building a network of YAF chapters in Florida from the high school and college levels to the young adult level. Jones drew his adult chapter in part from the St. Petersburg Jaycees, including a young trusts and estates attorney, Phillip O'Connell, an A.G. Edwards & Sons stock broker, William Wright, and a dentist then establishing his practice, Dr. Laurent Belanger, and others. While he was organizing that chapter, I was organizing the Pinellas County chapter with students. Florida YAF soon had an office at 710 Central Avenue in downtown St. Petersburg. Jones was the state chairman before becoming southern regional chairman and thereby serving on its national board, becoming in 1963 its executive director in Washington. I followed him in each of those positions.

Taking the Florida Helm

Jones attended YAF's March 1962 "Rally for World Freedom" in New York City's Madison Square Garden. Arizona senator and the

225

Republican Party's next nominee for president Barry M. Goldwater, Sen. John Tower of Texas, who had won Lyndon Johnson's open seat after he became Jack Kennedy's vice president, former secretary of the navy, and Democratic governor of New Jersey, as well as Thomas Edison's son Charles Edison, author Jon Dos Passos, economic guru Ludwig von Mises, and others addressed the cheering crowd of 18,000-plus. The rally garnered reluctantly written, printed, and aired coverage in the national news. It gave notice of YAF's arrival on the national political scene and that the conservative wings of student activism and the national Republican Party would no longer be ignored. In Buckley's words, YAF had become "a presence in the room" of national debate. In Jones's thoughts, Florida YAF needed to do something like that rally.

Jones needed visibility for Florida YAF because as a new organization it had no name recognition. He also needed to raise funds, not just in the St. Petersburg area but more widely in order to sustain its intended activities. In order to attract statewide attention, including from news media, he developed the ideas that there should be a fall 1962 awards dinner, and it should honor widely respected US senator Spessard L. Holland.

Holland had been a youth leader himself, graduating from Emory College in Atlanta and becoming the first elected student body president at the University of Florida. He qualified for a Rhodes Scholarship at Oxford University, but that opportunity fell to his World War I service. He received the Distinguished Service Cross for extraordinary heroism from no less than General of the Armies John J. Pershing. He returned to the law and soon became a member of the Florida Senate and then the state's governor. His Holland & Bevis law firm grew into the national and international law firm of Holland & Knight. He was a conservative Democrat because in his lifetime a person could be one in the Democratic Party and the Senate, serving there from 1946 until his 1971 retirement.

Jones's September 22 dinner achieved his objectives of garnering statewide media attention and getting YAF into the state's political discussions. At the same time, it gave him significant visibility within

YAF's national leadership, signaling him to them as a person of creativity and energy.

The New York City rally and the Orlando dinner were career-tipping points for Jones. When his call to Washington came, it was for him to be at YAF national headquarters relocated from Manhattan to Stanton Park on Washington's Capitol Hill. Jones's resignation from his teaching position upset his parents for one reason and his Northeast High principal for another. His parents did not understand why such a dramatic career change was needed, jumping from the certainty of career teaching in a public school system to the uncertainty of politics. It was an act not seen as sufficiently thoughtful. Northeast High's principal knew a broken contract when he saw it, but Jones did not care as to its consequences, for he never intended to return to teaching in Florida and never did.

YAF's new headquarters were only three blocks from the Supreme Court of the United States and four blocks from the Capitol's Senate side and another to its House of Representatives. Within months, Jones would become executive director upon the incumbent Richard Viguerie's departure to form his direct marketing firm within which direct mail was a core business. Additional words are required about this remarkable man. He was always Richard, and no one in the conservative movement has ever undertaken direct mail as effectively for more candidates and organizations than has he. No one has ever been lied to more by a client who lost, otherwise failed, or even won about being paid than Viguerie. His mastery of direct marketing/direct mail earned him the Funding Fathers sobriquet from Young America's Foundation's president Ron Robinson and Nicole Hoplin in their *Funding Fathers* chapters on the fundraising gurus and funders of the conservative movement.

The Fund for American Studies

Following his arrival in Washington, Jones observed defining differences between youth organizations on the political left and others. He concluded there were far more on the left than on the conservative and libertarian side of philosophical divides. He also concluded some on that left not only assured tax deductibility of funds contributed to them but also received funds from US government agencies to support their work. He rejected outright the notion of receiving such funds because accepting them would run a high risk of having to accept those agencies' directives. However, he did believe there should be equal footing in respect to tax-exempt statuses and the deductibility of contributions. These observations energized him to undertake the many tasks of bringing a new organization together at the university level.

Five leaders became the core of chartering the new organization. They were Jones and Charles Edison, the son of Thomas Alva Edison and a former secretary of the navy and New Jersey governor as well as a New York City business leader; Congressman Walter H. Judd of Minnesota, a medical doctor and former missionary in war-torn China; William F. Buckley Jr., editor of *National Review* and the brightest star within conservatives' intellectual firmament; and New York City–based fundraiser and publicist Marvin Liebman.

That core was reinforced by a circle of additional leaders: Young Americans for Freedom's national chairman, Tom Charles Huston of Indiana, who was involved in organizing the Fund and attended its initial meetings with that core; Georgetown University Economics Department chairman and author of the Captive Nations Week Resolution and that community's spokesperson in Washington, Dr. Lev E. Dobriansky, also a future Reagan ambassador to the Bahamas; then Georgetown University student and now president of Education Enrichments among other distinctions, Dr. Robert A. Schadler; and others. After months of gestation, the Charles Edison Youth Fund came into its nonprofit corporate existence on February 6, 1967, coincidentally then-California governor Ronald Reagan's birthday. After Governor Edison's 1969 death, the Fund was renamed the Charles Edison Memorial Youth Fund, and it began in 1986 a two-year transition to the Fund for American Studies.

The Fund, known also as TFAS, "is an educational nonprofit that is changing the world by developing leaders for a free society." Its "transformational programs teach the principles of limited government, free-market economics and honorable leadership to students and young professionals in America and around the world." It accomplishes that mission through weekend, one-week, two-week, eight-week, and semester-long institutes on comparative political and economic systems, journalism, business and government affairs, philanthropy and voluntary service, and foreign affairs. Since its 1970 inauguration of its first institute, it has had "more than 17,000 students, representing 144 countries" "live, learn and intern" through these programs. It now "reaches more than 60,000 young people annually" through fellowships, seminars, and educational videos. These programs inspire these future leaders to make a difference in their communities and throughout the world "by upholding the values essential to the preservation and success of a free society." The Fund has added high school programs through its affiliated Foundation for Teaching Economics' offerings to teachers and students, and its legal studies institute now achieves its reach into graduate-level education.

I worked with Jones before and in the earliest years of the Fund, writing texts for its publications, went onto its board of trustees not long before I returned in 1981 to Washington from Boston, and became the chairman of that board in 1998. The Fund is one of Jones's legacies, as it is now its president Roger Ream's. Ream is a Vanderbilt University and TFAS alumnus in whom Jones first entrusted the Fund's vice presidency and whose deliberative mind and hands as its president following Jones's death have assured its management, program, fundraising, alumni, and other successes at those high school, university, and graduate levels. Tracing "his passion for the ideas of freedom and free markets to his father, a minister who stressed the moral underpinnings of individual liberty and the connections between freedom and human flourishing," Ream has served as president of the Philadelphia Society, the Foundation for Economic Education, and the Foundation for Teaching Economics and in other capacities to assist young persons and others to understand and appreciate ideas of liberty.

23

Awaiting My Call to Washington

DAVE JONES'S DEPARTURE FOR WASHINGTON BROUGHT me into responsibility for Florida YAF's programs, membership, and financial base. I was apprehensive about becoming state chairman, but I was strengthened by the fact that he was never more than a telephone call away when questions arose about matters. His departure from YAF's governing board moved me onto it, including as its southern regional chairman. Given that the board met face-to-face with scheduled frequency and that Alexander Graham Bell's invention worked in both directions, Jones and I stayed in contact from big-picture questions to the daily logistics of implementing their answers.

The Florida YAF office moved to 7128 Central Avenue within several blocks of the causeway that linked St. Petersburg with St. Petersburg Beach and a half-dozen or so other mini-municipalities on the barrier islands between St. Petersburg and the Gulf. I have memories of our first office at downtown's 710 Central Avenue, but a vivid one at the successor office is of a winter afternoon in which it was snowing enough to need your windshield wipers on. One does remember such a day in the subtropics.

As state chairman, I had considerable shoe leather and elbow grease help from members at area colleges and tactical and financial help from Jones's Jaycees friends. We paid all our bills on time, which is not easy for a new organization or a youth organization and particularly if it is managed by a youngster. There's pride in that observation. Inasmuch as Jones had a successful event in centrally located Orlando for Sen. Holland, I reasoned we could have a successful West Coast event for Congressman Cramer. We worked on determining its feasibility.

A University of North Carolina and Harvard Law School–educated World War II navy veteran, Cramer had run for Congress in 1952 from the district that encompassed St. Petersburg's Pinellas County and several counties north of it. Its electorate voted heavily for General Dwight Eisenhower at the top of the ballot, and by doing so, they almost elected Cramer. Almost is not close enough in elections, so he continued to campaign over the next two years, and when 1954's ballots were counted, he had won.

The congressman had been targeted for defeat in 1962. He had been in office for eight years, and those encouraging an opponent against him reasoned that their intended biggest effort would defeat him. With Jones still in St. Petersburg, we organized Youth for Cramer. While elderly voters were more naturally seen as part of his base, youth were not. We worked far into many nights and early mornings to show that he had support from young people. Youth for Cramer signs went up throughout the district. Placard-carrying young people were wherever he appeared. Our teams walked precincts and distributed literature extolling his achievements and goals for another term. With his voting record and broad name recognition, he secured a 35,551 majority when ballot counting concluded. Our work had been needed, welcomed, and serious and a valuable experience for future campaigns. To where did this work lead?

On October 5, 1963, Florida YAF honored Cramer at a testimonial dinner at the Jack Tar Harrison Hotel in Clearwater. Congressman Edward Gurney from Florida's Orlando and Winter Park district introduced the featured speaker, national columnist, and commentator Fulton Lewis, Jr., as well as YAF national chairman and future congressman Robert Bauman, who presented the National YAF Award. I presented the Florida YAF Award. Former Cramer aide, already state senator, and future congressman C. W. "Bill" Young masterfully handled the introductions. In 1970, Young succeeded Cramer, and after years of accumulating seniority and the Newt Gingrich–led Contract with America 1994 recapturing of a House majority, he became chairman of the House Committee on Appropriations after having been chairman of its Subcommittee on Defense. President Eisenhower had given our 1963 dinner a helpful quote, which we featured prominently:

> Since 1954, when he was elected to the 84th Congress, he has not spared himself in the discharge of his duties and responsibilities as a legislator.
>
> Always a dedicated and ardent supporter of sound and progressive government and the free enterprise system under which our nation has prospered, I hope that Bill Cramer will long have the opportunity to serve his constituency in the Congress.

Our featuring of this on the front page of the printed dinner program was an intended pushback against the John Birch Society and others who were attacking Eisenhower, and as William F. Buckley Jr. and others were striving successfully to expel Birchers from the conservative movement.

I served as the dinner's general chairman from conceptualization to completion, but I was assisted by many who made it the success that it became. The November 3 Sunday edition of the *St. Petersburg Times* gave the dinner nearly three pages of coverage under the title "Old Guard's New Wave: A strong conservative tide is rising among students. YAF is riding the crest," with the second page's subtitle "Randy Teague has politics in his blood – and Washington in his eyes." Under some circumstances, that second-page title might have raised an eyebrow, even though I had nothing to do with scripting it, but it locked in with Congressman Cramer what my expectation was without me needing to say it.

24

The Washington Years Begin

THE END OF FEBRUARY 1964 OPENED THE FIRST OF MANY doors for me. It was an exciting but hectic final week for me in St. Petersburg. I had had an expectation of moving to Washington. It was tied to the possibility of being asked to become a member of Congressman Cramer's Washington staff. It weighed heavily in my not accepting the National Defense Education Act loan to study at the University of Miami and its expected commitment to a career in marine biology.

Cramer had by the spring of 1964 won four reelections and was seeking his sixth two-year term. He had climbed the seniority ladder faster than would have been possible in the House's larger Democratic majority. He was serving on both the House Committee on the Judiciary and the House Committee on Public Works. That double duty was a recognition of the House's partisan apportionment of committee seats and his Republican colleagues' positive assessment of his abilities and his value to them.

A Life-Changing Telephone Call

During the last week of February, I received a telephone call early one evening from the congressman. He said he had a position for me, if I wished to accept it, on the House Committee on Public Works staff. We discussed its nature and his expectations of the job and me, and I agreed in principle to the proposition. I asked when I would begin, expecting it to be some weeks or even months ahead, and he gave a one-word response, "Monday," with no change in the tone of his voice but with a near explosion within my head. I accepted the offer with thanks for it, hung up the receiver, and sought to control the near panic on what had to be done in only a few days. Amid packing clothing and other effects, I went to my bridge-in-time St. Petersburg College and withdrew. I made arrangements with my brother to drive me and my few possessions to Durham, from which Dad would drive me to Washington. David and Corinne Jones said I could stay in the guest room in their apartment at 3850 Tunlaw Road in northwest Washington until I could find other lodging, which took about two weeks after arrival. Several days later, I hugged farewell to a tearful mother. It was years, by then a parent myself with a parent's perspective and emotions, before I began working through how she must have felt when her youngest left for his own adult world and with the expectation on both our parts of returning only on holidays and vacations. It left her alone on Thirty-Seventh Avenue North, but it did not leave her alone in St. Petersburg, for my brother remained, as did eventually his wife and her son in its suburbs, followed after his wife's death by his wife Barbara and their son Frank.

There were remnants of a snowfall in the late-winter forests as my brother and I approached Durham. I recall thinking that the snow was dramatic evidence that I was leaving Florida behind me. It was to be permanent, and as I was driven to Durham and then to Washington, often in long silences, my twenty years ran through my mind like chapters of life.

Durham in 1964

What was Durham, the city I had left ten years earlier when we moved to Chapel Hill, like in early 1964?

It had not changed much. Relatives ahead of and roughly beside me in age were still living although not necessarily there. Its cigarette plants were still producing millions of them daily. Erwin Mills, now as Burlington Mills, was still producing seemingly endless sheets and pillowcases. Ruby's café was still doing an appreciable business from those mills' and other customers. Ninth Street had not much changed, even though it badly needed a facelift. Duke's East Campus was still within its defining granite walls with few new buildings. The West Durham churches were still full on Sunday mornings and nearly so on Wednesday nights during summers. Durhamites still had Easter Monday off as a weekend-extending holiday, and many a round of golf was played on them to experience firsthand God's creation of nature's beauty amid trees, grasses, pine needles, and sand. Durham's politicians were still too slowly adjusting to post–World War II changes, but the interstate highways leading out and into it were changing their constituencies whether they knew it or not. How do we know this latter point? During the early 1950s, Durham, Charlotte, Raleigh, and Winston-Salem had nearly equivalent populations of about 75,000, but Durham by 1964 was falling behind the other cities. What the raw number of its own population did not tell the uninformed was that much of it was attributable to its annexations. Dad's Hillandale golf course had been reconfigured by pushing it somewhat further north and west. Durham Dairy's buildings had not yet been demolished, and our Eighth Street duplex was still its shabby self and not to be bulldozed until after August 2014 to make room for a Ninth Street apartment and retail complex that was to reach back to our renamed Iredell Street. The pine trees of my dream about Hugo Street were still there. Durham's racial tensions had grown for decades, gradually in the wake of the sit-ins of the sixties and explosively in the wake of the assassination of

Martin Luther King, Jr., proving the point that the root causes of those tensions had not been addressed effectively nor permanent solutions advocated, adopted, and implemented by mutual understanding and cooperation.

St. Petersburg in 1964

What was the St. Petersburg I was leaving like in early 1964?

Our house on Thirty-Seventh Avenue North was pretty much as it had been when we moved into it in 1957, but after Mumsie's move from it, it would be remodeled into a duplex, and over time its cosmetic needs were ignored until it became and remains an eyesore in a neighborhood of eyesores. Lealman Junior High was soon to become the county's education department's headquarters. Northeast High was soon to experience a major expansion of its buildings and athletic fields. The Science Center was to relocate and change its name.

Downtown continued its decline into parking lots covering entire city blocks, paradoxically as parking space needs declined as those blocks emptied retail stores headed to the rapidly expanding suburbs. Doc Webb's multi-block Webb City department store was soon to collapse financially as far better designed shopping centers attracted his and other customers. The Million Dollar Pier was to be redone at far greater expense as salt water continued to erode its metal and concrete pilings. The "old St. Petersburg" of the Spanish-American War to World War I period was restored with New Orleans–styled wrought iron railings for several Central Avenue blocks leading up from the Bayfront.

Not by 1964, but in the decades that followed, the badly declining Bayfront area at the eastern end of downtown at Tampa Bay's water edge was revitalized into a "new St. Petersburg" with the always-present St. Petersburg Yacht Club, improved municipal marinas, the long-vacant Vinoy Hotel's rebirth as a five-star hotel and spa, as well as the designs, financings, constructions, and grand openings of its Museum of Fine Arts, the Mahaffey Theater, and the Salvador Dali Museum. The construction of top-tier condominium complexes overlooking the

Bayfront improved this part of the city and expanded its tax base. Even Northeast High's and other students' favorite places to neck along Tampa Bay's shores north of the city have been supplanted by the Weedon Island Preserve, on which island movies were attempted by studios before Hollywood was discovered in the 1920s to have more sunlight, read that as far less rain, for filming.

Washington in 1964

What was the nation's capital to which I was moving like in 1964, a move that preceded my twentieth birthday by twelve weeks?

The president of the United States of America, John F. Kennedy, had been assassinated less than one hundred days earlier, and Dallas, Texas, the nation, and the world were asking why and by whom. It remains an unsatisfactorily answered question over fifty years later. Kennedy's youthful vibrancy had generated ideas and expectations for his successors to finish, and Lyndon Johnson was doing his best to capitalize on them as Kennedy's and his shared legacies. He was running for his first election as president in his own name.

The US economy was sputtering along in its attempt to recover fully from President Eisenhower's second-term recession. Kennedy's initiative to add a badly needed spark to that economy by reducing marginal federal individual tax rates in order to leave more money in the private economy was looked upon within his own party as a Republican-like strategy. He stuck with it, and those rates were reduced. His leadership on this issue, including his weekend sailor's phrase, "A rising tide lifts all boats," and its consequences became a reference point in Congressman Jack Kemp's 1970s' attempts to cut those tax rates even further. Kemp's leadership on the tax rate issue was recognized most effectively through the enactment of President Reagan's first tax act in 1981 in that it embodied modifications of Kemp's proposed tax rate reductions. I had no idea in 1964 that I would be the one who was to research and compile at Kemp's request, as his 1973–1979 chief of staff and legislative counsel, the provisions that became his early legislative bills embodying tax reforms that, in turn, became his Jobs Creation Act and his Kemp-Roth tax rate reduction proposals. In 1964, I had never heard of Jack Kemp, then a professional football quarterback, and I knew Ronald Reagan's name only from his acting career. Kemp was to become another mentor, not replacing but rather alongside David Jones, as well as the best man at Jessica's and my 1978 wedding.

It was left to Kennedy's vice president, Lyndon Johnson, to close out the Kennedy-Johnson four-year term to which they had been elected on November 8, 1960. Johnson was to assure the enactment of many of Kennedy's ideas and his legislative proposals, while adding his own, especially his Great Society, during the inherited and his own 1965–1969 terms. He was challenged in his first election for the presidency in his own name by Republican senator Barry Goldwater of Arizona. Goldwater was championed by his party's conservatives over the vehement opposition of the its liberals masquerading as moderates, even though Goldwater was primarily a libertarian committed to limited government and expanded personal freedoms. His nomination at San Francisco's Cow Palace arena in mid-July culminated the ascendency of the intellectual conservative movement inspired before World War II but not a political force to be reckoned with until after 1964.

While Goldwater went down to predicted defeat on November 3, his ideas found other voices in its wake. His presidential election went down, but he did not. Not recognized for its significance until after that loss, Reagan's October 27 nationally televised speech in support of Goldwater, known as his "A Time for Choosing" speech, bolstered postelection excitement within the conservative movement and within the Republican Party, which was then and remains two different forces no matter how much overlap at times. The speech had the effect of launching Reagan's California gubernatorial ambitions and his two terms as governor, two terms as president of the United States, and the end of the Cold War "without the firing of a shot" as the Soviet Union collapsed under the weight of the coordinated political and budgetary attacks of the United States and Mikhail Gorbachev's recognition of that weight. Reagan had joined in alliance with the United Kingdom's prime minister Margaret Thatcher, Germany's chancellor Helmut Kohl, and the moral pinnacle of the Vatican's John Paul II, himself a refugee of sorts in Rome from Soviet-occupied Poland. All that lay years ahead.

Five years after my 1964 move, David Jones resigned as executive director of Young Americans for Freedom in order to become the president of the Charles Edison Youth Fund, later the Charles Edison Memorial Youth Fund, and later the Fund for American Studies. At YAF's early summer of 1969 farewell event for him, I had assembled and had bound a book of scores of letters from famous and other conservatives, libertarians, and fusionists, each in his or her own way thanking David for his service to YAF. In my letter within that collection, I sought to make this point to him and other readers:

> There are those whose deepest fulfillment lies in their work. But that can too easily be work for work's sake. You have not confused your means with your ends. These successes you have given to YAF would be shallow were they just fulfillment for fulfillment's sake, were they just executive-level responsibilities dutifully discharged. Your fulfillment has meant more, much more. It has meant that a high school or college student somewhere knows that classical liberalism exists today. It has meant that someone who has lost faith in freedom's force has found renewed inspiration. Our end is the end of tyranny through enlightenment as to liberty. It is a world free from the fear of the knock on the door.

It would be an absurdity for me to compare my approach to Washington by cars driven by my brother and father with Abraham Lincoln's approach to Washington by train in February 1861, so I do not. I was simply heading in February 1964 to the nation's political capital to work in and around its Capitol. I would seek with whatever competence and energy that I could muster to mesh politics, law, and government into my career and the life encapsulating it. I did know that

I was first going to work as an entry-level congressional staffer. I had no way to know in 1964 that I would work in the House of Representatives twice and in between serve in the executive office of the president of the United States and thereafter before the nation's federal courts, being a small part of each of the three branches of government set forth in our nation's Constitution of 1787.

But, as my own move to Washington was in part on a February 27, another February 27 emerged from my readings of American history. It was the date of Abraham Lincoln's 1860 Cooper Union address in New York City to a standing-room-only crowd of 1,500 or more. It more assuredly moved him to the nomination for president of the United States of the relatively new Republican Party more than any other appearance or speech, even more than his debating points in the two-years-prior Lincoln-Douglas debates in their Illinois campaigns for the US Senate. As I made my physical and mental journey to the same nation's capital, his words echoed in my head:

> Let us have faith that right makes might, and in that faith, let us, to the end, care to do our duty as we understand it.

It seemed then, as now, a thoughtful instruction.

25

1964 and Beyond

T HE YEARS AFTER I ARRIVED IN WASHINGTON MOVED
forward in expected and unexpected ways.

Educationally, I earned my bachelor of arts degree at American
University in Washington and my juris doctor and master of laws
degrees from George Washington University there in 1971 and 1972
respectively, the second with highest honors. I was conferred an honorary
doctor of laws from Allen University, an historically black university
in Columbia, South Carolina, in 1973, and an honorary doctor of
humanities from Universidad EARTH in Costa Rica in 2012. Given
how much I realized I did not know, I continued to add knowledge,
especially by reading and listening to others' perspectives on what they
believed and why.

Professionally, at the beginning of March 1964, I joined the
Minority, meaning Republican, staff of the House of Representatives'
Committee on Public Works, later renamed Committee on Public
Works and Transportation, and still later renamed the Committee on
Transportation and Infrastructure. I elaborate on the beginning of this
employment because it was borderline bizarre and demonstrates what

bipartisan cooperation can sometimes achieve. Moving parts to its complexity were plentiful. First, the offeror to me of the staff position, Congressman Bill Cramer, was not yet the ranking Republican on the committee, but he was at least next in line to become it. Representative James C. Auchincloss of New Jersey, a former governor of the New York Stock Exchange but more widely known as the lawyer and novelist Louis Auchincloss's and Standard Oil heir Hugh Auchincloss's cousin, the latter being Jacqueline Bouvier Kennedy Onassis's stepfather, held that position. Second, when I arrived to complete and sign the required paperwork, Cramer was startled that neither he nor Auchincloss had a Minority staff slot available. What was Cramer to do if not return me to St. Petersburg? He went with credible explanation in hand to the Democratic chairman of the committee, Congressman Charles A. Buckley, also the head of New York City's infamous Tammany Hall Democratic political machine, and negotiated a place for me to work for the remainder of 1964. It was on the committee's Subcommittee on Watershed Development, whose ranking Republican was Congressman Fred Schwengel of Iowa. They agreed, and I signed on. Third, unexpected fate was to intervene as we proceeded through spring. Congressman Buckley was challenged for reelection in the Democratic primary by Jonathan Brewster Bingham, a Connecticut well-born diplomat and son of the US senator and Yale-educated explorer Hiram Bingham, III, who discovered the Incas' Peruvian capital of Machu Picchu and a great-grandson of the missionary Hiram Bingham who helped translate the Bible into Hawaiian. In the news media coverage of the campaign between these two enormously different persons and backgrounds, I surfaced. On the morning of May 14, the committee's Minority Counsel, that being my boss Cliff Enfield, walked up to my end table-sized desk with an indecipherable expression on his face and said something to the effect that after only three months on the staff, I had made the news in a really big way. Puzzled and feeling more than merely apprehensive, I asked how so, to which he responded that I was in the news pages and on the editorial page of the *New York Times,* not to mention also in the *New York Herald Tribune* and the *New*

York Journal American. Bingham had accused Buckley of packing his committee payroll with friends and political cronies instead of hiring full-time qualified employees in Washington, but Bingham had not done his homework accurately in the including of fellow Republican staffer Paul Yates and me in the list he slipped to reporters. To the newspapers' immediate inquiries, Schwengel reported that "I never knew Mr. Teague until he applied for the job," to which he added, "The taxpayers never got more for their money." In its lead editorial, entitled "The Boss and His Pie," the *Times* averred "The Republican nominees were reported yesterday to be on the job in Washington doing nonpolitical work assigned by the committee." Occurring five days short of my twentieth birthday, I quietly regarded the matter's conclusions without wounds to me as an early birthday present. Fourth, on June 2, Bingham defeated Buckley, a consequence of which was Buckley's disinterest in committee's staffing on either side of the political aisle. His gift to me as his staff later cleaned out his office was a complete set of *Congressional Directories* reaching back to the First World War, the earliest of which must have been passed to him by his predecessor. Fifth, Congressman Auchincloss had announced his retirement in advance of President Lyndon Johnson's November 3 coattails sweeping thirty-six Republicans from the following Congress; sixth, Congressman Cramer was handily reelected, but, seventh, Congressman Schwengel was among those defeated although his resulting founding and presidency of the United States Capitol Historical Society continued his presence in Washington until his 1993 death. Eighth and as a consequence of those seven outcomes and while not yet twenty-one, I became in January 1965 the Minority clerk of the full committee.

On the first day of 1968, I moved to Young Americans for Freedom as its director of state and regional activities on its Washington-based headquarters staff, later succeeding David Jones as its executive director through late October 1971. These 1964–1971 years on the Hill and at YAF generated and nurtured friendships that endure to this day as we then-youngsters in law, journalism, business, government, politics, education, religion, and organizational management became in many cases nationally prominent in those fields. The cycles of life measured by educations, careers, marriages, births, christenings, children's marriages, and grandchildren, occasionally marked by divorces and deaths, knitted us together in often simple but sometimes complex ways. I value now with treasured depth seeing them and their families at reunions, receptions, dinners, theaters, restaurants, graduations, church services, and, yes now, funerals and memorial services.

In November 1971, I moved to the executive office of the president of the United States. It was not to a key policy or political position in the White House within shouting distance of the president's eyes and ears but rather to join a team of persons addressing policies designed to benefit persons and families with low incomes by restructuring the Office of Economic Opportunity, an undertaking accomplished by disaggregating its programs and sending them to the departments purportedly more competent to administer them.

In September 1973, I returned to Capitol Hill to become Congressman Jack Kemp's chief of staff, a position then known as administrative assistant, and legislative counsel as he was accelerating his economic agenda and its proposed reductions in marginal individual income tax rates. It took several days to effect my coming into that position because, when Kemp made me the offer during a discussion in the House Gallery, he had not yet created the vacancy. Several years later, he was my best man at my and Jessica Townsend's wedding in Shawnee Mission, Kansas, in the greater Kansas City area. Kemp rose in the leadership ranks of House Republicans and in 1988 ran unsuccessfully for the Republican nomination for president, losing along with others, including colleagues and friends, to Vice President George H. W. Bush. The next year, he became that President Bush's secretary of housing and urban development, and in 1996, he was chosen by the Republican National Convention in San Diego to be presidential nominee Senator Bob Dole of Kansas's vice presidential running mate. As a former college and professional quarterback, Kemp demonstrated leadership skills in everything he did. He died in 2009, the excitement and fulfillment of working with him and of his historic accomplishments in changing the course of the nation's economy by reducing its tax burdens will never be forgotten by me and many others. He accelerated and heightened the trajectory of our country's economy growth and for the benefit of persons and families across its economic spectrum.

In early 1979, Jessie, our infant Cornell, and I departed Washington for me to join the law department of the Boston-based Cabot Corporation, a global oil and gas, performance chemicals, and specialty metals company owned and managed in part by the Cabots of the John Collins Bossidy toast given at a Holy Cross College alumni dinner in 1910:

And this is good old Boston
The home of the bean and the cod.
Where the Lowells talk only to Cabots,
And the Cabots talk only to God.

I learned much from and enjoyed this corporate law practice and its workings with highly respected business leaders and other lawyers, the addressing of legal issues from local to global, working in historic Boston, living in suburban Wellesley Hills, vacationing throughout New England's spectacular four seasons, and downing its always available fresh seafood, especially lobsters and oysters. Those enjoyments notwithstanding, we returned to Washington to be closer to the incoming Reagan administration.

In early 1981, Jessie, our Cornell, and newborn Townsend and I returned to Washington at the suggestion of Peter McPherson, not to join the Reagan administration as some expected but rather to join the Washington office of the predominantly Midwestern law firm of Vorys, Sater, Seymour and Pease, organized in 1909. McPherson was the firm's manager of its Washington office after which he became White House legal counsel, administrator of the US Agency for International Development, executive vice president of Bank of America, president of Michigan State University, and is now president of the Association of Public and Land-grant Universities, among other distinctions. I retired from the firm and law practice altogether at midnight, December 31,

2014, after thirty-three years with this highly regarded firm whose mistake was, in my opinion, to have an age-based mandatory retirement policy, albeit a forewarned, consented, and eased one. I enjoyed and learned much from law practice, my fellow attorneys, our clients, their matters, and our collaborative resolutions of issues.

I worked during these Washington years with a number of nonprofit organizations. Some have been discussed in preceding pages, and the Salesians Missions of Saint Giovanni Bosco are discussed below. In addition, I chaired the US Agency for International Development's Advisory Committee on Voluntary Foreign Aid during the administrations of Presidents Ronald Reagan and George H. W. Bush from 1987 into 1991, seeking to reduce government subsidies but increase private sector support for humanitarian and development initiatives abroad. Another was the 1947-founded Salzburg Seminar in American Studies, now the Salzburg Global Seminar and self-described as embodying "a Marshall Plan for the Mind," and that moved beyond its Cold War roots to a globally recognized convener of rising leadership on important global, regional, and local public policy issues. Add to these, Health and Development International in Oslo and its US-support organization and their "aim to free populations of debilitating diseases which are deemed to be eradicable as public health problems, but insufficiently addressed" in Africa. Its concentrated focuses and diligent work under the stewardship of its Dr. Anders Seim, a self-described Norwegian "country doctor," has contributed substantially to the eradication of guinea worm and reductions in the scourges of obstetric fistula, elephantiasis (the distorting disease depicted in *The Elephant Man*), sleeping sickness, and other maladies in the tropics. Add to those my service with the US-based Friends of Mengo Hospital in Kampala, Uganda, and its work in dental care and HIV/AIDS prevention and palliative care. And there are others.

Familywise, I won and lost in three marriages yet managed to cultivate respectful and enduring friendships with each and fathered with the last four bright, caring, and now adult children who are sharing with others the love given to them and giving themselves and their parents the next generation. No words could capture the immenseness of my love, respect, and aspiration for each of them and for the significant other, Darlene McKinnon, with whom I am now sharing exciting times and plans for our future together.

Russia

I do not have the pages here necessary to relate in detail all of my work in respect to the Soviet Union and its mothership Russia. Suffice it for here and not unlike most Americans, I first learned about both from family attitudes, books, news accounts, and classrooms. Knowing Young Americans for Freedom's Sharon Statement warning that "the forces of international Communism are, at present, the greatest single threat" to liberties known to Americans and others and Moscow's management of that threat added to those awarenesses. Living in central west Florida only several hundred miles from Fidel Castro's Cuba and its installation of Soviet missiles and Russian support of many natures added another. Structured, in-depth knowledge was a consequence of Congressman Jack Kemp's service on the House Committee on Appropriations' Subcommittee on Defense.

I first became aware in 1975 of the work of the American Council of Young Political Leaders as it then related to the Soviet Union. Its bipartisan and bilateral work had begun about a decade earlier. It was ACYPL's 1977 exchange that first took me to Soviet Russia as well as to its Azerbaijan, Kazakhstan, and Ukraine. Over the decades that followed, I counseled Rodale Inc., the Salesian Missions of Saint Giovanni Bosco, Smith Corona Corporation, and other US corporations and nonprofit organizations in regard to the Soviet Union and its former republics. I discontinued all of this work after the rise to power of Vladimir Putin. I may author accounts in the years ahead of these ventures, adventures, and peradventures in *Dancing with the Bear: Recollections of Russia*. For now, let's simply discuss several of them.

In the late 1980s, Smith Corona Corporation was considering strategies to sell memory typewriters with alphabet-modified keyboards in Russian language markets. Memory typewriters, limited in their memory retention to about five lines of text, immediately preceded the advent of personal computers and laptops. Discussion of their objective was coordinated with our law firm by Howard A. Vine, for he had brought Smith Corona to the firm. I was asked to participate because I was an attorney with experience in Russia. The work we undertook with Smith Corona was a gallant effort, one built on high-awareness relationships fostered through my ACYPL relations with the Committee of Youth Organizations of the USSR and other entities in Moscow. The desired joint venture was cautiously pursued but came to naught for reasons out of Smith Corona's and its prospective partner V/O Vneshtorgizat's (VTI meaning Foreign Trade Publishing House Association) controls. Early sales opportunities were frustrated by Russian customers' lack of access to hard currency, forcing them to propose instead barter trades for mink oils, marmalades, and other products, collectively a nonstarter. After VTI and others were granted access to their own hard currency earnings, IBM had the competitive edge. It was moving rapidly to computerize electric typewriters even though it missed seeing broader sales potential in PCs. Smith Corona did not have access to, nor could it gain access to, IBM's patented technologies. An additional factor was worsening macroeconomic uncertainties as the Soviet Union was moving erratically through its breakup and Russia was emerging as erratically into its new status. On the heels of decades of ethical contamination by its Communist regime, Russia's business culture was already becoming a pay-to-play one incompatible with the mandates of US law, and this became the final straw.

At nearly the same time, Rodale Inc. and its partnered organizations sought to open a Russian door for their educational programs directed at better health and improved agriculture. Rodale sought to begin this process by having relevant Rodale's magazines published in the Russian language by VTI and distributed to health and agricultural agencies, institutes, organizations, leaders, and other readers. Robert Rodale was a successful publisher (*Prevention*, *Men's Health*, *Organic Gardening*, and others), but he was a determined idealist, one under no illusion about the steep slope ahead, for Russia's health and agricultural problems were systemic, massive, ill-informed, cultural, and resistant to change. His ideas seemed a natural fit, including undertaking the initial measures through the VTI publishing house, a business association of its own determined leadership. Despite the thin opening already under way, a tragic fate intervened. Robert Rodale was killed together with VTI employees in a vehicular accident on September 20, 1990, near the entrance to Moscow's Sheremetyevo international airport. A bus crossed the median and crashed head-on into their vehicle. I was supposed to be in that vehicle but had followed a different flight plan, first into Frankfurt to overnight and take a flight to Moscow the following morning. I learned of the accident upon my arrival at a Frankfurt hotel. It was a stunning moment and a terrible blow to the Rodale family, its organizations, and their families. Russia and its people could have learned much if this project had been undertaken.

Salesian Missions

My work with the Salesian Missions of Saint Giovanni Bosco began in 1981. Giovanni Bosco translates into English as John Wood, much as his contemporary fellow northern Italian Giuseppe Verdi translates into Joseph Greens. While those translations take a tad bit of the mystery out of their names, they help us sense them in additional ways. Giovanni Bosco is often referred to as Don Bosco, not because he was a Donald but rather because Don is a term of respect for Father in that he was a highly respected priest, as well as educator and writer, of the nineteenth century. His mission's Salesian appellation was of his choosing because Saint Francis De Sales was his patron saint.

An attorney in New York with whom I had worked in Washington and with whom I had served on a nonprofit board inquired of me as to my knowledge of the work of the Salesians. In furtherance of our shared objectives, James J. O'Neill and I further confirmed his conclusions on the demonstrated values of their work in bringing new meanings to the lives of millions of children and their families in over 130 countries.

Consisting of nearly 30,000 priests, brothers, sisters, and novices, they were then and are now the second largest order in the Roman Catholic Church, yet too little is known in the United States about their work except in the few locations where they administer vocational, college preparatory, and other training. This is to say most of their work is outside the States. O'Neill and I responded to this call by adding our time, talent, energy, and networks to theirs.

Over nearly twenty years, I worked with Fr. Edward Cappelletti and Fr. James Chiosso at the Salesians' mission office in New Rochelle, New York, and with others to help achieve the order's objectives. Our work began in qualifying them as a private and voluntary organization (PVO) with the United States Agency for International Development to receive funds for their work overseas. The first success of that registration was USAID assistance to Miguel, Cardinal Obando y Bravo of Nicaragua, himself a Salesian, for their humanitarian work there. Fathers Cappelletti and Chiosso have passed to other lives, but I think of them often, especially when I recall the depths of their commitments and capabilities or read or hear accounts of Salesians' work here or in distant lands, and their work has been continued by Fr. Mark Hyde and others. My recalls of this work would fill another book, and some day it might, but let me share several of them.

After our earliest meetings in New Rochelle and Washington, O'Neill's and my first overseas trip to experience Salesian work firsthand was to the Caribbean island of Hispaniola, the site of the first permanent European settlement in the Americas, one founded by Christopher Columbus on his voyages in 1492 and 1493. We know Hispaniola as the island on which are the Dominican Republic at its east and Haiti at its west. Those two countries are so distinct in their economic development that astronauts can ascertain their shared border by the Dominican Republic's green and Haiti's reddish-brown terrains. Our visits to the Salesians' work and the neighborhoods in which it was undertaken were what we needed to experience, given the relative prosperity in the Dominican Republic and deep poverty in Haiti. We observed in each country the witness of the Salesians to assist the poor through jobs-focused education and spiritual growth. I continued this work in respect to Colombia, Costa Rica, Cuba, Czechoslovakia before its partition, Hungary, the Holy Land, Poland, Russia, Uganda, Venezuela, and elsewhere.

Nearly immediately, I accompanied Fr. Chiosso for meetings with Fr. Javier De Nicolo, whose successful work with street children in Colombia was widely recognized in Latin America and globally. We discussed in Bogota how Father Javier's early concepts had matured into viable programs, and we walked through drug-gang controlled streets in which we were safe only because we were with him. We flew by single-engine plane to the Salesians' camp on the Oronoco River on the border of Colombia with Venezuela, to which he transported youngsters who chose to leave lives of crime and nearly certain early death behind them for opportunities of transformation through a system of mutual trust, respect, education, and job skills. Fr. De Nicolo's March 2016 death at age eighty-eight received international attention focused on his vision and dedication, his hard work but generosity, and his achievements in elevating work with the poor to human rights stature. He and his confreres helped large numbers of youth move themselves from the jaws of hell on earth to precincts near the gates of heaven.

One of my early trips to better understand the work of Don Bosco fathers and Mary Help of Christian sisters was to Poland. It held an array of recognitions of the Salesians' half century of relationships with Karol Wojtyla as a youth, seminarian, priest, bishop, archbishop of Krakow, and cardinal elevated at the second Papal Enclave of 1978 to be their holy father as Pope John Paul II, now known as Saint John Paul the Great. As a youngster, he had become acquainted with the Salesians in his native Wadovice. He later attended their St. Stanislaus Kostka Church in Krakow from the age of eighteen to twenty-four, often praying in its chapel of Mary Help of Christians. It was there that he met Jan Tyranowski, a Salesian "living the Gospel message in the spirit of Saint John Bosco while choosing to live in the world," meaning not living as an ordained priest. Tyranowski had what has been described as an enormous effect on the young Wojtyla. It was during these years that Wojtyla made friends within Poland's large Jewish population, particularly with Jerzy Kluger, who became a close lifelong friend and accompanied him to Rome to reinforce this new pope's desire for Catholic and Jewish reconciliation. The Salesians had secretly supported Wojtyla's clandestine seminary studies during the Nazi occupation of Poland, and after the war's end, one of his first Masses in 1946 was celebrated in their church. By then, its occupation by Germany had become its occupation by the Soviet Union. Decades later and as the holy father, he was deeply involved in the 1988 events celebrating the centennial of Father Bosco's birth, visiting the shrine and other sites honoring Bosco's life, as did his proclamation the next year of Bosco as Father and Teacher of Youth.

While I was undertaking this 1989 assessment of their funding needs, several priests expressed their wish for me to see firsthand some of what Catholic, Jewish, and other Poles, as well as other Europeans, had experienced during the tyrannical 1939–1945 Nazi occupation of Poland. I concurred and accompanied Fathers Marian Dziubinski and Tadeusz Biesaga to Oswiecim, the Polish town known by Germans and to the world as Auschwitz. It is the most widely known of the Nazi concentration and extermination camps, one at which civilians were imprisoned to die from disease, exhaustion, starvation, or execution. It was June 14, the forty-ninth anniversary of the first prisoners arriving there, consisting that 1940 day of 728 Poles of which twenty were Polish Jews. Over the next nearly five years, over a million Jews, as well as other Poles, Gypsies, Soviet POWs, political dissenters, and religious opponents were imprisoned, murdered, or otherwise died there. The Jewish numbers grew exponentially in the wake of the Nazis' January 1942 conference in Wanasee, a suburb of Berlin, at which the "Final Solution of the Jewish Question" policy was adopted and from which Nazi practices worsened. Poland suffered losses at their hands because it had been the first country to be hostilely invaded by them, Austria and Czechoslovakia having been political arrangements, had high battlefield and later underground casualties in vigorous opposition to its subjugation, and a large Jewish population in the prewar years, of which the Warsaw Ghetto was only one. As Auschwitz grew from its 1940 origins, it was conjoined with Birkenau, and they became the largest extermination camp in Europe. They were the end point of forty-eight subcamps. My day's images of what happened there will remain forever with me, that being the postwar intent of the site's preservation. Advice on how to internalize this tyranny was to set aside for the moment the one million or more number in order to imagine myself arriving at this site in those years. The advice rested on the expectation that a million cannot be easily grasped by the mind for the magnitude of its horror. But, arriving, being forcibly taken by heavily armed soldiers with barking guard dogs out of the train cars, separated from spouse, children, grandchildren, and others, and marched in different directions, publicly stripped of clothing, and forced into filthy prison garb with nothing any longer certain except hope against despair can be more readily grasped. I held myself together as well as I could, but in the museum housing relics and evoking memories, after the room showing a mound of luggage and other baggage, another with piles of clothing, another with an array of eyeglasses, I lost it altogether in the room behind whose glassed exhibit were the shoes of tens of thousands of children. You never forget any or all of this, nor should you. We must never forget the lessons learned from such hatred. Karol Wojtyla didn't. Perhaps it was within God's call to his ministry.

In January 1998, I considered myself blessed to accompany the United States delegation to join John Paul II and his delegation in Cuba. This was tied in key ways to the Salesians, for they were the largest Catholic vocational order in Cuba at the time of the Fidel Castro–led armed Cuban Revolution's ouster on January 1, 1959, of Fulgencio Batista's government. Suppression of religion within the broader suppressions of free assembly, press, and speech had reduced Salesian numbers from more than three hundred to only thirty-plus, for, in that as priests died, none from outside Cuba were allowed to replace them, and there was no functioning Catholic seminary there to educate students for the priesthood. It required years of negotiations at the highest levels in the Holy See and Havana for a papal trip to occur. The Vatican agreed to undertake it only after Castro's government agreed to reopen the Catholic seminary in Havana so additional priests could be educated and allowed priests outside Cuba to join their orders in Cuba. Those negotiations were against the deep backdrop of Cuba having been a predominant Catholic nation before Castro's Revolution. They were also against a more circuitous progress, components of which were Fidel's 1979 discussions with Catholic priests in Nicaragua as to Christ's teachings addressing the plight of the poor, his post-1989 recognition that the world's ideological forces had changed significantly and against communism, including and following the liberation of Central and Eastern Europe from Soviet Communist domination, the 1991 reversion of the Soviet Union to Russia and its other republics, Fidel's own rescinding in 1991 of the ban against Christians joining the Communist Party, and his declaration the following year that Cuba was a secular state, not an atheist one.

On the afternoon in which we returned from Havana, departure delay followed delay after delay. We assumed negotiations had needed to be continued. In the meantime, the beautiful morning had given way to the afternoon storm clouds of the subtropics. As our chartered Boeing 747 finally lifted skyward in the direction of south Florida, we flew into the teeth of what my father's father would have referred to as Old Testament weather, lightning flashing and thunder roiling all about us. This produced a tight grip on both arms of my aisle seat. The monsignor sitting next to me and calmly reading a newspaper, perhaps an account of the papal trip, and without looking in my direction, quietly observed, "You look nervous, my son," to which I replied that I just did not like the level of turbulence, to which he responded, "Given who's on this airplane, do you really think we are gonna crash?" Before I could respond, he added, "Besides, if you die while on a pilgrimage, it's automatic salvation," to which I exclaimed with near glee, "That's great, Father, for my whole life's been a pilgrimage!" to which he as calmly responded, "I don't think it works quite that way." We continued onward, beyond the storm's reach, to John F. Kennedy International

Airport, where we were met with Customs officers, nearly all of whose family names began with an O'.

I had traveled to Cuba before the papal trip to meet with Salesians as to their needs and limited expectations within the severe contextual restraints surrounding them and their work. As to the holy father's January 21–25 trip, I accompanied the US delegation of all but one of the American cardinals, as well as numerous archbishops, bishops, and other clerical and lay leaders. It was an enlightening experience to be there for such a momentous week. Instead of the holy father traveling from one city to the next and then to the next, he travelled each day from Havana and back to it at the end of that day. This strategy brought the Word to believers and nonbelievers in Santiago de Cuba in Fidel's Oriente Province, Santa Clara, the site of Che Guevara's first successful attack on Baptista's armed forces, and other cities, culminating with his celebration of Mass in Havana's Plaza of the Revolution near the José Marti Memorial and under the glaring image of the face of Che Guevara on the neighboring Ministry of Interior headquarters. I was right behind the platform of the dignitaries at that Mass.

Two years later, I was blessed to be able to return to the Holy Land on the occasion of John Paul II's March 21–26, 2000, visit to Jordan, Israel, and Palestine. I had been there before in various capacities and nearly annually and was to do so in the future. Salesian experience in this region was important, for they had long worked with youth in the Holy Land and especially in Bethlehem at its vocational training school. In the modern age, it is only a few hours' flight from Rome to Tel Aviv, but John Paul was only the second pope to visit Jerusalem, Pope Paul VI having spent one day there in January 1964. Thirty-six years later, John Paul's pilgrimage seemed to have established a new tradition in that both of his successors, Benedict in 2009 and Francis in 2014, undertook pilgrimages to the holy sites of Israel. Together, these four visits over decades represented prodigious amounts of highly sensitive work and its progress, badly needed following the Second World War and its deep scars. Could one have imagined in 1945 or 1948 that international news media would report in 2000 that a holy father had "reached out to both Jews and Muslims" in Israel and Palestine and been "warmly embraced." John Paul's most remembered presences were during his moments of prayerful silence at Jerusalem's Yad Vashem Holocaust Memorial and his placing of his prayer into the crevices of the Temple Mount's Western Wall:

> God of our fathers, you chose Abraham and his descendants to bring Your name to the nations: we are deeply saddened by the behavior of those who in the course of history have caused these children of Yours to suffer, and asking Your forgiveness we wish to commit ourselves to genuine brotherhood with the people of the Covenant. Jerusalem. 26 March 2000. Johannes Paulus II.

In the otherwise ordinary course of life, a "chill bump" experience sometimes occurs, and, for me, there have been more than one while in the Holy Land, actually many. One occurred when my dear friend Leslie Israel, whom I had known since 1967 as her husband, Fred, sought to expand my knowledge of contracts law in order to succeed in my first year of law school and with whom I had worked later on democracy-building initiatives abroad, invited me to accompany her to a Shabbat (Sabbath) meal in Jerusalem with her close friends, Rabbi David Rosen and his wife, Sharon, and members of their family. Rabbi Rosen held a number of positions that brought him into decades-long experiences in seeking reconciliation between the Jewish people and Catholic officialdom. Among them, this former chief rabbi of Ireland and professor of Jewish studies at the Jerusalem Center for Near Eastern Studies served on the permanent bilateral commission of the State of Israel and the Holy See and on the International Jewish Committee for Interreligious Consultations where much of his life has been focused on that reconciliation. His wife, Sharon, was serving in similarly directed work. In recognition of his work and its successful consequences, he was in November 2005 made by Pope Benedict a knight of the Order of St.

Gregory the Great for his contribution to promoting Catholic-Jewish reconciliation and in 2010 was made by H.M. Queen Elizabeth II a commander of the British Empire for his contributions to interfaith relations. I saw in him how a framework for reconciliation among peoples and faiths could emerge from personal awareness, determination, and energy. I felt blessed to be in his and their presence. Their daughter Gabriella attended the Fund for American Studies' 2001 International Institute for Political and Economic Systems in Chania on the Greek island of Crete.

A further experience involved Salesians amid tensions with the Soviet Union and then Russia. The Russian Orthodox Church's origins lay in the Greek Orthodox Church, whose priests bought it to the lands of the Rus and others beginning in AD 988. In doing that, the Great Schism between the Holy See and the Eastern Orthodox was brought to the Russia church with its animosities toward Rome. Move forward a thousand years, and that tension had continued but with the addition of more recent tensions between Orthodox Russia and the Roman Catholic nations within Central and Eastern Europe. Add to them the startling occurrence of a cardinal from Krakow, Poland, being elected by the College of Cardinals as the holy father of that Catholic Church, one who helped lead the emancipation of Poland from the most recent post–World War II occupation by Soviet Russia. John Paul II brought hope to scores of foreign lands, but he was never extended an invitation to celebrate Mass in Russia, even at the most obvious of churches to do so, the Cathedral Church of the Immaculate Conception in Moscow. Before the Soviet era, it had been the principal place of worship for Poles living in Moscow. Following the Russian Revolution of 1917, the Soviet government confiscated it, erected floors within its space, and used it as an office building and storage warehouse. Somehow, someone in authority was able to hedge the bet on which faith, Roman or Marxist, was going to win in the long run, for the church was neither destroyed, as many were by Stalin under the guise of widening streets to accommodate modern vehicular traffic, an effective demolition strategy in that churches are most often at intersections, nor was it desecrated within, as icons and statuary were boarded up before it became an office building and warehouse. A Polish priest particularly close to John Paul II from the pope's years as archbishop of Krakow, Augustyn Dziedziel (pronounced jeyd-jel'), was named Salesian vicar in and vice provincial for Russia, Ukraine, Belarus, Lithuania, and Georgia, among other tasks to see to the restoration of this church. I visited this church during the intermediate period of its restoration, and while I was impressed by the progress shown in Catholic-Orthodox relations generally, I was deeply moved by Father Dziedziel's work with the street children of Moscow. There were lessons in it learned from Fr. De Nicolo in Bogota and others. I have in the ensuing years seen the Russian doors blocking the Church in Rome gradually opening wider, not only in its western regions but even in its Vladivostok oblast on the Pacific. Perhaps some year a holy father will celebrate Mass in this Moscow cathedral or another Roman Catholic Church in Russia.

IFES

Whether and how the United States should support democracy-building in foreign lands has been foreign policy questions for the length of our democracy. Our young nation addressed it when France overthrew its monarchy in hopes of creating democracy instead of the French Revolution's reign of terror and its later turn to the new monarchy that it presaged. We cheered when the United Mexican States won their long struggle for a democracy independent of European powers. President Woodrow Wilson's intent for the United States to enter a World War I already under way in Europe but with its outcome in doubt was to make the world safe for democracy. Yet Russia's Bolshevik Revolution, Germany's Nazi period, China's Maoist revolution, the partitions of Korea and Vietnam, and Cuba's alignment with the Soviet Union occupied much of the twentieth century.

In seeking to support pro-democracy ideas instead of only opposing antitotalitarian ones, Florida congressman Dante Fascell, a Democrat, introduced in April 1967 a measure to create an Institute of International

Affairs to provide a louder voice to democratic ideas. In a speech fifteen years later in London's Palace of Westminster, President Ronald Reagan proposed an initiative "to foster the infrastructure of democracy—the system of a free press, unions, political parties, universities." His United States Agency for International Development (USAID) responded and contracted with the American Political Foundation to study the history of and prospects for democracy promotion abroad, an end of which was a proposed Democracy Program. Its findings in turn recommended creation of a bipartisan, private, nonprofit corporation to be known as the National Endowment for Democracy. Fascell of Florida, Democratic National Committee chairman Charles T. Manatt, Republican National Committee chairman Frank Farenkopf, and others worked for its enactment, and it became law. Five entities were created by it, and three of them are now known as the National Endowment for Democracy (NED), the National Democratic Institute (NDI), and International Republican Institute (IRI). Reagan, British prime minister Margaret Thatcher, German chancellor Helmut Kohl, Pope John Paul II, and others across broad and bipartisan political spectrums continued their push for a world of more broadly shared democratic values.

It did not take long for those within USAID, the NED structures, and others to realize that a major element of the democratic process was missing. That element needed to be harnessed within an organization that would transfer competencies in technical election contexts and skills required to assure free and fair elections, the "where the rubber hits the road" part of democratic processes, to others abroad. An additional study was commissioned on how to do this, and it was headed by Eddie Mahe, an organizational structures authority with election experience. Grounded upon its recommendations, there was organized in 1987 the International Foundation for Electoral Systems (IFES). F. Clifton White was chosen by USAID to devise and direct the formidable tasks of getting IFES organized, which meant organizing and incorporating it and obtaining a tax-exemption status. It also meant naming a bipartisan governing board and selecting competent administrators, devising revenue strategies and budget controls, securing an office, and hiring staff. With a handful of persons selected from both US political parties' and others' competencies, it became a success and celebrated in 2017 its first thirty years. I served as its legal counsel from 1987 until 2015 and have served on its governing board from 2017. IFES posthumously recognized White's contributions through the creation and naming of its F. Clifton White Research Center, which name was later changed to reflect the substantive content of its actual work. White had died in 1993 at the age of seventy-five.

White's reputation as a political campaign consultant overshadowed his earlier career as a university professor in Upstate New York. I recall an observation he made to me in Budapest when I was working with him years later on the formation of the Association of Central and Eastern European Election Officials, now the Association of European Election Officials but still using the ACEEEO acronym. It was about a perception he had and expressed in his professorial years. Reflecting on when the United Nations came into operational existence, intending as it did to unite the nations of the world within a single body devoted to addressing shared issues, he recalled there were only fifty-one nations at the April-June 1945 San Francisco Conference to complete the proposed Charter of the United Nations. A larger number of nations grew in the decades that followed. Why? Following the war, European powers granted independence to their colonial territories. Years later, the dissolution of the Soviet Union caused fifteen to come into being, and the dissolution of Yugoslavia caused eight to come into being. Czechoslovakia split into the Czech Republic and Slovak Republic. Now, some in Belgium wish to divide it, the Catalonians are demanding independence from Spain, Greenland wants independence beyond just territorial autonomy from Denmark, and the tribes of northwest Canada have accepted semi-independence as a political compromise but may seek in years to come their sovereignty. By 2017, there were 193 members not including two nonmember permanent observer states, nominated members, and non-UN members of the UN's specialized agencies. What is a discernible consequence from globalization? It is the point related by White to me: globalization's gravitational force toward one world generated a counterforce, a centrifugal one, in which peoples sought to preserve their own identities, heritages, languages, and so on. To the extent an action generates a reaction, the action of the world becoming smaller provoked the reaction of searches for preserving national neighborhoods. It is a process that has not and will not stop, and IFES remains engaged in providing technical elections assistance to nations and their voters.

EARTH University

I became aware in late 1986 of the mutual interests of the United States, Costa Rica, W.K. Kellogg Foundation, and others in the creation of a university in Costa Rica to deliver agriculturally focused higher education there and more widely in the humid tropics of Latin America. I was asked to consider serving on its board of trustees, which was being organized to manage its funds, while the board of directors would manage its academic programs in all other ways. I attended a meeting at the W.K. Kellogg Foundation's headquarters in Battle Creek, Michigan, to learn more about the proposal, the likelihood of it coming into existence, and its organizers' expectations for its earliest years. After presentations and much discussion, I agreed to do so on one condition: I would serve as a trustee but for only several, perhaps two or three, years. We shook hands on this understanding. As the meeting ended, it began snowing outside, and the Costa Ricans hurried out to have their photographs taken in the snow for their families at home in the hot and humid tropics. In March of the following year, the Costa Rican legislature enacted the enabling statute, and the many follow-on tasks of the proposed school of agriculture of the humid tropics region began. The formal name of Escuela de la Agricultural de la Regional Tropical Humeda produced an appropriate acronym of EARTH.

Moving from those earliest years to my 2014 retirements from both boards, I had served twenty-six years instead of the two or three to which I had initially committed. I had served as chairman of its board of trustees in the years following its founding chairman, Dr. Norman

A. Brown, president and CEO of the W.K. Kellogg Foundation, and had served also on its board of directors. References to the words school and college had ended because EARTH was truly a university, and its early narrow focus on the humid tropics had become its broader focuses on humid and dry tropics. Its students no longer came just from Latin America but also from Africa and other continents, and the EARTH model of hands-on delivery of higher education had become widely known and globally valued.

I treasure my years at EARTH, appreciating the uniqueness of a place where students and alumni, faculty, administrators and staff, trustees and directors, and donors pull in the same directions. They do so through cooperation and collaboration, not compulsion or coercion, in order to achieve sustainable development, appreciating that no treaties, laws, or government regulations will ever protect nature's heritage as promptly and effectively as the commitments of people, communities, and institutions when they understand that doing so is in their best mutual interests. I treasure its graduation ceremonies, for they are events at which students end their classroom and field studies to begin new relationships as alumni based on what they know of EARTH's mission, their own remaining educational, career, and other goals.

The Holy Land

I began travel to the Holy Land in 1995. Known as the Levant, the land where the rising of the sun begins, we know it as the Eastern Mediterranean. My travels were in respect to the Fund for American Studies' organizing its Georgetown University–accredited summer program for top-tier university students from throughout the Middle East. It began the next summer as the International Institute for Political and Economic Studies (IIPES). One half of its first institute was held at the Agricultural Bank of Greece's training facility in Kastri in Athens' northern neighborhoods, and its second was at the International Olympic Committee's campus in ancient Olympia on the western Peloponnesian fields where the ancient city-states' top athletes competed for honor and olive wreath crowns two millennia before the reintroduction of the Olympics. The Fund recruited students from universities around the eastern rim of the Mediterranean, that is, from Italy, Slovenia, and other countries that emerged from the breakup of Yugoslavia, further to Greece, Turkey, and Cyprus, to Syria, Lebanon, and Jordan, thence Israel, Palestine, Egypt, and, skipping Libya, to Tunisia. We comingled those students with those from the United States and Europe. In its later years, we added countries further east, including those proximate to the Arabian Gulf. For budgetary considerations, we consolidated IIPES with our American Institute on Political and Economic Systems (AIPES) at historic Charles University, founded in 1348 in Prague in what is now the Czech Republic. After that merger, IIPES gradually lost its uniqueness but not its AIPES-connected reasons for existing. If the Fund had new funds to do so, I would ask its governing board to authorize restarting, enlarging, and lengthening IIPES.

One of the students who attended IIPES and later one of its Georgetown institutes was from Bethlehem University, a Roman Catholic university in the Palestinian territory between Jerusalem and the desert south of Herod's Herodian fortress that is on the cusp of the Judean desert. The student is Ra'id Shomali. Both his parents, Augustyn (Qustandi in Arabic pronunciation) and Sawsan, were professors at that university. Visit after visit, each time bringing friends with me, his father would drive us to the escarpment overlooking Shepherd's Field. We would walk and stand, sometimes sit, in this natural stone shelter with soot from scores of centuries of warming winter fires and later votive candles caked on the overhead stone. One did not touch that soot, for it was too sacred a place to mar. It was here that is set forth in the Gospel according to St. Luke:

> And there were in the same country shepherds abiding
> in the field, keeping watch over their flock by night.
> And, lo, the angel of the Lord came upon them, and
> the glory of the Lord shone round about them: and they
> were sore afraid. And the angel said unto them, Fear

not: for, behold, I bring you good tidings of great joy, which shall be to all people, For unto you is born this day in the city of David a Savior, which is Christ the Lord. And this shall be a sign unto you; Ye shall find the babe wrapped in swaddling clothes, lying in a manger. And suddenly there was with the angel a multitude of the heavenly host praising God, and saying, Glory to God in the highest, and on earth peace, good will toward men.

Ra'id's mother would drive us to its many historic sites. She would also show to us how the area had been cut off from both Israel and the tourists who used to come to Bethlehem on their pilgrimages or just out of historic curiosity. The downturned economic consequences from the loss of those tourists' spending were obvious. We would walk to the Church of the Nativity and enter through its narrow doorway, built that way to require dismounting from a horse before entering holy space, in order to climb down to the grotto once sheltered by an inn's stable and in which Jesus was born in about 4 BCE.

One afternoon in June 2009, Brian Waidmann, a personal friend and a professional acquaintance of many years and at that time the chief of staff to the secretary of the US Department of the Interior, Dirk Kempthorne, and I were sitting in their living room with Prof. and Prof. Shomali when their son Ra'id was in the States earning his PhD at Southern Illinois University. We had had a splendid midday repast, and in the summer air, I may have been imitating sleep. As Waidmann was looking from where we were sitting, through the open doors and across their balcony, he asked what the open field immediately behind their home was, one not in some way built upon as was the nearly every other square meter of Bethlehem. Dr. Shomali responded, "It is the field of Ruth," and that is why to this day it has been hallowed. It is the physical manifestation of the story of three thousand years ago of Naomi's daughter-in-law Ruth. I understood my father's mother's name as never before.

26

What's Next for Me and for You?

Wʜᴀᴛ'ꜱ ɴᴇxᴛ ꜰᴏʀ ᴍᴇ? Aꜱ ꜰᴏʀ ᴡʀɪᴛɪɴɢ, I ɪɴᴛᴇɴᴅ ᴛᴏ undertake at least three additional books.

The first's working title is *Encounters* and is about 90 percent complete in its present draft. It is a compilation of excerpts from my published and a few unpublished writings, tied together by my and others' commentaries on the subjects addressed. Its chapters are focused on thinkers and doers, their ideas and other achievements, economic freedom and its calculations, family, organizations, and lands afar. Choosing what to excerpt from the past for a current audience and describing why and their connections to me has been a surmountable challenge.

The second's working title is *Dancing with the Bear: Recollections of Russia* and is a multifaceted report on my decades of work as to and in Russia as the central control room of the Soviet Union and now as a post-Soviet Russia seeking to regain and surpass its Soviet era power within the world community, in short what was and is Russia and why and what we should know about it.

The third's working title is *Shadows at the Back Door* and is beginning to take shape among my readings and thoughts. It will speak to Durham's failures to address its racial issues through examinations of what were the wrongs, how remedial strategies have not overcome them, and what proposals for the mutual benefits of those living, working, and knowing about Durham should be considered and sought. It will be a massive assignment in access, research, conversation, introspection, and articulation.

Write Your Memoirs!

What's next for you? Permit me this opportunity to persuade you to write your memoirs. If you do, you will learn more about yourself, and your family will learn more about you. Learning more about both will inform in ways known, suspected and unexpected, and that will be exciting for you and instructive to others. Examining them now in hindsight, what were my starting points, expectations, and surprises?

This memoir was drawn from three sources: me, others' perspectives on me and their shared knowledges of contexts surrounding me, and my and others' research in the digital age in which billions of facts, circumstances, and much else are accessible online.

I knew that much research would be required. Without it, there would have been erroneous information, inadequately understood contexts, and missed narratives. My desire for both accuracy and thoroughness drove the research. Even during the times when it was tedious and extraordinarily time-consuming, it was enjoyable because of the work product emerging from it.

I had little expectation that this undertaking would expand my knowledge of myself in such large measure. How much it did was the most far-reaching of all the surprises.

I had less expectation that some of the knowledge I had learned within my family would be wrong. At first, I wondered how this could happen, yet information thought to be accurate, but was not, had been passed from generation to generation in the same ways in which correct information had been passed. A reverse of that was the loss of knowledge important to families' understandings of themselves.

I had little expectation that the research and writing would, sometimes more than others, become deeply emotional. It did. It brought back to my daytime consciousness and to my nighttime dreams arrays of thoughts about family members and others. That ushered in nostalgia, some of which involved regrets and a tied sense of wanting to communicate with persons no longer among the living. In this, I was reminded of Norman Maclean's *A River Runs Through It* in which the wife-to-be, Jessie, poses this profound question:

> Why is it that people who need the most help won't take it?

After which Maclean recounted in that adaptation the last sermon he heard his Presbyterian minister father give, in which his father observed to his family and his congregation:

> Each one of us here today will, at one time in our lives, look upon a loved one who is in need and ask the same question. "We are willing to help, Lord, but what, if anything, is needed?" It is true we can seldom help those closest to us. Either we don't know what part of ourselves to give or more often than not, the part we have to give is not wanted. And so it is those we live with and should know who elude us, but we can still love them. We can love completely without complete understanding.

After which, Maclean surpassed in both logic and emotion those observations when he added this epilogue:

> Now nearly all those I loved and did not understand
> in my youth are dead. Even Jessie. But I still reach out
> to them. Of course, now I'm too old to be much of a

fisherman. And now I usually fish the big waters alone, although some friends think I shouldn't.

But when I am alone in the half-light of the canyon, all experience seems to fade to a being with my soul and memories, and the sounds of the Big Blackfoot River and a four-count rhythm and the hope that a fish will rise.

Eventually, all things merge into one, and a river runs through it. The river was cut by the world's great flood and runs over rocks from the basement of time. On some of the rocks are timeless raindrops. Under the rocks are the words and some of the words are theirs.

We may have here an observation of life likened to a stream, a life lived in the narrowness of time and place between unknown sources upstream, passing us quickly and ever changing to equally unknown places and times downstream. This is my summary of these thoughts—certainly not his and those of literary scholars.

My writing of this memoir took the overcoming of hurdles not to undertake it. In the end, which is to say at its beginning, I thought my children, grandchildren, and others whom I will never meet had their rights to know this part of their ancestry.

It is a certainty that my needs to know more about matters would have been much easier had I undertaken this writing years or even decades earlier when its central figures were alive for discussions. This point's lesson? Don't wait to ask questions and get as many answers as you can!

If there was ease during this writing, it lay in how memories brought forward additional memories. It's a process captured in Marvin Hamlisch, Marilyn Bergman, and Alan Bergman's lyric "Memories light the corners of my mind" from the soundtrack of the movie *The Way We Were*. Yet memories alone do not assure a wholly factual account.

"Why write much about persons not known personally to me or not in the family?" can certainly be asked. How can a person write only about their self? What a narrow and inadequately informed recitation that would be. Facts and contexts about others and their achievements and failures were essential. Not only does no one live in a single moment, but we are each a collage of them. I came to enjoy the weaving of persons, families, institutions, cities, states, and even the nation into our family's fabric.

If there were difficulties in this writing, some lay in the tedium of research, for there was a self-determined necessity that it be factually accurate. I attempted to discover the underlying truth amid incompatible facts and to distill and reconcile differing points of view. When facts could not be nailed with certainty to the proverbial wall, they are described in a manner that notes their uncertainty.

In respect to that necessity of truth and in practicing law for over forty years, I know the oath or affirmation that is taken before judge and jury by a witness preceding testimony at a trial. The reader knows it too, if not from being an attorney, then from watching television shows or movies involving courtroom proceedings. While it differs to some extent from jurisdiction to jurisdiction, the oath or affirmation is:

> I do solemnly swear (or affirm) to tell the truth, the
> whole truth and nothing but the truth.

There should be no equivocation in taking or adhering to that oath at a trial, an event where lives, properties, and reputations hang in the balance. Only truth should be before judge and jury in the reaching of a courtroom verdict. While a memoir is not a judicial proceeding, my pledge here was to tell the truth and nothing but the truth. This pledge did not, however, include all truths, because I was not free on my own motion to tell all the truths known to me, and other truths exist that are unknown to me. That point was set forth in the summer of 2015 when biographer William Novak wrote:

> St. Augustine notwithstanding, not every memoir has
> to be confessional, and no rule, heavenly or human,
> requires us to disclose every detail of our lives.

Or to disclose every detail of others' lives.

Beyond those expectations, surprises, observations, and recommendations, there was an overarching intent. This memoir is an attempted loud shout-out against a paragraph in the *Washington Post* of January 6, 1998. Peter Carlson had written a review of Annie Dillard's "The Wreck of Time" essay in *Harper's* magazine in which she had propounded:

> You've got a few minutes or a few decades to horse around and then you'll be gone, dead and buried, along with all your friends and family; soon not a living soul will remember you, and the indifferent world will go on as if you'd never been here. We arise from dirt and dwindle to dirt and the might of the universe is arrayed against us.

This is not a new observation, and furthermore, it is true, even if the more widely recited expression is "from ashes to ashes." But it is not the whole story. Whole truth encompasses the fact that books and other forms of written communication can transcend lives and centuries and carry memories into the future, and often as guidance for that future. They have done so for ages, and if humans continue far into the future, we should assume writings in whatever formats will continue to do so. You can recount the past as an additional guide for those whose eventual past is still in front of them as their present and their future. If the world is in balance, there should be as much optimism as there is pessimism, maybe a little more optimism than pessimism, for optimism's edge accounts in part for marginal improvements in the future. Further and quoting the poet Linda Pastan, I acknowledge that this effort has been for me an attempt to "find the pure center of light within the dark circle" of my own doubt. I hope so because life is a fabric, and a fabric is woven, one thread over and under another that, after thousands of times, becomes a strong piece of cloth. The combined strength of woven silk is said to be stronger than steel. The weaving of muscles, organs, blood, and nerves becomes a physical life, and here, a human life had to be stronger than either silk or steel in order to grow. This phenomenon works outside of a straight-lined chronology, for a geometrically straight-lined life does not exist. We are each woven, from the uniting DNA in our conception to the total experiences of our life. Certainly, we are more complete at the end, whether it ushers in a renewed beginning someplace else or not.

As I worked toward this memoir's completion, I became increasingly aware of an important consequence of it: it had become therapeutic. Mistakes in my life remained mistakes, as did regrets and doubts. Some were within the range of remedy, but others were not. In that last realization, time alone does not heal all wounds. I made amends when there were possibilities for them. Quite obviously, if a person was no longer among the living, I could not tell them how much I loved, treasured, or appreciated them, but I could still communicate with their family and friends. I could also make a charitable gift in their memory, an atonement of sorts.

I had a low expectation, but a great hope, that those persons whom I would ask to review drafts from a single paragraph to its entirety would be as willingly helpful, sometimes enthusiastically so, as they were. Aside from structural, grammatical, spelling, and punctuation errors, they pointed out inconclusive facts; gave different interpretations of circumstances; offered different opinions of persons' motivations and attitudes; filled in years not known to me; and much more. My work alone would have been questionable had they not done so. This book's text matured from their reviews and comments and my required revisions.

Lastly, I felt this writing's contents' receding distances, and that feeling became a powerful motivation to conclude it. Composer and conductor Leonard Bernstein once observed that some of the best work of anyone lies in a plan to do it but not enough time to do it. That means there's no better time than now to plan and start your undertaking of your own memoir. Take it!

Recognized and Recorded Spellings of "Tadhg"

TadhG, TADG, TADIG
TEEG, TEGG, TEEGE
TEIG, TEIGE, TEIGS
TIGHE, McTIGHE
MacTEIG, MacTIEG
TEECH, TEACH
TEAGG, TEAGH, TEGG, TEGGS
TEAGLE
TAGUE, TEAGUE *
McTEAGUE, MacTEAGUE, McTEIGUE
MonTEAGUE
O'TAGHA, O'TEAGUE
O'TADLEY

The spelling Teague was recognized by grant of Henry III of England (1207–1272 and reigned 1216–1272) as an anglicized spelling of "tadhg" (with the "d" and the 'h' on the same stem).

John Teague Line

John Teague + Martha and Betty
(1635–1677)

Edward Teague + Susan Smith
(b. 1660 at Tegg's Delight, Cecil County, MD) + (b. 1663)
(d. March 09, 1695/96) + (d. April 13, 1741, in Harford County, MD)

William Abel Teague + Isabelle Loftin
(b. August 23, 1693) + (b. December 19, 1693, in
St. George Parish, Baltimore City, MD)
(d. 1775 in Rowan, Chatham County, NC) + (d.
1762 in Rowan, Chatham County, NC)

Moses Teague + Elizabeth Loftin (his first cousin)
(b. March 3, 1718, Chatham County, NC) + (b.
January 1, 1713/14 in Frederick, VA)
(d. 1799 in Chatham County, NC) + (d. after
1759 in Chatham County, NC)

Issac Newton Teague + Mary (and Judith)
(b. 1748, d. UNK) + (b. UNK, d. UNK)

Jacob Teague + Mary Nall
(b. 1786, d. 185_) + (b. UNK, d. UNK)

William Teague + Anna Caviness
(b. 1819 d. 1882) + (b. 1820 d. UNK)

William Swaim Teague + Mary Frances Durham
(b. 1852, d. 1931 nr. Rockingham. NC) + (b.
1851 d. 1934 nr. Rockingham, NC)

Richard Monroe Teague + Naomi Iola Lasater
(b. November 1, 1887; d. July 30, 1965, in Durham,
NC) + (b. September 12, 1886, in Elam, NC; d.
December 17, 1976, in Durham, NC)

Roy Merle Teague (Sr.) + Lottie Mae Rhew
(b. December 19, 1917, in Durham, NC) + (b.
August 10, 1916, in Durham County, NC)
(d. August 27, 1970, in Durham, NC) + (d.
June 30, 2000, in St. Petersburg, FL)

Randal Cornell Teague + Jessica Townsend
(b. May 19, 1944, in Durham, NC) + (b.
January 19, 1954, in Hinsdale, IL)

Randal Cornell Teague Jr.
Robert Townsend Teague
Mary Robb Durham Teague (now Wilson)
James Keller Burke Teague

Randal Teague's Descent
from
Henry Soane

Confirmed by February 13, 2013, Acceptance of Enrollment
as a Member in the Jamestowne Society

Randal Cornell Teague Sr. (b. 1944 –) >

Roy Merle Teague Sr. (b. 1917 – d. 1970) >

Richard Monroe Teague (b. 1887 – d. 1965) + Naomi Iola Lasater (b. 1886 – d. 1976) >

Robert Artemus Lasater (b. 1855 – d. 1888) + Jeannette Jackson Burke (b. 1856 – d. 1941) >

Millender Burke (b. 1835 – d. btw. 1858–1864) >

James C. Burke (b. 1801 – d. 1864) + Winifred W. Clark (b. 1807 – d. 1880) >

William Clark (b. 1775 – d. 1852) >

Alexander Clark (b. 1747 – d. 1783) + Phoebe Jefferson (b. 1743 – d. 1830) >

Field Jefferson (b. 1702 – d. 1765) >

Thomas Jefferson[1] (b. 1677 – d. 1731) + Mary Field (b. 1679 – d. 1715) >

Peter Field[2] (b. 1642 – d. 1707) + Judith Soane (b.)

Henry Soane[3] (b. 1622 – d. abt. 1661)

Note: Wives are listed above when lineage shifts from prior generation by the maternal line.

---

[1] A grandfather of President Thomas Jefferson.

[2] Member of Virginia House of Burgesses, 1688 and 1693.

[3] The younger Henry Soane was christened on November 17, 1622, at St. Nicholas, Brighton, Sussex County, England, and died in 1661 and is interred at an unknown location on Hoggs (now Hog) Island, James River, Virginia. He was the son of Henry Soane (1594–1632) and Elizabeth Worger (1592–1633) and immigrated to James City County, Virginia, in 1651. He was first granted 297 acres along the Chickahominy River for importing six persons (himself and his family), after which he acquired additional land holdings and became an elected public official serving in the Virginia House of Burgesses in 1652–55, 1658, 1660, and 1661 and serving as its Speaker in his last session. He is the great-great-grandfather of President Thomas Jefferson and therefore the grandfather of "the original" Thomas Jefferson.

Henry Soane[4] (b. 1594 – d. 1632) >
Edward Soane (b. 1562 – d. 1593) >
Edmund Soane (b. 1530 – d. 1561) >
Edward Soane

---

[4] The elder Henry Soane was born on May 7, 1594, in Rottingdean, Brighton, Sussex, England, and died on March 16, 1632, in Rottingdean. He married Elizabeth Worger on November 5, 1621, in Brighton, and she was the daughter of Richard Worger and Mary Humphrey.

Sons of the American Revolution
and
Sons of the Revolution

Confirmed by February 1, 2011, Admission to Membership
in the
National Society of the Sons of the American Revolution
and
Confirmed by February 21, 2015, Admission to Membership
in the
Sons of the Revolution

In respect to Sons of the American Revolution

Moses Teague + Elizabeth Loftin (his first cousin)
(b. March 3, 1718, Chatham County, NC) + (b.
January 1, 1713/14, in Frederick, VA)
(d. 1799 in Chatham County, NC) + (d. after
1759 in Chatham County, NC)

Issac Newton Teague + Mary (and Judith)
(b. 1748, d. UNK) + (b. UNK, d. UNK)

Jacob Teague + Mary Nall
(b. 1786, d. 185_) + (b. UNK, d. UNK)

William Teague + Anna Caviness
(b. 1819, d. 1882) + (b. 1820, d. UNK)

William Swaim Teague + Mary Frances Durham
(b. 1852, d. 1931 nr. Rockingham, NC) + (b.
1851 d. 1934 nr. Rockingham, NC)

Richard Monroe Teague + Naomi Iola Lasater
(b. November 1, 1887, d. July 30, 1965, in Durham
NC) + (b. September 12, 1886, in Elam, NC, d.
December 17, 1976, in Durham, NC)

Roy Merle Teague (Sr.) + Lottie Mae Rhew
(b. December 19, 1917, in Durham, NC) + (b.
August 10, 1916, in Durham County, NC)

(d. August 27, 1970, in Durham, NC) + (d.
June 30, 2000, in St. Petersburg, FL)

and

In respect to Sons of the Revolution

Alexander Clark + Phoebe Jefferson
(b. 1747, d. 1783) + (b. about 1743 on or near Farrar's
Island on the James River in Henrico County, VA,
d. June 29, 1830, in Chatham County, NC)

Their son William Clark + Susannah Bell
(b. June 7, 1747, in Chatham County, NC, d. September 5, 1783, in
Chatham County, NC) + (b. September 24, 1784, d. July 23, 1870)

James C. Burke + their daughter Winifred W. Clark
(b. 1801 and d. October 10, 1864, in Chatham County,
NC) + (b. December 10, 1775, in Chatham County,
NC, d. after June 1880 in Chatham County, NC)

Their son Millender Burke + Martha Ann Womble
(b. about 1835 in Chatham County, NC, d. between
1858 and 1864 in Chatham County, NC) + (b.
April 12, 1843, in Chatham County, NC)

Robert Artemus Lasater + their daughter Jeannette Jackson Burke
(b. December 19, 1855, d. June 20, 1888) + (b. August 15, 1856, in
Chatham County, NC, d. February 15, 1941, in Durham, NC)

Richard Monroe Teague + their daughter Naomi Iola Lasater
(b. November 1, 1887, d. July 30, 1965, in Durham,
NC) + (b. September 12, 1886, in Elam, NC,
d. December 17, 1976, in Durham, NC)

Their son Roy Merle Teague (Sr.) + Lottie Mae Rhew
(b. December 19, 1917, in Durham, NC) + (b.
August 10, 1916, in Durham County, NC)
(d. August 27, 1970, in Durham, NC) + (d.
June 30, 2000, in St. Petersburg, FL)
Their sons Roy Merle Teague (Jr.) and Randal Cornell Teague

Phoebe Jefferson was the daughter of Field Jefferson, a brother
of Thomas Jefferson's father, Peter, and as such, Field was Thomas
Jefferson's uncle, and Phoebe was Thomas's first cousin. Alexander
Clark was the son of William Clark and his wife, Winifred. William
Clark was a prominent planter as well as friend and neighbor of the
Jeffersons. Phoebe was raised on her father's Occoneechee plantation,
named after the indigenous population residing along and on both sides
of the Virginia-North Carolina border, and was situated in presently
named Cumberland County. Phoebe and Alexander were married
in 1769 or 1770 at Peter Jefferson's estate, Shadwell, where Thomas
had been born and not far distance from his son's Monticello, under
continued construction at the time of the wedding. The Clarks settled
in Chatham County, NC, shortly after its establishment in 1770.

ACKNOWLEDGMENTS

I express my deep appreciations to Cory M. Amron, Carol Croley Aregood, John M. Bridgeland, Don V. Cogman, D. W. Duke, Lee Edwards, Neal A. Freeman, Nancy O'Briant Glenn, Karen and Sarah Huntley, John Lake Jones, June A. Leonard, Luis G. Lobo, Joseph D. Lonardo, Christopher Malagisi, Darlene B. McKinnon, M. Peter McPherson, M. Sean Purcell, Richard W. Rahn, Roger R. Ream, Lois Rhew, Kathleen Rothschild, Arnold Steinberg, Jeff D. Stevens, Jessica Townsend Teague, R. Cornell Teague, Townsend Teague, James K. B. Teague, Roy M. (Jr.) and Barbara Teague, Michael and Katharine Thompson, Richard and Carrie Tucker, Teri Watkins, Karen Jones Whelan, Mary Robb Durham Teague Wilson, and any others if I have failed to recall them by name for their giving of their time and talent in bringing this book to publication.

Their values to this product ranged from encouragement to undertake it, to technical assistance on how to navigate search engines and my laptop's software, and much in between. None should be identified with the opinions expressed here by me, and several could be appalled if they were. Some offered thoughts on facts and circumstances and the necessity of intense scrutiny of what turn out to be family mythology. Some reviewed draft texts and gave instructive advice on additions, deletions, and other revisions as this work moved from an idea, through drafts, to a published work. Others guided me through the processes, also known as landmines, of moving the text to publication and distribution. Any mistakes of circumstances or facts still within this published text are solely mine.

I express my deep appreciation for the hard copy and digital worlds in which we live and those who brought them into existence and nurtured and matured them. I chose to set out sources throughout the book as they occurred rather than in footnotes or endnotes, and I did so to avoid wrongful allegations of plagiarism within the narrative. I wish to thank the Library of Congress, the departments of vital statistics of a number of states and counties, Duke University, the city and county of Durham and the latter's library, and Preservation Durham for being valuable sources of information. I thank Ancestry.com for its inclusions made by professionals and amateurs, each in their own way offering hints toward verified answers, Google for its portals, and Wikipedia for its e-encyclopedia and the Wikipedia Foundation for its maintenance of that website.

Special shout-outs go to several persons and organizations in more or less this chronological order of appearance of their material.

That first and second persons are Jean Bradley Anderson and Jim Wise for her 596-page 2011 magnum opus *Durham County: A History of Durham County, North Carolina* and his 2002 *Durham: A Bull City Story* and his additional books on the county and city of Durham. Through their respective extended and more summary texts, they offered to me opportunities to correct my prepublication mistaken facts and circumstances. I am particularly grateful for their and Andre. D Vann's *African Americans of Durham County* for bringing forth accounts on the protracted avoidance of Durham leaders in acknowledging African American achievements and addressing racial issues in continued need of resolution and on the social, economic, and political prices paid for that delay in comparison to cities that more readily addressed them.

The fourth is Preservation Durham for the product of tens of thousands of hours that go into its website and the ease of access to its texts and photographs, a project funded by contributions to it. It is an Internal Revenue Code section 501(c)(3) nonprofit organization to which charitable contributions are tax deductible and welcomed by it. For those wishing to make a gift, it is found at Preservation Durham, P.O. Box 25411, Durham, NC 27702 and at www.preservationdurham.org.

The fifth is Brock and Lisa Bierman of Civic Ancestry for their encouragement, genealogical research, corrections, and suggestions, which together connected the proverbial dots in ways that provided valuable insights, corrected wrong information, and overcame family mythology with family facts. For the benefit of readers who wish to explore their own genealogy, Civic Ancestry can be reached at 845 Chinquapin Drive, Lyndhurst, VA 22952 and www.civicancestry.com.

The sixth is Margaret Jones, not only for the contextual and specific biographical information on country music colossus Connie B. Gay found in her 1995 biography, *Patsy: The Life and Times of Patsy Cline*, but also for her instructive advice on the development of that subchapter in this work and the eventual marketing of this memoir.

The seventh is my deepest gratitude to the Salesian Missions for their consent to the disclosures set forth in the subchapter in "1964 and Beyond" as to their transformative work. For those further interested in their work, it can be obtained from Salesian Missions, 2 Lefevres Lane, New Rochelle, NY 10801 or www.salesianmissions.org. For the work of Fr. Javier de Nicolo with street children in Colombia and its critically important lessons for such work elsewhere, please go to https://www.youtube.com/watch?v=pBwwGfO6MOE.

REQUEST

Any errors of circumstance or fact within this published text are solely mine. I will regret each. In that spirit, I invite any reader who wishes to inform me on anything written here to email me at randal.c.teague@ gmail.com. Do not do so on a social media site, for I seldom review them. This input will be helpful to me, particularly if there is ever a second edition revised in part by those inputs.

BIBLIOGRAPHY

Abbott, R. Tucker. *Indo-Pacific Mollusca: Monographs of Marine Mollusks of the World with Emphasis on Those of the Tropical Western Pacific and Indian Oceans.* 1959.

———. *Kingdom of the Seashell.* New York: Crown Publishers, Inc., 1974.

———. *Seashells of South East Asia.* 1991.

———. *Sea Shells of the World.* 1968.

Anderson, Jean Bradley. *Durham County: A History of Durham County, North Carolina*, 2nd ed. Durham and London: Duke University Press, 2011.

Andrews, Matthew Page. *Virginia, the Old Dominion.* New York: Doubleday & Company, Inc., 1937.

Brown, Brené. *The Gifts of Imperfection.* Center City, MN: Hazelden, 2010.

Carlson, Rachel. *The Edge of the Sea.* Boston: Houghton Mifflin, 1955.

———. *The Sea Around Us.* UK: Oxford University Press, 1951.

———. *Under the Sea Wind.* New York: Simon & Schuster, 1941.

Catton, Bruce. *Prefaces to History.* New York, 1969.

———. "The Real Michigan." In *Holiday Magazine.* Philadelphia: Curtis Publishing, 1957.

———. *Waiting for the Morning Train: An American Boyhood.* New York: Doubleday & Company, Inc., 1972.

Cunningham, Agnes Teague. *History and Genealogy on Teague Pioneers of Christian County, Kentucky.* 1971.

Deans, Bob. *The River Where America Began: A Journey Along the James.* Lanhan, MD: Rowman & Littlefield Publishers, Inc., 2007.

Dragovich, Alexander, and John A. Kelly Jr. "A Biological Study and Some Economic Aspects of Squid in Tampa Bay, Florida." In *Proceedings.* Gulf and Caribbean Fisheries Institute, 1962.

Duke, D. W. *The Duke Legacy.* Bloomington, IN, and New York: iUniverse, 2014.

Durden, Robert F. *The Dukes of Durham, 1865–1929.* Durham: Duke University Press, 1975.

Glymph, Minnie, Chris Hildreth, Les Todd, and Lacey Chylack. *Duke Chapel Illustrated.* Durham, NC: Duke Stores, 2001.

———. *Hills Durham City (NC) Directories.* 1905 et seq.

Jones, Margaret. *Patsy: The Life and Times of Patsy Cline.* New York: HarperCollins Publishers, 1994.

Kars, Margaret. *Breaking Loose Together: The Regulator Rebellion in Pre-Revolutionary North Carolina.* Chapel Hill and London: University of North Carolina Press, 2002.

Kukla, Jon. *Speakers and Clerks of the Virginia House of Burgesses 1643–1776.* Richmond, VA: Virginia State Library, 1981.

Kwitny, Jonathan. *Man of the Century: The Life and Times of Pope John Paul II.* New York: Henry Holt and Company, 1997.

Maclean, Norman. *A River Runs Through It.* University of Chicago Press, 1976.

McCartney, Martha. W. *Jamestown People to 1800: Landowners, Public Officials, Minorities, and Native Leaders.* Baltimore, MD: Genealogical Publishing Company, 2012.

Nugent, Nell Marion. *Cavaliers and Pioneers: Abstracts of Virginia Land Patents and Grants 1623–1800.* Richmond: Virginia State Library, 1934.

O'Brien, Darcy. *The Hidden Pope.* New York: St. Martin's Press, 1998.

Paul, Hiram Voss, and James Dike. *History of the Town of Durham, N.C.* Charleston, SC: American Chronicles, 2016.

Porter, Florence Collins, and Clara Wilson Gries. *Our Folks and Your Folks*. Los Angeles, CA: 1919.

Preservation Durham. www.opendurham.com. Durham, NC: 2015 et seq.

Schnur, James Anthony. *St. Petersburg Through Time*. Oxford, UK, and Charleston, SC: Fonthill Media LLC, 2014.

Shank, Henry Mercer III. *Genealogy of John Shank, Ariaen Degoede, Elijah Teague and Thomas Swann*. 1960.

Smith, Captain John. *The General Historie of Virginia, New-England, and the Summer Isles with the names of the Adventurers, Planters, and Governours from their first beginning An. 1584 to the present 1624*. London: 1624.

Smith, James Leonard Brierley. *The Search Beneath the Sea: The Story of the Coelacanth*. New York: Henry Holt and Company, 1956.

Smyth, Samuel Gordon. *A Genealogy of the Duke-Shepherd-Van Metre Family*. Lancaster, PA: 1909.

Steinbeck, John, and Edward F. Ricketts. *Sea of Cortez*. New York: Viking Press, 1941.

Steinbeck, John. *The Log from the Sea of Cortez*. New York: Penguin Books, 1951.

Stix, Hugh and Marguerite, and R. Tucker Abbott. *The Shell: Five Hundred Million Years of Inspired Design*. New York: Harry N. Abrams, Inc. Publishers, 1968.

Storck, John, Walter Dorwin Teague, and Harold Rydell. *Flour for Man's Bread*. Minneapolis: University of Minnesota Press, 1952.

Taylor, Sharon. *The New World Teague Family Album and Complete History*. 1989.

Teague, Bob. *Letters to a Black Boy*. New York: Lancer Books, Inc., 1969.

Teague, Charles Collins. *Fifty Years a Rancher*. Santa Paula, CA: 1944.

Teague, Ellen. "Mount Washington Railway Company: World's First Cog Railway, Mount Washington New Hampshire." New York, Dowington, Princeton, and Portland: 1970.

Teague, Hon. Olin E. "A Survey of Views of Leading Industrial Executives on the National Space Program." Washington, DC: US Government Printing Office, 1968.

Teague, Hon. Olin E., and Hon. Donald L. Jackson. "National and International Political Movements: Report Relative to the Situation in Greece." Washington, DC: US Government Printing Office, 1948.

Teague, Walter Dorwin. *Design This Day*. New York: Harcourt, Brace and Company, 1940).

————. *Land of Plenty*. New York: Harcourt, Brace and Company, 1947.

Vann, Andre D. *African Americans of Durham County*. Charleston, SC: Arcadia Publishing, 2017.

Vickers, James. *Chapel Hill*. Charleston: Arcadia Publishing, 1996.

Wescott, Dusty, and Kenneth Peters. *Historic Photos of Raleigh-Durham*.

Wikipedia. 2015 et seq.

Wise, Jim. *Durham: A Bull City Story*. Charleston, SC: Arcadia Publishing, 2002.

————. *Durham County*. Charleston, SC: Arcadia Publishing, 2000.

————. *Durham Tales*. Charleston, SC: History Press, 2008.

bold denotes photo

A

Abbott, R. Tucker, 195, 196, 197
Abney Mills, 81
ACEEEO (Association of Central
    and Eastern European Election
    Officials), 260
Advisory Committee on
    Voluntary Foreign Aid (US
    Agency for International
    Development), 246
Agutter, Jenny, 82
Allen University, 241
American Council of Young Political
    Leaders (ACYPL), 42, 91,
    220, 247
American Institute on Political
    and Economic Systems
    (AIPES), 263
American Tobacco Company, 39, 40
American University, 241
Amley, Robert (Rob), 184, 211
Amos 'n' Andy's, 133
ancestry, understanding, 23
Andre the Giant, 5

Andrews, Matthew Page, 16
Angus Barn, 134
Anthony, Susan B., 42
Aregood, Charles, 190
Aregood, Frances Carol Croley
    (Carol), 188, 189–190
Asbury Methodist Church, 45, 46, 47
Ascophyllum nodosum, 207
Ashbaugh, V.J., 8
Assateague National Seashore, 16
Association of Central and Eastern
    European Election Officials
    (ACEEEO), 260
Astor, Nancy Viscountess, 5, 27
Ataturk, Mustafa, 5
Auchincloss, James C., 143, 242, 243

B

Bagley, Maybelle, 77
Bagsby, Mrs. English, 155–156
Ballard, Robert, 196
Barefoot, Mrs., 147
BAT (British-American Tobacco),
    39, 40
Battle of Alamance, 15
Bauman, Robert, 232

Beck, Calvin, 38
Beck, Charles, 38
Belanger, Laurent, 225
Bennett, James, 26
Bennett, Nancy, 26
Bernstein, Leonard, 271
Bierman, Brock, 15
Biesaga, Tadeusz (Fr.), 252
Bingham, Jonathan Brewster,
    242–243
Biscuit King, 129
Blank, Deborah (author's cousin), 94
Blank, Gary, 94
Blumberg, Robert, 189
Boleyn, Anne, 5
Bonsack, James Albert, 39
book of Ruth, 68–69
Boone, Richard, 82, 83
Bosco, Giovanni (Don Bosco),
    249, 252
Bossidy, John Collins, 245
Bovier, Jacqueline Lee, 143
Branch, Christopher, 23
British-American Tobacco (BAT),
    39, 40
Britt
    more on family of, 50, 52, 53, 56
    religion among family of, 45–49
Britt, Martha Ann Lasater (Aunt
    Matt or Mattie) (author's great-
    aunt), 46, 50, 52, 53
Britt, Mary Verna (Verna), 53, 56
Britt, Robert Mullen, 50, 52, 53
Broad Street Drug, 62
Brown, Norman A., 261–262
Brown & Williamson, 39
Brown's Schoolhouse, 41
Buckley, Charles A., 143, 242, 243

Buckley, William F., Jr., 221, 224,
    226, 228, 232
"Buffalo Bill's Wild West," 5
Bullock's Barbeque, 133–134
Bunker, Chang, 60
Bunker, Eng, 60
Burke, James C., 276, 279
Burke, Martha Ann Womble, 279
Burke, Millender, 276, 279
Burke, Winifred W. Clark, 276, 279
Burlington Mills, 235
Busch, August (Gussie) Anheuser,
    III, 218

C

Cabot Corporation, 245
California Fruit Growers
    Exchange, 21
California Walnut Growers
    Association, 21
Cape Haze Marine Laboratory, 198
Cappelletti, Edward (Fr.), 250
Cardon, Carson, 38
Cardon, Virginia, 38
Carlson, Peter, 270
Carlton, Wade, 128
Carnegie, Andrew, 51
Carolina Beach, 162–163
Carr, Julian, 29, 41, 42–43
Carson, Rachel, 206–207
Carter, Stella Ruth, 171
Cates, Eliza, 87
Catherine of Aragon, 5
Cavaliers and Pioneers, 12
Cayton, Lawrence, Jr., 38
Cayton, Sylvia, 38
Chapel Elementary School, 146–148

Chapel Hill, NC
  author's home on Hillview Road
    in, 116, 135, 145, 150
  compared to Durham, 144
  Dairy Bar, 116, 144, 150, 151
  photo of, **140**
  as place of author's
    adolescence, 144
  University Baptist Church, 48
Chapman, Thomas Robert Tighe, 11
Charlemagne (Charles the Great), 110
Charles Edison Memorial Youth
    Fund, 228, 239
Charles Edison Youth Fund, 228, 239
Cherokee, NC, 160–161
Chiosso, James (Fr.), 250, 251
Christ Church, 46
Church of Ascension and St.
    Agnes, 48
Churchill, Winston, 5
City Dairy, 121
Clark, Alexander, 276, 279, 280
Clark, Eugenie, 196, 198
Clark, Phoebe Jefferson, 276, 279
Clark, Susannah Bell, 279
Clark, William, 276, 279, 280
Clark, Winifred, 280
Cline, Patsy, 100
Coastal Research Laboratory (Bureau
    of Sport and Commercial
    Fisheries), 204–209
Cody, Buffalo Bill, 5
Cold Mountain (Frazier), 60, 61
Collins, Charles, 19, 20
Collins, Susan M., 19
Columbus, Christopher, 5
Columbus, Diego, 5
Committee of Youth Organizations of
    the USSR, 248

contract labor system, 13, 14
Cornell, as author's middle name, 8
Cornell University, 8–9
Correll, Charles, 133
Couch's furniture store, 75, 78, 79
country music careers, 96–105
Cramer, William (Bill), **142**, 143, 177,
    214, 231–232, 233, 242, 243
Croley, Carol, 198–200, 201–202. *See
    also* Aregood, Frances Carol
    Croley (Carol)
Croley, Nell Rodgers, 188–189, 191
Crowell, John, 41
Crum, Daniel (Dan), 182, 211, 215
Custis, Mary Anna Randolph, 46

D

Dairy Bar (Chapel Hill), 116, 144,
    150, 151
David R. Jones (Edwards), 216
Davis, Archie, 33
Davis, Jefferson, 5
De Nicolo, Javier (Fr.), 251, 258
Dean, Jimmy, 98, 99, 100, 105
DeWitt, William A., 110
Diamond Crystal, 121
Dickens, Annie Bell (A.B.) Rhew
    (author's aunt), 94
Dickens, Tammy (author's cousin), 94
Dillard, Annie, 270
Dobriansky, Lev E., 228
Doris Duke Charitable
    Foundation, 44
Dragovich, Alexander, 207
Duke

contribution of to Trinity College
and Duke University,
51–52
emergence of family of, 27–29
growth and breakup of empire of,
39–41
Duke (Teague family dog), 158
Duke, Angier Biddle, 44
Duke, Benjamin Newton, 28, 30–31,
32, 44
Duke, Brodie Leonidas, 28
Duke, Buchanan, 43, 44, 52
Duke, Doris, 44
Duke, George Washington
(Washington), 27–29, 43, 51
Duke, James Buchanan ("Buck"),
28, **139**
Duke, Sarah, 58
Duke Endowment, 39, 43, 52
Duke Energy, 43
Duke Forests, 43
Duke Power, 43
Duke University, 29, 41–44
Duke's Woman's College, 53
Dunham, Stanley Ann, 15
Dunlop, William, 171
Durham, Bartlett, 24–25
Durham, Eliza Hall (author's great-
great-grandmother), 61
Durham, Nathan (author's great-
great-grandfather), 61
Durham, NC
in 1964, 235–236
author's birth in, 2, 4
author's family's home in.
See Eighth Street
(Durham, NC)
brightleaf tobacco of, 27
Civil War's end near, 25–26

demise of tobacco empire in,
40–41
eateries in, 132–134. *See also*
Ruby's café
events of May 1944 in, 1–2
origin of name of, 24
Durham, Polly Snipes, 24
Durham, William, 24
Durham: A Bull City Story (Wise), 24,
25, 27
*Durham City Directory 1905–
1906*, 116
Durham City Directory 1934, 76, 116
Durham Dairy, 8, 57, 117–118, 121,
129, 159, 235
Durham Recorder, 28, 89
Durham Station, 25, 28, 37
Durham Sun, 124
Durhamville, 25
Dziedziel, Augustyn (Fr.), 258
Dziubinski, Marian (Fr.), 252

E

EARTH University (Escuela de la
Agricultural de la Regional
Tropical), 261–262. *See also*
Universidad EARTH
The Ed Sullivan Show (TV
program), 81
The Edge of the Sea (Carson), 206
Edison, Charles, 228
Edwards, Lee, 216
Eighth Street (Durham, NC), author's
home on, 2–3, 45, 88, 111,
121, 126, 127, 129, **139**, 148,
161, 235
Eisenhower, Dwight D., 232

E. K. Powe School, 37, 108, **140**
Elizabeth I (Queen), 5
E.M. Holt Plaid Mills, 29
emotional depression, 87
Enfield, Cliff, 242
Ephron, Nora, 5
Episcopal Cathedral Church of St.
    Peter, 48
Episcopalian, 46, 47
Erwin, Jesse Harper, 32
Erwin, William A., Sr., 29–30, 31,
    32, 47
Erwin Auditorium, 32, 37
Erwin Chatter, 50
Erwin Mills, 2, 29, 30–32, 50, 59,
    80–81, 115, 235
Erwin Mills Village, 32, 76
Eugene III (Pope), 5
Evans, Faye Dean, 112–113
Evans, M. Stanton, 222
Every Man (play) (later *The
    Summoning of Everyman)*, 82

F

Farenkopf, Frank, 259
Farrand, George E., 21
Fascell, Dante, 258, 259
Faulkner, Helen, 171
Ferrentino family, 38
Field, Judith Soane, 276
Field, Peter, 276
Fifty Years a Rancher (Teague), 20,
    35–36, 148
Flack, Marjorie, 109
Florida, author's family's move
    to, 164–171. *See also*

Thirty-Seven Avenue North
    (St. Petersburg, FL)
Florida Foundation for Future
    Scientists, 204
Florida Junior Academy of
    Science, 204
Follansbee family, 216
Foundation for Teaching
    Economics, 229
Frank, Anne, 6
Frazier, Charles, 60, 61
Freewill Baptist, 45
Friends of Mengo Hospital
    (Uganda), 246
Fund for American Studies (TFAS),
    42, 49, 177, 216, 220, 227–229,
    239, 257, 262–263
Funding Fathers (Robinson and
    Hoplin), 227

G

Gaither, Allan, 183
Galicia, Bille mac, 10
Gallico, Paul, 82
Gant, Roger, 30
Gay, Connie B., 96–105
*Genealogy of Duke-Shepard-Van Metre
    Family* (Smyth), 13
General Electric Theater, 82
George II, 5
George Washington University, 241
Germino, Hugo, 124–125
Gilbert, Eli Karen (Karen), 9–10
Glenn, Nancy (author's cousin), 50,
    52, 56, 65
globalization, 260–261

God and Man at Yale (Buckley), 221, 222

Goldwater, Barry, 226, 238

golf, importance of to author's father, 122–125, 126

Gorbachev, Mikhail, 238

Gosden, Freeman, 133

Gould, Jay, 20

Gracilaria verrucosa, 207

Graham, Barrett, 145

Grant, Ulysses S., 26

Green, Paul, 161

Greystone Baptist, 47, 81

Gries, Clara Wilson, 10, 19

Grunert, Donald, 133

Guest, Romeo, 33

Guild, William (Uncle Bill), 186–188, 191, 193, 194, 198

Gulf Coast Marine Biology Company, 204, 210

Gurney, Edward, **142**

H

Hallmark Hall of Fame, 82

Handel, George Frederick, 48

Hanes, Robert M., 33

Hardison, Wallace, 19, 22

Hardison-Stewart Oil Company, 22

Harris, Frederick Brown, 214

Harris, Richard, 82

Harrison, Agnes Gant, 30

Harrison, Burr Powell, Jr., 30

Harvey's Cafeteria, 129

Haynes, Charles, Jr., 132

Health and Development International, 246

Healy, Jim, 218

Henry III, 9

Henry VIII, 5

Herr, Evelyn, 190

Herr, Judith, 190, 202

Herr, R.T. ("Tex"), 190

Herr family, 179

Hill, George Watts, Sr., 33

Hill, John Sprunt, 133

Hillandale Golf Course, 59, 62, 122–123, 126, 131, 168, 235

Hill's Durham City Directory 1905–1906, 57

Hill's Durham City Directory 1934, 76, 116

Hillview Road (Chapel Hill), author's family's home on, 116, 135, 145, 150

History Detectives (TV series), 13

History's Hundred Greatest Events (DeWitt and Nisenson), 110

Ho Chi Minh, 5

Hodges, Luther, 33

Hofmannsthal, Hugo von, 82

Holland, Spessard L., 226

Holloway, Elizabeth Caine (author's great-great-grandmother), 85

Holloway, William F. (author's great-great-grandfather), 85

Holt, E.M., 29

Holy Land, author's travels to, 262–264

Homestead Act, 5

Hook, Jane, 148, 149

Hopkins, Johns, 4

Hoplin, Nicole, 227

Horne, Martha J., 46

Hoskins, Anthony, 12

House Committee on Public Works, 234, 241

House Committee on Public Works and Transportation, 241
House Committee on Transportation and Infrastructure, 241
Huston, Tom Charles, 228
Hyde, Mark (Fr.), 250

I

Imperial Tobacco, 39–40
indentured persons, 13, 14
Institute of International Affairs, 258–259
International Foundation for Electoral Systems (IFES), 259–261
International Institute for Political and Economic Studies (IIPES), 262
International Oceanographic Foundation, 196, 204
International Republic Institute (IRI), 259
Iredell, James, 2–3
Iredell Street (Durham, NC), 2
Israel, Leslie, 256
It's All Relative: Adventures Up and Down the World's Family Tree (Jacob), 23

J

Jackson, America, 59
Jackson, Andrew, 137
Jackson, Henry W., 86, 88
Jackson, John Henry, 59
Jackson, Mary Susan, 59
Jackson, Samuel, 59
Jacob, A.J., 23

James I (King), 69
Jamestown, 69–72, 110
Jamestowne Society, 70
Jeannette (author's aunt), 62, 73, 74, 80–81, 115
Jedermann (play), 82
Jefferson, Field, 276, 280
Jefferson, Mary Field, 276
Jefferson, Peter, 280
Jefferson, Thomas, 276, 280
Jenkins, Mrs. W.M., 112
Jobs Creation Act, 238
John (King), 71
John 13:34, 47
John Birch Society, 224, 232
John Paul II (Pope), 239, 251–252, 253, 255–256, 257, 259
Johnson, Lyndon, 237, 238
Johnston, Joseph E., 26
Jones, Corinne Adele Watts, 219, 234
Jones, David R., Jr., 215, 216
Jones, David Richard, III, 215–220, 222, 225, 226–228, 229, 230, 234, 238, 239
Jones, Doris Lake, 217
Jones, Grace, 5
Jones, John Lake, 216
Jones, Margaret, 100, 102, 103, 104
The Journals of Captain John Smith (Smith), 71
Judd, Walter H., 228

K

"Kay Kyser's Kollege of Musical Knowledge," 150
Kelly, John, Jr., 207
Kemp, Hal, 150

297

Kemp, Jack F., 220, 237–238, 244–245, 247

Kemp-Roth tax rate reduction proposals, 238

Kempthorne, Dirk, 264

Kennedy, John F., 143, 237

Kluger, Jerzy, 252

knotted wrack, 207

Kohl, Helmut, 239, 259

Kyser, Kay (James Kern Kyser), 150

Leonard, June Alice (author's wife), 214

Lewis, Fulton, Jr., 231

Liebman, Marvin, 228

Liggett and Myers, 39

Limoneira Company, 21

Lois (author's aunt), 62. *See also* Rhew, Ruby Lois (Lois) (author's aunt)

Long Meadow Farms, 128, 129

Lyon, Mary Elizabeth Duke, 51

L

The Lady and the Sharks (Clark), 198

Lady With a Spear (Clark), 198

Lake, John B. (Jack), 218–219

Langhorne, Chiswell Dabney, 27

Langhorne, Nancy, 27

Lasater, Jeannette Jackson Burke (author's great-grandmother), 45, 56–57, 59, 67, 68, 69, 276, 280

Lasater, religion among Lasater family, 45–49

Lasater, Robert Artemus (author's great-grandfather), 56, 59, 67–68, 276, 280

laudanum, 87

Lawrence, John, 14

Lawrence of Arabia, *see* Lawrence, T. E.

Lawrence, T.E. (Thomas Edward), 11

Lealman Junior High, 170–171, 181–182, 184, 213, 236

Lee, Robert E., 26, 46

Leigh, Hezekiah Gilbert, 41

Leister, George, 67–68

Leister, Thomas, 67–68

M

Maclean, Norman, 267–268

Magna Carta, 71, 110

Mahe, Eddie, 259

Major League Baseball's spring training, 168–169

Malcolm X, 5

Manatt, Charles T., 259

Manning, Archie, 5

marine algae, 206–207

marine sciences, author's interest in, xiii, 4, 141, 165, 170, 181, 183–184, 189, 190, 193, 195, 198, 200, 202, 204–209, 233

Mark 10:43, 47–48

Martel, Charles (Charles the Hammer), 110

Martin, C.B., 8

Mary Help of Christian sisters, 251

Mary Queen of Scots, 5–6

May 19, 1944, important events happening on, 4–6

McBride, Angus, 36

McGraw Tower (Cornell University), 8

Mckevett Corp., 22

McKinnon, Darlene, 110, 163, 197, 247
McPherson, Peter, 245
McTeague (Norris), 11
McVeigh, George, 94
McVeigh, Sara Jean Sherr (Jeannie) (author's cousin), 94
memoir
    author's experience of writing as therapeutic, 271
    encouragement for writing of, 266, 271
    telling of truth in, 269
memories
    as bringing forward additional memories, 268
    reasons for trying to recollect, xii
Methodist, 45
Meyer, Frank, 224
Miami, FL, 161–162
Milesius of Spain, 10
Mirror Lake Junior High, 170, 181–182, 184, 211, 213
Missouri-Kansas-Texas Railway Company (Katy), 19–20
Moore, Joe, 145
More, Sir Thomas, 5
Morehead, John M., III, 152
Morehead Planetarium and Science Center, 150, 151–152
Morocco, author's father work in, 118–121, 126
Mote, William R., 198
movies, author's watching of on television, 82
Mt. Washington Cog Railway, 18–19
Munroe, Andrew, 14

N

names, history of author's names, 7–11
National Democratic Institute (NDI), 259
National Endowment for Democracy (NED), 259
National Football League, 5
National Society of Magna Charta Dames and Barons, 71
Nellie (author's aunt), 62. *See also* Rhew, Nellie Rivers (author's aunt)
Nello L. Teer Company, 118
The New World (movie), 72
Ninth Street (West Durham), 75–80
Nisenson, Samuel, 110
Norris, Frank, 11
Northeast High School (NEHI), 181–183, 184, 210, 211–214, 236
Norweigian kelp, 207
Novak, William, 269

O

Obama, Barack Hussein, 15
Obolensky, Sergei Alexandrovich, 55
O'Brian, Paul Linwood, Jr. (Linwood) (author's cousin), 73, 74
O'Briant, Amanda Tucker (author's cousin), 79
O'Briant, Nancy (author's cousin), 38–39, 73, 74, 75, 77, 78, 80, 133
O'Briant, Paul (author's uncle), 73, 74, 76
O'Briant, Paul Linwood, Jr. (Linwood) (author's cousin), 76, 77

O'Briant, Ruby (author's aunt), 73–74, 75, 76–77, 78, 79, 83
O'Connell, Phillip, 225
Office of Economic Opportunity, 244
Ohio Company, 5
Olsen, Oliver J., 188–189
O'Neill, James J., 249, 250
Operation Fortitude, 5
Order of Legion d'Honneur, 6
OSS: The Secret History of America's First Central Intelligence Agency (Smith), 54–55
Our Folks and Your Folks (Porter and Gries), 10, 19

P

P. Lorillard Co., 39, 40
Pal (Teague family dog), 158
Parker, John Dyas, 193–195, 197–198, 199
Pastan, Linda, 270
Patent Book No. 3, 12
Patsy: The Life and Times of Patsy Cline (Jones), 100, 102, 103, 104
Patten, Lord, 40
Paul's Place, 76
Pearl Cotton Mill, 28
Peewee (Teague family dog), 158
Philip Morris, 39
Pin Hook (a.k.a. Pinhook), 30
Pol Pot, 5
Porter, Francis Collins, 10, 19
Portugal, author's visit to (1962), 202–203
Powe, Edward Knox (E.K.), 29, 32, 33
Powe, E.K., III, 33, 34

Preservation Durham, 30, 43, 79
Price, Richard, 14
Pride, Charley, 100–101
Proceedings of the Gulf and Caribbean Fisheries Institute, 207
Pullen Park (Raleigh), 136–137
Putin, Vladimir, 247

R

racism, 42–43, 265–266
Rainey, Lawyer J., 93
Ralston, Earl, 176–177
Randal, as author's first name, 7–8
Rape, Harvey, 129
Reagan, Ronald, 228, 237, 238, 259
Ream, Roger, 229
red tide, 205–206, 207
Reed, Stanley Forman, 21, 123
Reinhardt, Max, 82
religion, among Teague, Lasater, and Britt families, 45–49
Research Triangle Park (the Triangle), 33–34
Revell, Edward, 12, 13, 16
Revell, Randall, 16
Revolt on the Campus (Evans), 222
Revolutionary War–era lineal societies, 15, 70
Reynolds, Mary Katherine Smith (Katherine), 58, 59
Reynolds, R.J., 58
Reynolds, William Neal, 58
Rhew
  burials of, 89–90
  origin of name, 86
Rhew, Annie Bell (A.B.) (author's aunt), 88, 94

Rhew, Artelia Browning (author's great-great-grandmother), 85

Rhew, Bertha Mae Rippey (author's grandmother), 62, 85, 86–87, 88, 90–91, 92

Rhew, Butch, 38

Rhew, Elizabeth Frances (Fannie) Holloway (author's great-grandmother), 85

Rhew, Elizabeth Frances (Fran) (author's aunt), 94

Rhew, Irby A. (author's great-great-grandfather), 85

Rhew, Jefferson J., 89

Rhew, Lottie Mae (author's mother), 47, 92–93, 95–96, **139**. *See also* Teague, Lottie Mae Rhew (author's mother) (Mom/Mother)

Rhew, Nellie Rivers (author's aunt), 88, 91, 93. *See also* Nellie (author's aunt)

Rhew, Ruby Lois (Lois) (author's aunt), 88, 90, 93, 95. *See also* Lois (author's aunt)

Rhew, Wiley Preston (author's grandfather), 85, 86, 89

Rhew, William L. (author's great-grandfather), 85

Ringling Brothers Circus, 5, 134

Rippey, Daniel (author's great-grandfather), 87

Rippey, Geneva Couch (author's great-grandmother), 87

A River Runs Through It (Maclean), 267–268

R.J. Reynolds Tobacco Company, 39, 40, 58

Roan, Henry, 58

Roberts, John M., Jr. ("Buddy"), 53–57

Roberts, Margaret, 55

Robinson, Ron, 227

Rockefeller, John D., 51

rockweed, 207

Rodale, Robert, 248–249

Rodale Inc., 247, 248–249

Rogers, Elizabeth, 61

Roosevelt, Franklin, 5

Rosen, David, 256–257

Rosen, Gabriella, 257

Rosen, Sharon, 256

Ruby (author's aunt), 73–74, 75, 76–77, 78, 79, 83, 115. *See also* O'Briant, Ruby (author's aunt)

Ruby's café, 61, 62, 77, 78, 235

Russia, author's work in respect to, 247–249

S

Saddle & Fox, 132–133

Salesian Missions, author's work with, 49, 246, 249–258

Salzburg Seminar in American Studies (now Salzburg Global Seminar), 246

Sarah P. Duke Gardens, 43

Sargassum, 206

Schadler, Robert A., 228

Schwengel, Fred, **143**, 143, 242, 243

Science Center of Pinellas County, 188, 189, 202, 236

Science Center of St. Petersburg, 183, 186–192

The Sea Around Us (Carson), 206

Seim, Anders, 246

Sharon Statement, 222–224, 247

Sherman, William Tecumseh, 26

Sherr, Earle J. (author's uncle), 94

Sherr, Elizabeth Frances Rhew (Fran)
    (author's aunt), 94

Shomali, Augustyn, 263, 264

Shomali, Ra'id, 263–264

Shomali, Sawsan, 263, 264

Simpson, George, 33

Smiley, Barbara D., 113

Smith, F.G. Walton, 196

Smith, John, 71–72

Smith, R. Harris, 54–55

Smith, Zachary Taylor, 58

Smith Corona Corporation, 247–248

Smith Corona typewriter, 66

Smyth, Samuel G., 13

The Snow Goose, 82

Soane, Edmund, 277

Soane, Edward, 277

Soane, Elizabeth Worger, 276, 277

Soane, Henry, Jr., 23, 70, 276

Soane, Henry, Sr., 70, 276, 277

Sons (and Daughters) of the American
    Colonists, 70

Sons (and Daughters) of the American
    Revolution, 70

Sons of the American Revolution, 15,
    278–279

Sons of the Revolution, 279–280

Soong, Charles, 42

Souchak, Michael, 123

Southern Baptist, 45, 47

Southern Dairy, 117, 129

Southern Power Company, 43

Spain, author's visit to (1962),
    202–203

Spotsylvania Court House battle
    (Civil War), 5

St. Andrews Church (Wellesley,
    MA), 48

St. George's Hanover Church, 48

St. James Church (Leesburg, VA), 48

St. John's Church (Church of the
    Presidents), 48

St. Joseph's Episcopal Church (St.
    Joe's), 46–47

St. Petersburg College, 210

St. Petersburg, FL, 165–168, 170,
    236–237

St. Petersburg's Fifth Avenue Baptist
    Church, 48

St. Philip's Episcopal Church, 47

Stamper, Helen, 182

Stanford, Leland, 51

Stanton, Edwin, 26

Stanton, Elizabeth Cady, 42

The Story About Ping (Flack and
    Wiese), 109–110

student council, author's participation
    in, 184–185, 210, 211–214

Subcommittee on Watershed
    Development, 242

Sullivan, Ed, 81

Sun, Dr., 42

Sunkist Growers, Inc. (Sunkist),
    22, 148

T

Tadhg, as spelling for Teague, 9, 273

Taylor, Issac (Ike), 149

Taylor, James, 149

Teagg, John, 14

Teague
    as author's last name, 9–11

earliest Teagues to America, 12–22

humor regarding, 16

more on family of, 50, 56, 57–66

northern Teagues, 12, 18–22

photo of, **140**

religion among Teague family, 45–49

southern Teagues, 12–18

Teague, Anna Caviness, 274, 278

Teague, Arthur S., 19

Teague, Barbara (author's brother's wife), 95, 178, 234

Teague, Barbara (author's father's second wife), 129

Teague, Betty, 20

Teague, Charles, 17

Teague, Charles Collins, 19, 20, 21–22, 35–36, 116, 148

Teague, Charles McKevett, 22

Teague, Claude Edward, 152

Teague, Daniel, 18

Teague, Dennis, 14

Teague, Edward, 14, 60, 274

Teague, Elizabeth Loftin, 15, 274, 278

Teague, Ellen Crawford, 19

Teague, Evaline Morse, 19

Teague, Frank (author's brother's son), 234

Teague, George, 14

Teague, G.F., 18

Teague, Harry, 17–18

Teague, Henry N., 18

Teague, Isaac Newton, 15, 274, 278

Teague, Isabella Mary, 15

Teague, Isabelle Loftin, 274

Teague, Jacob, 274, 278

Teague, James Keller Burke (author's son), 9, 275

Teague, Jessica Townsend (author's wife), 9, 128, 177, 275. *See also* Townsend, Jessica (author's wife)

Teague, John, 14, 60

Teague, John (1635–1677), 12–13, 14–18, 274

Teague, J.R., 18

Teague, Judah Dana, 19

Teague, Judith, 274, 278

Teague, Lottie Mae Rhew (author's mother) (Mom/Mother), 92–93, 102, 104–105, 106–107, 121, 127, 144, 155, 158, 172–174, 176–179, 234, 275, 279, 280. *See also* Rhew, Lottie Mae (author's mother)

Teague, Mary, 274, 278

Teague, Mary Frances Durham (author's great-grandmother), 60, 61, 274, 278

Teague, Mary Jeannette (Jeannette) (author's aunt), 57

Teague, Mary Kathleen King (author's wife), 224

Teague, Mary Nall, 274, 278

Teague, Mary Robb Durham (author's daughter), 275. *See also* Wilson, Mary Robb Durham Teague (author's daughter)

Teague, Milton, 22

Teague, Moses, 13–14, 274, 278

Teague, Myra Jane (M.J.) (author's great-aunt), 57

Teague, Naomi Iola Lasater (author's grandmother), 45, 50, 56, 58,

59, 63, 64–65, 67, 68, 275, 276, 279, 280

Teague, Narcissa, 20

Teague, Olin Earl ("Tiger"), 17, 18, 22

Teague, Randal Cornell
adolescence of, 144–158, 179–180
birth of, 2, 4
as Boy Scout, 154–155
childhood memories of, 35–39
childhood vacations of, 159–163
cotillion participation of, 155–156
creation of Gulf Coast Marine Biology Company by, 204, 210
descent of from Henry Soane, 276–277
education of, 108–113, 146–149, 170–171, 181–183, 210, 241
European trip of (1962), 202
family finances in childhood of, 126–127
family's move to Florida, 158, 164–171
future book plans, 265–266
and girls, 156
grandfather's gift of typewriter to, 65–66
health issues of, 127–128, 156–157
history of names of, 7–11
homes of. See Eighth Street (Durham, NC); Hillview Road (Chapel Hill); Thirty-Seven Avenue North (St. Petersburg, FL)
interest of in marine science. See marine sciences, author's interest in
in John Teague line, 275
marriages of, 246. See also Leonard, June Alice (author's wife); Teague, Jessica Townsend (author's wife); Teague, Mary Kathleen King (author's wife)
memories of Morocco, 120–121
memories of Raleigh's Pullen Park, 136–137
1964 and beyond, 241–264
parents of. See Rhew, Lottie Mae (author's mother); Teague, Lottie Mae Rhew (author's mother) (Mom/Mother); Teague, Roy Merle, Sr. (author's father) (Dad)
pets of, 158
photos of, **138**, **141**, **142**, **143**
repetitive nighttime dreams of, 134–136
science expedition possibilities for, 193–197
science fair participation of, 191–192, 201
shift in focus of from marine biology to government, 209–210
sports participation of, 156–157
student council participation of, 184–185, 210, 211–214
summer employment at Coastal Research Laboratory, 204–209
travels to Holy Land, 262–264

as vacation baby, 4

war games of, 152–154

Washington, awaiting call to, 230–232

Washington, first job in, 143

Washington, move to, 240

Washington years, beginning of, 233–240

work of in respect to Soviet Union/Russia, 247–249

work of with Salesian Missions, 49, 246, 249–258

and Young Americans for Freedom. *See* Young Americans for Freedom (YAF)

Teague, Randal Cornell, Jr. (Cornell) (author's son), 9, 40, 245, 275

Teague, Richard Monroe (author's grandfather), 45, 59–60, 62–64, 275, 276, 279, 280

Teague, Robert Townsend (Townsend) (author's son), 96, 245, 275

Teague, Roy, Jr. (Merle) (author's brother), 36, **141**, 158, 174–175, 179

Teague, Roy Merle, Sr. (author's father) (Dad), 8, 21, 36, 46, 47, 57, 59, 73, 88, 91, 92, 114–131, **139**, 144, 151, 159–162, 164, 165, 172–173, 178, 179, 181, 191, 275, 276, 279, 280

Teague, Ruby Beatrice (author's aunt), 57, 115

Teague, Susan Smith, 274

Teague, TX, 20

Teague, W. Dorwin, 16–17

Teague, Walter Dorwin, 16–17

Teague, William, 13, 274, 278

Teague, William Abel, 274

Teague, William Swaim (author's great-grandfather), 60, 274, 278

"Teague Special," at Republican's Capitol Hill Club, 22

Teague-McKevett Co., 22

Tegg's Delight, 14–15, 60

television, 81–82, 83

Tenney, Percy, 77

TFAS (Fund for American Studies), 42, 49, 177, 216, 220, 227–229, 239, 257, 262–263

Thatcher, Margaret, 239, 259

Thirty-Seven Avenue North (St. Petersburg, FL), author's home on, 155, 164, 170, 176, 179, 190, 203, 234, 236

Thomas Jefferson Institute on Public Policy, 70

Thompson, John S., III, 207–208

Thompson, Katharine, 60–61

Thompson, Michael, 60–61

Tidewater Osyter Gardeners Association, 72

Tiegs, Cheryl, 11

Tilley, Doris, 89

The Toast of the Town (TV program), 81

tobacco. *See also specific tobacco companies*

brightleaf tobacco of Durham, 27

smoking habit, 44

technological innovations in tobacco industry, 58

US war on, 40

Tobacco Trust, 39

Townsend, Abram R., 9

Townsend, Harold, 9

Townsend, Jessica (author's wife), 46, 244, 245. *See also* Teague, Jessica Townsend (author's wife)

Townshend, Pete, 5

Treaty of Guadalupe Hidalgo, 5

Trinity and Brazos Railway, 20

Trinity College, 29, 41, 42, 51, 53

TRW, Inc., 175–176

Tucker, Andrew Leon (Leon) (author's cousin), 83–84

Tucker, Andrew Lyon ("Tuck") (author's uncle), 73, 81, 84

Tucker, Carrie (author's cousin), 84

Tucker, Jeannette (author's aunt), 73, 74, 80–81, 84, 115

Tucker, Richard (author's cousin), 84, 162, 163

Tucker, Robert (author's cousin), 84, 163

Turner, Andrew, 25

Turner, Stansfield, 9, 10

Tyranowski, Jan, 251–252

U

Ulva lactuca, 206

Under the Sea Wind (Carson), 207

Underwood typewriter, 65–66

Union Oil Company of California (UNOCAL), 22

Universidad EARTH, 241. *See also* EARTH University (Escuela de la Agricultural de la Regional Tropical)

University Baptist Church (Chapel Hill), 48

University of North Carolina, 144, 147–152, 157

Unto These Hills (play), 161

Urban Dictionary, 11

V

Viguerie, Richard, 227

Vine, Howard A., 248

Virginia Institute of Marine Sciences (VIMS), 200–201

Virginia Theological Seminary (VTS), 46

Virginia—The Old Dominion (Andrews), 16

Vorys, Sater, Seymour and Pease, 245–246

VTI (Foreign Trade Publishing House Association), 248, 249

W

W. Duke Sons & Company, 28

Waidmann, Brian, 264

Washington, DC
  author awaiting call to, 230–232
  author's first job in, 143
  author's first years in, 233–240
  author's move to, 240
  in 1964, 237–240

Watts, Corinne Adele, 218

Watts, George W., 28, 30, 31

Watts Hospital (Durham, NC), 3–4

West Durham, NC, 29–34, 75–76

West End Lunch, 76

White, F. Clifton, 259, 260

White, James Blair, 191–192

White, Rebecca A., 146–147

Wiese, Kurt, 109

Wilde, Oscar, 6

William the Conqueror, 110

Wills, Catherine Mary Hamilton, 40

Wills, Hugh David Hamilton (Sir
    David), 40

Wilson, Elizabeth, 111–112

Wilson, Mary Robb Durham Teague
    (author's daughter), 74, 275

Wise, Jim, 24, 25, 26, 27, 28

W.K. Kellogg Foundation, 261

Wolfe, Thomas, 55–56

women's rights, 42–43, 51

Worger, Mary Humphrey, 277

Worger, Richard, 277

Worger, Thomas, 70

"The Wreck of Time" (Dillard), 270

Wright, William, 225

Y

Yankees spring training, 169

Yates, Paul, 243

Yoakum, Benjamin Franklin, 20

Young, C.W. ("Bill"), 177, 232

Young Americans for Freedom
    (YAF), 216, 220–227, 239,
    243, 247

Youth for Cramer, 231

Z

Zaglul, Jose Antonio, 10

ABOUT THE AUTHOR

RANDAL TEAGUE was raised near Duke University and UNC and graduated from American and George Washington Universities in the nation's capital. He abandoned aspirations in marine biology to become an attorney and a giver of time, talent, and treasure through commitments to nonprofit organizations. He is an avid fisherman and a lover of plump oysters and fine scotches, and he is known as Papa Randy to his grandchildren. An inquisitive traveler to more than 100 countries and more than 280 national park sites, he calls Alexandria, Virginia his home.

Printed in the United States
By Bookmasters